Related Books of Interest

Disciplined Agile Delivery
A Practitioner's Guide to Agile Software Delivery in the Enterprise

By Scott W. Ambler and Mark Lines

ISBN-13: 978-0-13-281013-5

It is widely recognized that moving from traditional to agile approaches to build software solutions is a critical source of competitive advantage. Mainstream agile approaches that are indeed suitable for small projects require significant tailoring for larger, complex enterprise projects. In *Disciplined Agile Delivery*, Scott W. Ambler and Mark Lines introduce IBM®'s breakthrough Disciplined Agile Delivery (DAD) process framework, which describes how to do this tailoring. DAD applies a more disciplined approach to agile development by acknowledging and dealing with the realities and complexities of a portfolio of interdependent program initiatives.

Ambler and Lines show how to extend Scrum with supplementary agile and lean strategies from Agile Modeling (AM), Extreme Programming (XP), Kanban, Unified Process (UP), and other proven methods to provide a hybrid approach that is adaptable to your organization's unique needs.

A Practical Guide to Distributed Scrum

By Elizabeth Woodward, Steffan Surdek, and Matthew Ganis

ISBN-13: 978-0-13-704113-8

This is the first comprehensive, practical guide for Scrum practitioners working in large-scale distributed environments. Written by three of IBM's leading Scrum practitioners—in close collaboration with the IBM QSE Scrum Community of more than 1,000 members worldwide—this book offers specific, actionable guidance for everyone who wants to succeed with Scrum in the enterprise.

Readers will follow a journey through the lifecycle of a distributed Scrum project, from envisioning products and setting up teams to preparing for Sprint planning and running retrospectives. Using real-world examples, the book demonstrates how to apply key Scrum practices, such as look-ahead planning in geographically distributed environments. Readers will also gain valuable new insights into the agile management of complex problem and technical domains.

Related Books of Interest

Being Agile
Eleven Breakthrough Techniques to Keep You from "Waterfalling Backward"

By Leslie Ekas, Scott Will
ISBN-13: 978-0-13-337562-6

When agile teams don't get immediate results, it's tempting for them to fall back into old habits that make success even less likely. In *Being Agile*, Leslie Ekas and Scott Will present eleven powerful techniques for rapidly gaining substantial value from agile, making agile methods stick, and launching a "virtuous circle" of continuous improvement.

Ekas and Will help you clear away silos, improve stakeholder interaction, eliminate waste and waterfall-style inefficiencies, and lead the agile transition far more successfully. Each of their eleven principles can stand on its own: When you combine them, they become even more valuable.

Patterns of Information Management

By Mandy Chessell and Harald Smith
ISBN-13: 978-0-13-315550-1

Use Best Practice Patterns to Understand and Architect Manageable, Efficient Information Supply Chains That Help You Leverage All Your Data and Knowledge

In the era of "Big Data," information pervades every aspect of the organization. Therefore, architecting and managing it is a multi-disciplinary task. Now, two pioneering IBM® architects present proven architecture patterns that fully reflect this reality. Using their pattern language, you can accurately characterize the information issues associated with your own systems, and design solutions that succeed over both the short- and long-term.

Related Books of Interest

Common Information Models for an Open, Analytical, and Agile World

By Mandy Chessell, Gandhi Sivakumar, Dan Wolfson, Kerard Hogg, Ray Harishankar
ISBN-13: 978-0-13-336615-0

Maximize the Value of Your Information Throughout Even the Most Complex IT Project

Five senior IBM architects show you how to use information-centric views to give data a central role in project design and delivery. Using Common Information Models (CIM), you learn how to standardize the way you represent information, making it easier to design, deploy, and evolve even the most complex systems.

Using a complete case study, the authors explain what CIMs are, how to build them, and how to maintain them. You learn how to clarify the structure, meaning, and intent of any information you may exchange, and then use your CIM to improve integration, collaboration, and agility.

In today's mobile, cloud, and analytics environments, your information is more valuable than ever. To build systems that make the most of it, start right here.

Implementing the IBM® Rational Unified Process® and Solutions

A Guide to Improving Your Software Development Capability and Maturity

Joshua Barnes

ISBN-13: 978-0-321-36945-1

Software Test Engineering with IBM Rational Functional Tester

The Definitive Resource

Davis, Chirillo, Gouveia, Saracevic, Bocarsley, Quesada, Thomas, van Lint

ISBN-13: 978-0-13-700066-1

Enterprise Master Data Management

An SOA Approach to Managing Core Information

Dreibelbis, Hechler, Milman, Oberhofer, van Run, Wolfson

ISBN-13: 978-0-13-236625-0

An Introduction to IMS

Your Complete Guide to IBM Information Management Systems, 2nd Edition

Barbara Klein, et al.

ISBN-13: 978-0-13-288687-1

Outside-in Software Development

A Practical Approach to Building Successful Stakeholder-based Products

Carl Kessler, John Sweitzer

ISBN-13: 978-0-13-157551-6

Practical
Software
Architecture

Practical Software Architecture

Moving from System Context to Deployment

Tilak Mitra

IBM Press
Pearson plc
New York • Boston • Indianapolis • San Francisco
Toronto • Montreal • London • Munich • Paris • Madrid
Cape Town • Sydney • Tokyo • Singapore • Mexico City

ibmpressbooks.com

IBM Press Program Managers: Steven M. Stansel, Ellice Uffer
Cover design: IBM Corporation
Editor-in-Chief: Dave Dusthimer
Marketing Manager: Stephane Nakib
Executive Editor: Mary Beth Ray
Publicist: Heather Fox
Editorial Assistant: Vanessa Evans
Managing Editor: Kristy Hart
Designer: Alan Clements
Senior Project Editor: Betsy Gratner
Copy Editor: Chuck Hutchinson
Indexer: Tim Wright
Compositor: Nonie Ratcliff
Proofreader: Debbie Williams
Manufacturing Buyer: Dan Uhrig

Published by Pearson plc
Publishing as IBM Press

For information about buying this title in bulk quantities, or for special sales opportunities (which may include electronic versions; custom cover designs; and content particular to your business, training goals, marketing focus, or branding interests), please contact our corporate sales department at corpsales@pearsoned.com or (800) 382-3419.

For government sales inquiries, please contact governmentsales@pearsoned.com.

For questions about sales outside the U.S., please contact international@pearsoned.com.

Library of Congress Control Number: 2015947371

ISBN-13: 978-0-13-376303-4
ISBN-10: 0-13-376303-X

Text printed in the United States on recycled paper at R.R. Donnelley in Crawfordsville, Indiana. First printing: December 2015

Dedication

I dedicate this book to my late father, Sri. Dibakar Mitra (1940–2015). My father left us earlier this year (2015) and has left a traumatic lacuna in my life, which I find increasingly hard to deal with and to accept its veracity. Baba (father) was my ultimate motivation in life— to believe in myself and go that extra mile to achieve anything to make him immensely proud of his only son—and proud he was! He used to carry my (not even his own) business card in his wallet and show it with immense amour-propre in his professional and personal circles.

Baba left us just 45 days shy of my becoming a Distin- guished Engineer at IBM®, an honor which he so desperately wanted to see happen; it remains as my single greatest regret that I could not pick up the phone and give him the news. His last words to me on his death bed were "Do not worry; your DE will happen this year." He was put on the ventilator shortly thereafter. He had fought so hard to not leave us but had to fall victim to some utter medical negligence and incompetency of one of the so-called best hospitals in Kolkata, India (my native place); the emotional rage inside me will never cease to burn.

Baba, I hope you are at peace wherever you are, and I pray that I can only serve you in some form in my remaining lifetime. Accept my love, forever.

Contents

Foreword

Ah. Software architecture. A phrase that brings delight to some, grumblings to others, and apathy to far too many, particularly those who are far too busy slamming out code to bother with design.

And yet, as we know, all software-intensive systems have an architecture. Some are intentional, others are accidental, and far too many are hidden in the constellation of thousands upon thousands of small design decisions that accumulate from all that code-slamming.

Tilak takes us on a wonderful, approachable, and oh-so-very pragmatic journey through the ways and means of architecting complex systems that matter. With a narrative driven by a set of case studies—born from his experience as a practical architect in the real world—Tilak explains what architecture is, what it is not, and how it can be made a part of developing, delivering, and deploying software-intensive systems. I've read many books and papers about this subject—if you know me, you'll know that I have a few Strong Opinions on the matter—but do know that I find Tilak's approach based on a solid foundation and his presentation quite understandable and very actionable.

Architecting is not just a technical process, it's also a human one, and Tilak groks that very important point. To that end, I celebrate how he interjects the hard lessons he's learned in his career as a practical architect.

Architecture is important; a process of architecting that doesn't get in the way but that does focus one on building the right system at the right time with the right resources is essential...and very practical.

Grady Booch
IBM Fellow and Chief Scientist for Software Engineering

Preface

Software architecture, as a discipline, has been around for half a century. The concept was introduced in the 1960s, drawing inspiration from the architecture of buildings, which involved developing blueprints that formulated designs and specifications of building architecture before any construction ever began. A blueprint of a building provides an engineering design of the *functional* aspects of the building—the floor space layout with schematics and measurements of each building artifact (for example, doors, windows, rooms, bathrooms, and staircases). The blueprint also provides detailed designs of the aspects needed to keep the building *operational*—the physics of the building foundation required to support the load of the building structure; the design of electrical cabling, water, and gas pipelines; and sewer systems needed for a fully operative and usable building.

True inspiration was drawn from the discipline of civil engineering (of building architectures) into information technology (IT); software architectures were broadly classified into *functional architecture* and *operational architecture*. The practice of software architecture started gaining momentum in the 1970s, and by the 1990s, it had become mainstream in the world of IT. At this time, architecture patterns were formulated. Patterns continue to evolve when recurrent themes of usage are observed; recurrences imply consistent and repeated application. Pattern development in software architecture presupposed that software architecture, as a discipline, was practiced enough to become mainstream and accepted as a formal discipline of study and practice.

With the complexity of IT Systems on the rise, IT projects have seen consistent and widespread use of software architectures. With more use comes diversity, or the emergence of various schools of thought that indoctrinate different views toward software architecture and popularize them through their adoption in the development of real-world software systems. With the growing number of variations and views toward software architectures, IT practitioners are typically confused about which school of thought to adopt. As a case in point, have you found yourself asking some of the following questions?

- Because I have read so many books on architecture and have devoured so many journals and publications, how do I put the different schools of thought together?
- Which aspects of which schools of thought do I like more than others?
- Can the aspects complement each other?
- Where should I start when tasked with becoming an architect in a time-constrained, budget-constrained, complex software systems implementation?
- Can I succeed as a software architect?

I too have been in such a confused state. One of the toughest challenges for software architects is to find the best way to define and design a system's or application's software architecture. Capturing the essential tenets of any software architecture is as much a science as it is an art form. While the science lies in the proper analysis, understanding, and use of an appropriate description language to define the software architecture of the system, the art form assumes significance in defining a clear, crisp, nonredundant depiction used for effective communication with the different stakeholders of the system's solution architecture. Software architects find it immensely challenging to determine how to capture the essential architecture artifacts in a way that clearly articulates the solution. While overengineering and excessive documentation add significant delays and associated risks to project delivery, a suboptimal treatment can result in the developer's lack of comprehension regarding the solution architecture. Understanding the architecture is critical to adhere to the guidelines and constraints of technology and its use to design and develop the building blocks of the system. This gap can only widen with progression in the software development life cycle.

In 2008, I started writing a series of articles in the IBM developerWorks® journal; the focus was on documenting software architecture. I published four parts in the series and then for some personal reason could not continue. For the next few years, above and beyond the standard queries and accolades on the series topics, I started to receive a class of queries that got me increasingly thinking. Here are some snippets from these queries:

- "Dear Sir, I am using your article series as a part of my master's thesis. May I know when your next set of articles is coming out?"
- "Mr. Mitra, We have embarked on an IT project in which we [have] adopted your architecture framework. Our project is stalled because the next article is not out. Please help."

One fine morning it dawned on me that there must be a serious need for an end-to-end architecture treatment, one that is simple, crisp, comprehensible, prescriptive and, above all, practical enough to be executable. IT professionals and students of software engineering would significantly benefit from such a practical treatise on architecting software systems. It took me a while to finally put ink on paper; *Practical Software Architecture: Moving from System Context to Deployment* represents all the collective wisdom, experience, learning, and knowledge in the field of software architecture that I have gathered in more than 18 years of my professional career. I have tried to write this book catering to a wide spectrum of readers, including

- Software architects, who will benefit from prescriptive guidance on a *practical* and repeatable recipe for developing software architectures.

- Project managers, who will gain an understanding and appreciation of the essential elements required to develop a well-defined system architecture and account for *just enough* architecture activities in the project plan.

- Graduate students, who will find this book relevant in understanding how the theoretical premises of software architecture can actually be translated and realized in practice. This book is intended to be their long-time reference guide irrespective of technology advancements.

- Professors, who will use the book to help students transition from the theoretical aspects of software architecture to its real-world rendition, assisting students to become practical software architects.

- C-level and senior-level executives, who will benefit indirectly by gaining an awareness and appreciation for what it takes to develop well-formed system architectures for any IT initiative. This indirect knowledge may allow them to better appreciate IT architecture as a fundamental discipline in their company.

I intend this to be a practical how-to book with recipes to iteratively build any software architecture through the various phases of its evolution. It shows how architectural artifacts may be captured so that they are not only crisp, concise, precise, and well understood but also are *just enough* in their practical application. Throughout the book, I have also used the terms "software," "systems," and "solution" quite liberally and interchangeably to qualify the term architecture. The liberal and interchangeable usage of the three terms is a conscious decision to work the mind into such acceptance; they are used quite loosely in the industry.

On a philosophical note, the East and the West have been historically divided in their acceptance of two forms of consciousness: the *rational* and the *intuitive*. Whereas the Western world believes in and primarily practices rational, scientific, and deductive reasoning techniques, the Eastern world places a premium on *intuitive* knowledge as the higher form in which awareness (which is knowledge) is gained by watching (and looking inside one's self; through self-introspection) rather than gained only through experimental deductions. Being born and raised in a culturally rich Bengali (in Kolkata, India) family, I firmly believe in the Eastern philosophies of religion and knowledge, one in which conscious awareness is ultimately obtained through the practice of conscious free will; the ultimate knowledge is gained through intuitive and inductive reasoning. However, having been in the Western world for close to two decades, I do value the scientific and rational knowledge form. I have come to believe that for us as mere mortals to survive in this world of fierce competition, it is imperative that we master the rational and scientifically derived knowledge, especially in the field of science, engineering, and IT. Once such a professional stability is attained, it is worthwhile, if not absolutely rewarding, to delve into the world of intuitive consciousness, of inductive reasoning—one through which we can attend *moksha* in life's existentialism.

In this book, I have tried to share a prescriptive technique to help master *practical* ways of developing *software architecture*, through deductive and rational knowledge reasoning. My hope is that, if you can master the rational knowledge, you can turn your inner focus into the more mystical world of intuitive knowledge induction techniques. Solving the toughest architecture challenges is the Holy Grail; to be able to intuitively derive aspects of software architecture is the higher-level *moksha* we should all aim to achieve!

By the time you have finished reading this book and consuming its essence, I envision a newly emerged practical software architect in you. At least you will be a master of rational knowledge in this fascinating discipline of software architecture, paving the way into the world of mystical intuition, some of which I have only just started to experience!

P.S. If you are curious about the epigraphs at the start of each chapter, they were conjured up in the mind of *yours truly*!

Acknowledgments

I would first like to thank my wife, Taneea, and my mom, Manjusree, for giving me the time and inspiration to write this book. My uncle Abhijit has been the most persistent force behind me to make me believe that I could complete the book. And to my one and only son, Aaditya, for having consistently expressed his wonder regarding how his dad can write yet another book.

On the professional side, I convey my sincere gratitude to Ray Harishankar for supporting me in this gratifying authoring journey, right from its very inception; he is my executive champion. I would also like to thank my colleague Ravi Bansal for helping me review and refine the chapter on infrastructure; I relied on his subject matter expertise. My colleague from Germany, Bertus Eggen, devised a very nifty mathematical technique to help design the capacity model for network connectivity between servers, and I would like to thank Bert for giving me the permission to leverage his idea in my book. My sincere thanks go out to Robert Laird who has, so willingly, reviewed my book and given me such invaluable feedback. Many thanks to Craig Trim for sharing some of the inner details and techniques in natural language processing.

I would like to sincerely thank Grady Booch. I cannot be more humbled and honored to have Grady write the foreword for my book.

And to the Almighty, for giving us our son, Aaditya, born in 2010, who brings me unbridled joy; he is the one I look forward to in the years to come. He is already enamored with my "high-flying" professional lifestyle and wants to become like me; it will be my honest attempt in guiding him to set his bar of accomplishments much higher.

About the Author

Tilak Mitra is a Chief Technology Officer at IBM, Global Business Services®. Tilak is an IBM Distinguished Engineer, with more than 18 years of industry experience in the field and discipline of IT, with a primary focus on complex systems design, enterprise architectures, applied analytics and optimization, and their collective application primarily in the field of industrial manufacturing, automation, and engineering, among various other adjacent industries. He is an influential technologist, strategist, well-regarded thought leader, and a highly sought-after individual to define and drive multidisciplinary innovations across IBM.

As the CTO, Tilak not only drives IBM's technology strategy for the Strategic Solutions portfolio but also spearheads transformative changes in IBM's top clients, developing innovative and new business models to foster their IT transformational programs.

Tilak is the co-author of two books—*Executing SOA* and *SOA Governance*—and has more than 25 journal publications. He is a passionate sportsperson, captains a champion cricket team in South Florida, and is also a former table tennis (ping pong) champion.

He currently lives in sunny South Florida with his wife and son. He can be reached at tilak_m@yahoo.com.

CHAPTER 1

Case Study

I only solve the toughest of cases. Bring it on!

Life without context is like a boat without sails. Context helps us focus on the work at hand; it gives us a sense of direction and a reason to achieve something worthwhile! Architecture, as it applies to the fields of information technology (IT) and computer engineering, also needs a reason for existence. It cries out loud to be instantiated, to be fulfilled, to see itself being realized—contributing to solve real-world problems.

In this chapter, I describe a fictitious case study to illustrate a problem statement. And although I will make no such claim, don't be surprised if you happen to bump into a similar challenge in the real world! A case study that describes a real-world problem will help provide some context against the backdrop of which the elements of IT or software architecture can see itself being brought to life—an objective raison d'être for software architecture!

The Business Problem

Best West Manufacturers (BWM), Inc., a heavy equipment manufacturing company, has primarily been in the legacy business of manufacturing machinery and heavy equipment with an established customer base.

The industry outlook and independent analyst research reports have predicted that BWM's opportunities to grow its market share, through the addition of new customer contracts for buying its equipment, may be quite limited in the coming years.

A concerned board of directors met behind closed doors for a significant portion of two consecutive weeks. After much deliberation and several brainstorming sessions, the outcome was summarized and communicated to the company's senior leadership as a business directive: focus on gaining significantly larger mind- and wallet-share of the aftermarket expenses of the current customer base.

The company's C-level executives analyzed the directive and deemed it critical to channel the focus on offering more services to the customers. This meant that BWM would be offering more value-added services along with the sales of the equipment itself. The value-added services would be targeted at helping the customers maximize their production through efficient use of the machines, reducing unplanned maintenance downtimes, and predicting failures well ahead of their actual occurrences.

The Technical Challenge

To support a set of high-valued services along with the fleet of machines, BWM needed a state-of-the-art IT System as a foundational backbone. There was a distinct lack of in-house IT expertise to conceptualize, formulate, architect, design, and build such a robust enterprise-scale system.

Some of the challenges that were immediately apparent were

- Lack of in-house software development skills and expertise
- Lack of exposure to the current state-of-the-art technologies
- Lack of exposure, experience, and expertise in software development methodologies
- Lack of an IT infrastructure to host an enterprise class system

The technical team, with sponsorship and support from the business, decided to hire a consulting firm to assist them in their transformation journey. And they did!

Focusing on the solution, the consulting firm started by picking up a set of usage scenarios, subsequently formalized into use cases, that would collectively provide appropriate understanding and appreciation of the complexity, criticality, and capabilities supported by the solution to be built.

Some of the key use cases are described in this chapter. However, the use cases presented here

- Are primarily business use cases
- Represent only a small subset of the actual number of use cases
- Are described in simple language, at a very high level, and do not include any technical manifestations or details

Use Cases

The following sections describe a few system features that characterize and define the core capability set that the system ought to support. The capabilities represent a fully functional IT System that in turn participates in an ecosystem that integrates the end-to-end supply chain—from equipment sell to aftermarket value-added services (the focus of this IT System) to an optimized inventory of parts supply.

I illustrate four use cases that will form the central theme of our case study.

Note: In this book, any reference to the "IT System" denotes the system or application that is being built. Any reference to "system" should be assumed to also mean the IT System. Also, in the context of our case study, machine and equipment mean the same thing and hence may be used interchangeably.

Real-Time Processing and Monitoring of Machine Operations

The system should be able to process the incoming stream of data from the instrumented machines in such a way that key performance and monitoring metrics are computed in real time—that is, as and when the data is emitted from the machine instrumentation, such as from digital machine sensors. Multiple metrics may constitute a critical mass of information and insight that collectively will determine the real-time processing and monitoring signature of any given machine type.

It is expected that the real-time processing happens before the data is persisted into any storage. The frequencies at which data may arrive from any given machine could be in milliseconds while data from multiple machines can also arrive simultaneously.

The computed metrics would be persisted into a persistent store and will also be made available on visual monitoring dashboards that can update information at the speed at which they are computed and generated.

The main actors intended to interact with the IT System in support of and to leverage this capability are Field Personnel and the Monitoring Supervisor.

Seamless Activation of Services for New Machines

The system should be able to on-board—that is, add—new machines to the system. Such an addition should not only be seamless and transparent to the end user but also quick in its execution.

When a new machine is sold to a customer, the buyer expects the offered services to be available and activated. Hence, the machine should be automatically registered with the IT System such that the services are active from the first time the customer starts using the machine and data is generated by the instrumentations on the machine.

Seamlessness, in this case, is characterized by the minimal need of user intervention to enable all aspects of the IT System to be aware of the introduction of the new machine(s). This includes gathering machine data from the fields to visualizing real-time monitoring metrics, proactive diagnostics, and automating the subsequent generation of work orders (to fix any upcoming equipment conditions).

The main actor intended to interact with the IT System in support of this system feature is the Power User.

Generation of Work Orders

The system should support proactive determination and generation of maintenance work orders. It should be able to identify faults in machine operations and should also be able to predict the imminent failure or breakdown of the machine or its component parts.

It should be able to intelligently assess the severity of the machine condition and determine whether there is a possibility for the required maintenance to wait until the next scheduled maintenance cycle. Upon determination, it should make a decision on whether to generate and initiate a work order or to wait for the next maintenance cycle, issuing a warning to the appropriate personnel in the latter case.

The entire workflow should be automated with a final validation step (by maintenance personnel) before the work order is initiated from the system.

The main actor intended to interact with the IT System in support of this capability is the Maintenance Supervisor.

Minimal Latency Glitches for Customers Worldwide

The system should not give its users an impression that it performs slowly. The user interactions and the corresponding system responses should be better than typical tolerable limits of any enterprise class system.

The system should not give an impression that its globally distributed nature of coverage is a reason for higher latency and lower throughput.

The system should categorize features based on time sensitivity and criticality and accordingly put a premium on minimizing latency and maximizing throughput for the more sensitive and critical features. For example, the "Real-Time Processing and Monitoring of Machine Operations" is a time-critical feature; therefore, it should not give an impression to the user that system response (that is, the display of performance and monitoring metrics) is slow and the information refresh does not occur in real time.

This system feature should be supported regardless of any specific human actor(s) interacting with the system.

The four use cases described here are best considered as some significant capabilities that the IT System must exhibit. Such capabilities are usually captured as business use cases.

Also, be aware that a *business use case* is different from a *system use case*. Without getting into "use case analysis paralysis," it is worthwhile to state that the essential difference between a business use case and a system use case is that the former illustrates "what" a system should provide in the form of capabilities, whereas the latter illustrates "how" the features ought to be implemented by the system. Use case definition is a discipline in its own right and constitutes the first phase of any software development life cycle—that is, Requirements Gathering.

Summary

The architecture of an IT System is arguably one of the most critical elements that shapes and holds all the software development pieces together.

There exists a common syndrome, even among the experts in software architecture and system developers, to theorize and generalize more than what is required to address the problem at hand. Having such a problem at hand often helps the software architect take a step back and reassess: *Am I making this too complex? Am I generalizing this more than what is required to solve the problem? Am I overengineering the IT System's architecture?*

A case study provides the context of the problem to solve and defines a set of boundaries that assist in focusing and addressing the problem at hand.

Such a focus marks the inception of a cult I aspire to start: *The Practical Software Architect*. (And if you are aspiring to be a practical software architect, you picked up the right book!)

CHAPTER 2

Software Architecture: The *What* and *Why*

Unless I am convinced, I cannot put my heart and soul into it.

If you're reading this chapter, I am going to assume that you are serious about following the cult of "The Practical Software Architect" and you would like to not only proudly wear the badge but also practice the discipline in your real-world software and systems development gigs and be wildly successful at it.

Software architects come in various flavors, and often they are interesting characters. Some architects work at a very high level engaging in drawing pictures on the back of a napkin or drawing a set of boxes and lines on a whiteboard, where no two boxes ever look the same. Others tend to get into fine-grained details too soon and often fail to see the forest for the trees; that is, see the bigger overarching architectural landscape. Still others are confused about what is the right mix. There is a need to level the playing field so that there is not only a common and comprehensible understanding of the discipline of software architecture, but also of what is expected of the role of the software architect, in order to be successful every time.

This chapter provides some background on the discipline of software architecture and some of the time-tested value drivers that justify its adoption. I end the chapter by laying some groundwork for the essential elements of the discipline that you and I, as flag bearers of the practical software architect cult, must formalize, practice, and preach.

How about a T*he* PSA (pronounced "thepsa") T-shirt?

Some Background

Software architecture, as a discipline, has been around for more than four decades, with its earliest works dating back to the 1970s. However, it is only under the pressures of increasing complexity hovering around the development of complex, mission-critical, and real-time systems that it has emerged as one of the fundamental constructs of mainstream systems engineering and software development.

Like any other enduring discipline, software architecture also had its initial challenges. However, this is not to say that it is free of all the challenges yet! Early efforts in representing the architectural constructs of a system were laden with confusing, inconsistent, imprecise, disorganized mechanisms that were used to diagrammatically and textually represent the structural and behavioral aspects of the system. What was needed was a consistent and well-understood pseudo- or metalanguage that could be used to unify all modes of representation and documentation of software architecture constructs and artifacts. The engineering and computer science communities, fostered by academic research, have made tremendous strides in developing best practices and guidelines around formalization of architecture constructs to foster effective communication of outcomes with the necessary stakeholders.

The What

Various research groups and individual contributors to the field of software engineering have interpreted software architecture, and each of them has a different viewpoint of how best to represent the architecture of a software system. Not one of these interpretations or viewpoints is wrong; rather, each has its own merits. The definition given by Bass, Clements, and Kazman (2012) captures the essential concept of what a software architecture should entail:

> The software architecture of a program or computing system is the structure or structures of the system, which comprise software components, the externally visible properties of those components, and the relationships between them.

Now what does this definition imply?

The definition focuses on the fact that software architecture is comprised of coarse-grained constructs (a.k.a. software components) that can be considered building blocks of the architecture. Let's call them architecture building blocks (ABB). Each such software component, or ABB (I use the terms interchangeably from here on), has certain externally visible properties that it announces to the rest of the ABBs. The internal details of how each software component is designed and implemented should not be of any concern to the rest of the system. Software components exist as black boxes—that is, internal details are not exposed—exposing only certain properties that they exhibit and that the rest of the software components can leverage to collectively realize the capabilities that the system is expected to deliver. Software architecture not only identifies the ABBs at the optimum level of granularity but also characterizes them according to the properties they exhibit and the set of capabilities they support. Capturing the essential tenets of the software architecture, which is defined by the ABBs and their properties and capabilities, is critical; therefore, it is essential to formalize the ways it is captured such that it makes it simple, clear, and easy to comprehend and communicate.

Architecture as it relates to software engineering is about decomposing or partitioning a single system into a set of parts that can be constructed modularly, iteratively, incrementally, and independently. These individual parts have, as mentioned previously, explicit relationships between them that, when weaved or collated together, form the system—that is, the application's software architecture.

Some confusion exists' around the difference between architecture and design. As Bass, Clements, and Kazman (2012) pointed out, all architectures are designs, but not all designs are architectures. Some design patterns that foster flexibility, extensibility, and establishment of boundary conditions for the system to meet are often considered architectural in nature, and that is okay. More concretely, whereas architecture considers an ABB as a black box, design deals with the configuration, customization, and the internal workings of a software component—that is, the ABB. The architecture confines a software component to its external properties. Design is usually much more relaxed, since it has many more options regarding how to adhere to the external properties of the component; it considers various alternatives of how the internal details of the component may be implemented.

It is interesting to observe that software architecture can be used recursively, as illustrated in Figure 2.1.

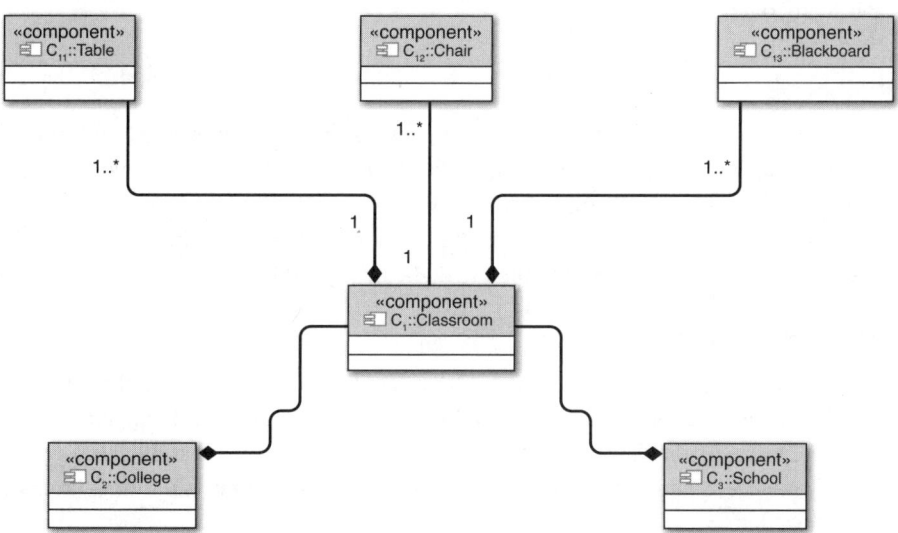

Figure 2.1   Illustrative example of recursive component dependencies.

Referring to Figure 2.1, consider a software component (C_1 representing a Classroom) that is a part of a system's software architecture. The software architect shares this software component (among others), along with its properties, functional and nonfunctional capabilities, and its relationships to other software components, to the system designer—the collection of ABBs along with their interrelationships and externally visible properties represents an *architecture blueprint*. The designer, after analyzing the software component (C_1), decides that it may be broken down into some finer-grained components (C_{11} representing a Table object, C_{12} representing a Chair object, and C_{13} representing a Blackboard object), each of which provides some reusable functionality that would be used to implement the properties mandated for C_1. The designer details C_{11}, C_{12}, C_{13}, and their interfaces. The designer may consider C_{11}, C_{12}, and C_{13} as architectural constructs, with explicitly defined interfaces and relationships, for the software component C_1. Then C_{11}, C_{12}, and C_{13} may need to be further elaborated and designed to address their internal implementations. Hence, architecture principles can be used recursively as follows: divide a large complex system into small constituent parts and then focus on each part for further elaboration.

Architecture, as mentioned previously, confines the system to using the ABBs that collectively meet the behavioral and quality goals. It is imperative that the architecture of any system under consideration needs to be well understood by its stakeholders: those who use it for downstream design and implementation and those who fund the architecture to be defined, maintained, and enhanced. And although this chapter looks more closely at this issue later on, it is important to highlight the importance of communication: architecture is a vehicle of communicating the IT System with the stakeholder community.

The Why

Unless I am convinced about the need, the importance, and the value of something, it is very difficult for me to motivate myself to put in my 100 percent. If you are like me and would like to believe in the value of software architecture, read on!

This section illustrates some of the reasons that convinced me of the importance of this discipline and led me to passionately and completely dedicate myself to practicing it.

A Communication Vehicle

Software architecture is the blueprint on which an IT System is designed, built, deployed, maintained, and managed. Many stakeholders expect and hence rely on a good understanding of the system architecture. However, one size does not fit all: a single view of the architecture would not suffice to satisfy the needs and expectations of the stakeholder community; multiple architecture viewpoints are needed.

Different views of the architecture are required to communicate its essence adequately to the stakeholders. For example, it is important to communicate with business sponsors in their own language (for example, a clear articulation of how the architecture addresses business needs). It should also communicate and assure the business stakeholders that it does not look like something that has been tried before and that has failed. The architecture representation should also illustrate how some of the high-level business use cases are realized by combining the capabilities of one or more ABBs. The representation (a.k.a., a viewpoint, which this chapter elaborates on later) and the illustrations should also focus on driving the value of the architecture blueprint as the foundation on which the entire system will be designed and built. The value drivers, in business terms, will ultimately need to ensure that there is adequate funding to maintain the vitality of the architecture until, at least, the system is deployed, operational, and in a steady state.

For the technical team, there should be multiple and different architecture representations depending on the technology domain. Following are a few examples:

- An application architect needs to understand the application architecture of the system that focuses on the functional components, their interfaces, and their dependencies—the *functional architecture* viewpoint.

- An infrastructure architect may be interested in (but not limited to) understanding the topology of the servers, the network connectivity between the servers, and the placement of functional components on servers—the *operational architecture* viewpoint.

- A business process owner would certainly be interested in understanding the various business processes that are enabled or automated by orchestrating the features and functions supported by the system. A business process is typically realized by orchestrating the capabilities of one or more business components. A static business component view, along with a dynamic business process view, would illustrate what business process owners may be interested in—the *business architecture* viewpoint.

Effective communication of the architecture drives healthy debates about the correct solution and approach; various alternatives and trade-offs may be analyzed and decisions made in concert. This not only ensures that the stakeholders are heard but also increases the quality of the architecture itself.

Communicating the architecture in ways that ensure various stakeholders' understanding of its value and what is in it for them, while also having their active participation in its evolution, is key to ensuring that the vitality of the architecture is appropriately maintained.

Influences Planning

Recall the fact that any software architecture can be defined, at a high level, by a set of ABBs along with their interrelationships and dependencies. Recall also that an ABB can be deconstructed into a set of components that also exhibit interrelationships and dependencies. In a typical software development process, the functionalities of the system are usually prioritized based on quite a few parameters: urgency of feature availability and rollout, need to tackle the tough problems first (in software architecture parlance, these problems often are called *architecturally significant use cases*), quarterly capital expenditure budget, and so on. Whatever the reason may be, some element of feature prioritization is quite common.

Dependencies between the ABBs provide prescriptive guidance on how software components may be planned for implementation (see Figure 2.2).

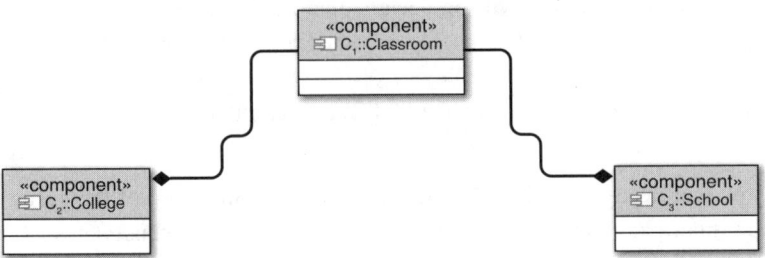

Figure 2.2   Illustrative example of intercomponent dependencies.

Consider a scenario (as in Figure 2.2) in which components C_2 and C_3 depend on the availability of C_1's functionality, while C_2 and C_3 themselves are independent of each other. The architect can leverage this knowledge to influence the project planning process. For example, the architect may perform the design of C_1, C_2 and C_3 in parallel if sufficient resources (designers) are available; however, he may implement C_1 first and subsequently parallelize the implementation of C_2 and C_3 (assuming sufficient resources are available). Proper knowledge of the architecture and its constituents is critical to proper project planning; the architect is often the project manager's best friend, especially during the project planning process.

Seeing the value the architect brings to the planning process, the planning team has often been found to be greedy for more involvement of the architect. The complexity of the architecture components influences how time and resources (their skill sets and expertise levels) are apportioned and allocated.

If the stakeholders do not have a thorough understanding of the architecture, subsequent phases—design, implementation, test planning, and deployment—will have significant challenges in any nontrivial system development.

Addresses Nonfunctional Capabilities

Addressing the nonfunctional capabilities of a software system is a key responsibility of its architecture. It is often said, and rightfully so, that lack of commensurate focus on architecting any system to support its nonfunctional requirements (NFR) often brings about the system's failure and breakdown.

Extensibility, scalability, maintainability, performance, and security are some of the key constituents of a system's nonfunctional requirements. NFRs are unique in that they may not always be component entities in their own right; rather, they require special attention of one or more functional components of the architecture. As such, the architecture may influence and augment the properties of such functional components. Consider a use case that is expected to have a response time of no more than one second. The system's architecture determines that three ABBs—C_1, C_2, and C_3—collectively implement the use case. In such a scenario, the nature and complexity of the supported features of the components dictate how much time each component may get to implement its portion of the responsibility: C_1 may get 300 milliseconds, C_2 may get 500 milliseconds, and C_3 may get 200 milliseconds. You may start finding some clues from here how ABBs get decorated with additional properties that they need to exhibit, support, and adhere to.

A well-designed and thought-out architecture assigns appropriate focus to address the key nonfunctional requirements of the system, not as an afterthought but during the architecture definition phase of a software development life cycle.

The risks of failure, from a technical standpoint, are significantly mitigated if the nonfunctional requirements are appropriately addressed and accounted for in the system architecture.

Contracts for Design and Implementation

One crucial aspect of software architecture is the establishment of best practices, guidelines, standards, and architecture patterns that are documented and communicated by the architect to the design and implementation teams.

Above and beyond communicating the ABBs, along with their interfaces and dependencies, the combination of best practices, guidelines, standards, and architecture patterns provides a set of constraints and boundary conditions within which the system design and implementation are expected to be defined and developed. Such constraints restrict the design and implementation team from being unnecessarily creative and channel their focus on adhering to the constraints rather than violating them.

As a part of the communication process, the architect ensures that the design and implementation teams recognize that any violation of the constraints breaks the architecture principles and contract of the system. In some special cases, violations may be treated and accepted as exceptions if a compelling rationale exists.

Supports Impact Analysis

Consider a situation, which presumably should not be too foreign to you, in which there is scope creep in the form of new requirements. The project manager needs to understand and assess the impact to the existing project timeline that may result from the new requirements.

In this situation, an experienced project manager almost inevitably reverts first and foremost to her lead architect and solicits help in exercising the required impact analysis.

Recall that any software architecture defines the ABBs and their relationships, dependencies, and interactions. The architect would perform some analysis of the new use case and determine the set of software components that would require modifications to collectively realize the new use case or cases. Changes to intercomponent dependencies (based on additional information or data exchange) are also identified. The impact to the project timeline thus becomes directly related to the number of components that require change, the extent of their changes, and also additional data or data sources required for implementation. The analyses can be further extended to influence or determine the cost of the changes and any risks that may be associated with them. Component characteristics are a key metric to attribute the cost of its design, implementation, and subsequent maintenance and enhancements.

I cited five reasons to substantiate the importance of software architecture. However, I am certain that you can come up with more reasons to drive home the importance of architecture. I decided to stop here because I felt that the reasons cited here are good enough to assure me of its importance. And, staying true to the theme of this book, when I know that it is *just enough*, it is time to move on to the next important aspect. My objective, in this book, is to share my experiences on what is *just enough*, in various disciplines of software architecture, so that you have a baseline and frame of reference from which you can calibrate it to your needs.

Architecture Views and Viewpoints

Books, articles, research, and related publications on the different views of software architecture have been published. There are different schools of thought that prefer one architecture viewpoint over the other and, hence, practice and promote its adoption. In the spirit of this book's theme, I do not devote a separate chapter to an exhaustive treatment of the different views of software architecture; rather, I present one that I have found to be practical and natural to follow and hence to use.

VIEWS AND VIEWPOINTS

Philippe Kruchten (1995, November) was the pioneer who postulated the use of views and viewpoints to address the various concerns of any software architecture. Kruchten was a part of the IEEE 1471 standards body, which standardized the definitions of *view* and introduced the concept of a *viewpoint*, which, as published in his paper (see "References"), are as follows:

- **Viewpoint**—"A specification of the conventions for constructing and using a view. A pattern or template from which to develop individual views by establishing the purposes and audience for a view and the techniques for its creation and analysis."
- **View**—"A representation of a whole system from the perspective of a related set of concerns."

IBM (n.d.) defined a set of viewpoints called the IBM IT System Viewpoint Library. I have found it to be quite complete, with appropriate coverage of the various facets of a system's architecture. The library consists of four basic viewpoints and six cross-cutting viewpoints. Figure 2.3 provides a pictorial representation.

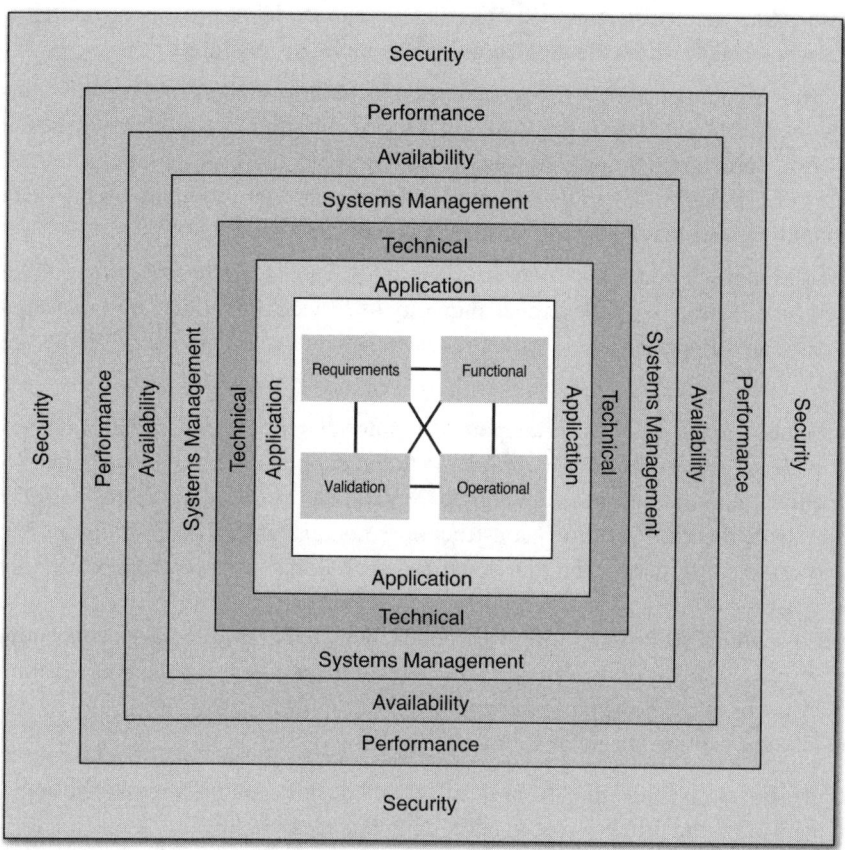

Figure 2.3   Viewpoints in the IBM IT System Viewpoint Library (see "References").

The four basic viewpoints of the IBM IT System Viewpoint Library are the following:

- **Requirements**—Models elements that capture all the requirements placed on the system, including business, technical, functional, and nonfunctional requirements. Use cases and use case models are the most common means of capturing the requirements viewpoint.

- **Solution**—Models elements that define the solution satisfying the requirements and constraints; further organized into two categories:

  - **Functional**—Focuses on the model elements that are structural in nature and with which the system is built by not only implementing the elements but also wiring the relationships between the elements (both static and dynamic). The functional architecture (the focus of Chapter 7, "The Functional Model"), broadly speaking, is the construct through which the details of this viewpoint are captured.

- **Operational**—Focuses on how the target system is built from the structural elements and how the functional view is deployed onto the IT environment (which consists of the network, hardware, compute power, servers, and so on). The operational model (the focus of Chapter 8, "The Operational Model") is the most common architecture construct through which the details of this viewpoint are captured.

- **Validation**—Models elements that focus on assessing the ability of the system to deliver the intended functionality with the expected quality of service. Functional and nonfunctional test cases are often used as the validation criteria to attest to the system's expected capabilities.

As shown in Figure 2.3, the four basic viewpoints are interrelated. The functional and operational viewpoints collectively realize (that is, implement and support) the requirements viewpoint; both the functional and operational viewpoints are validated for acceptance through the validation viewpoint. Note that the "solution" construct does not appear explicitly in Figure 2.3; for the sake of clarity, I have only shown the functional and operation constructs that collectively define the solution construct.

The library also contains six cross-cutting viewpoints, depicted in Figure 2.3 as concentric squares around the four basic viewpoints. The idea is to illustrate the point that the cross-cutting viewpoints influence one or more of the basic viewpoints.

The six cross-cutting viewpoints are as follows:

- **Application**—Focuses on meeting the system's stated business requirements. The application architect plays the primary role in addressing this viewpoint.

- **Technical**—Focuses on the hardware, software, middleware (see Chapter 5, "The Architecture Overview," for a definition), and packaged applications that collectively realize the application functionality and enable the application to run. The infrastructure and integration architects play the primary roles in addressing this viewpoint.

- **Systems Management**—Focuses on post-deployment management, maintenance, and operations of the system. The application maintenance and management teams play the primary roles in addressing this viewpoint.

- **Availability**—Focuses on addressing how the system will be made and kept available (for example, 99.5 percent uptime) per the agreed-upon service-level agreements. The infrastructure architect plays the primary role in addressing this viewpoint, with support from the application and the middleware architects.

- **Performance**—Focuses on addressing the performance of the system (for example, 400 milliseconds average latency between user request and the system response) per the agreed-upon service-level agreements. The application architect plays the primary role in addressing this viewpoint, with support from the middleware and infrastructure architects.

- **Security**—Focuses on addressing the security requirements of the system (for example, single sign-on, security of data transfer protocol, intrusion avoidance, among others). Some of the security requirements—for example, single sign-on—are addressed primarily by the application architect role, whereas other requirements such as data protocols (HTTPS, secure sockets) and intrusion avoidance are addressed primarily by the infrastructure architects.

There are many more details behind each of the basic and cross-cutting viewpoints. Each viewpoint has a set of elements that collectively characterize and define their responsibilities. Understanding them can provide key insights into how each viewpoint may be realized. Although there are many details behind each of the basic and cross-cutting viewpoints, the idea here is to acknowledge their existence and realize the fact that any system's overall architecture has to typically address most, if not all, of the viewpoints. Awareness is key!

After having personally studied a handful of viewpoint frameworks, I feel that most, if not all, of them have a degree of commonality in their fundamental form. The reason is that each of the frameworks sets about to accomplish the same task of establishing a set of complementary perspectives from which the software architecture may be viewed, with the goal of covering the various facets of the architecture.

The choice of adopting a viewpoint framework, at least from the ones that are also quite established, hardened, and enduring, depends on your level of belief that it addresses your needs and your degree of comfort in its usability and adoption.

Summary

As humans, we need to be convinced of the value of the work we are undertaking in order to put our mind and soul into it, to believe in its efficacy so that we can conjure up a passionate endeavor to make it successful.

In this chapter I shared my rationale for and belief in the value of a well-defined software architecture in relation to developing a successful software system. I defined a software architecture (that is, the *What*) while also emphasizing its value (that is, the *Why*).

The chapter also introduced the notion of architecture views and viewpoints and provided an overview of one viewpoint library that I tend to follow quite often.

The next chapter highlights the various facets of software architecture that are described in the rest of the book. The fun begins!

References

Bass, L., Clements, P., & Kazman, R. (2012). *Software architecture in practice*, 3rd ed. (Upper Saddle River, NJ: Addison-Wesley Professional).

IBM. (n.d.) Introduction to IBM IT system viewpoint. Retrieved from http://www.ibm.com/developerworks/rational/library/08/0108_cooks-cripps-spaas/.

Kruchten, P. (1995, November). Architectural blueprints—The "4+1" view model of software architecture. *IEEE Software, 12*(6), 42–50. Retrieved from http://www.cs.ubc.ca/~gregor/teaching/papers/4+1view-architecture.pdf.

CHAPTER 3

Capturing Just Enough

Define the boundaries, and I will show you how to flourish even within them.

The preceding chapter highlighted some of the considerations to ascertain the importance of architecture in the development of any nontrivial system. You may have gone through the views and viewpoints in more detail or may have read about different architecture schools of thought around some of its other facets. Now you may be thinking, "What are the most essential architecture aspects that I need to focus on? Where do I start? When time comes for my next architecture assignment, will I be well prepared?" If that's the case, I don't blame you for such questions and thoughts.

The pivotal theme of this book is seeded in practicality—specifically to identify the areas in software architecture that are critically important and within each area to determine what is *just enough* to capture the essence of the task at hand. Follow the The PSA cult with conviction, contribute to, and shape it for adoption en masse!

This chapter highlights the architecture aspects I feel are *just enough* to be captured with commensurate time, effort, and due diligence, such that the software architecture of any nontrivial IT System will be conspicuous in its value and outcome.

Architecture Aspects in Focus

Any software architecture has multiple aspects, some of which have the potential of going into excruciating, often unnecessary detail (from an architecture standpoint). The trick is to be able to choose those aspects that not only provide adequate coverage of the various facets of the solution but also satisfy the need for effective communication with all the involved stakeholders. The choice also depends on the inherent complexity of the system that is being built and, of course, on your personal preference.

As mentioned, the theme of this book is to focus on *just enough*—to concentrate the architecture work effort in only the areas that I have found to be necessary and sufficient even in building the most complex systems.

The facets covered in this book are as follows:

- **System Context**—Documents how the IT System, which is typically represented as a black box, interacts with external entities (systems and end users) and defines the information and control flows between the system and the external entities. It is used to clarify, confirm, and capture the environment in which the system has to operate. The nature of the external systems, their interfaces, and the information and control flows are inputs to the downstream specification of the technical artifacts in the architecture.

- **Architecture Overview**—Illustrates the main conceptual elements and relationships in any software architecture described through simple and clear schematic representations. The architecture overview diagrams can be produced at different levels: an enterprise-level view, an IT System-level view, and a layered architecture view. These views help in representing the architecture artifacts supporting an IT System. This artifact provides high-level schematics that are then further elaborated and captured in the form of functional and operational models. It also depicts the strategic direction that the enterprise may be taking as it pertains to building IT Systems, specifically the system under consideration.

- **Architecture Decisions**—Provides a single consolidated artifact in which all the architecturally relevant decisions are captured. Decisions are typically made around, but not limited to, the structure of systems, the identification of middleware components to support integration requirements, the allocation of functions to each architecture component (or architecture building block, ABB), allocation of ABBs to the various layers in the architecture, compliance and adherence to standards, choice of technology to implement a particular ABB or functional component, and so on. Any decision that is considered architecturally important to satisfy the business, technical, and engineering goals is captured. Documentation usually involves the identification of the problem; evaluation of the various alternative solutions with their pros and cons; and choice of the solution, supplemented by adequate justification and other relevant details that are expected to help downstream design and implementation.

- **Functional Model**—Also known as the component architecture or model. It describes, defines, and captures how the architecture is deconstructed into IT subsystems that provide a logical grouping of the software components. This artifact describes the structure of an IT System in terms of its software components with their responsibilities, interfaces, static relationships, and the mechanisms in which they collaborate to deliver the required functionality expected of the system. This artifact is developed iteratively through various stages of elaboration.

- **Operational Model**—Represents a network of computer systems that not only support some of the system's nonfunctional requirements (for example, performance, scalability, and fault tolerance, among others) but also run the middleware, systems software, and application software components. This artifact also defines the network topology that interconnects the computer systems. It is also developed iteratively through various stages of elaboration.

- **Integration Patterns**—Represents a set of most commonly used reusable patterns that focus on simplifying and streamlining the techniques by which the system under construction connects and communicates with other participating applications and systems. It leverages architecture patterns such as mediation, routing, transformation, event detection, message brokering, and service invocations.

- **Infrastructure Architecture**—Focuses on the development of infrastructure including servers, storage, hardware, workstations, nonapplication software, and the physical facilities that support the development, testing, deployment, management, and maintenance of the application.

It is critical to recognize that any system will render itself usable if it is right-performing. The infrastructure aspects must focus on making the system usable in relation to latency and turnaround time for user to system interactions, while ensuring that the computational capacity is right-sized to support both the functional and nonfunctional requirements.

Summary

The utopia of getting things to be *just right* eludes popular wisdom; it is something that is missing in most walks of life.

In this chapter I identified and described (albeit very briefly) only those aspects that are necessary and sufficient to develop any successful software architecture.

System Context starts by considering the IT System to be a black box and only depicts its connection and information exchange with other external applications and systems. Architecture Overview illustrates the architecture building blocks of the system, providing a first look at the system internals through the lens of an architect. The Functional Model provides a first look at a subsystem view of the architecture that not only describes a systematic grouping of functionality but also introduces the interfaces that each functional (that is, software) component exposes and consumes. The Operational Model addresses how the operational topology may be defined such that the functional components may be appropriately hosted on the operational runtime topology. Integration Patterns elaborates on the mechanisms and techniques for simplifying the integration with other applications, systems, and databases by identifying reusable and scalable techniques. Infrastructure Architecture focuses on the actual servers, hardware, networks, and their physical placement in data centers and facilities. Architecture Decisions is a critical piece of work that captures the thinking around the various alternatives considered during the problem-solving process of some specific areas of concern that require an architectural approach to problem solving.

Now it's time to get ready for the heavy lifting.

CHAPTER 4

The System Context

My context: my conscious mind, connecting me with the multiverse.

In the first chapter, which introduced the case study, I stated that setting the context is key; it helps bring focus to the task at hand. Metaphorically speaking, it is critical that any IT System knows its surroundings, particularly the systems and users with which it is expected to interact in its daily life and the specific languages it needs to speak to communicate effectively and to exchange relevant information with the external systems.

In tech speak, establishing the context in which an application or system will be developed is an important early step toward gaining a good understanding of the interaction and relationships that the evolving system or application will have with its environment (that is, the users and other systems). This insight assists the architect in gaining an understanding of how the system is going to coexist and interact with other entities that are outside the boundary of the application under development.

This chapter focuses on the System Context of an IT System. The System Context provides a catalog of systems (external to the system under consideration), the information flow with the external systems, the external events that the IT System needs to be aware of or respond to, along with a catalog of profiles of different types of user roles that will be accessing and interacting with the IT System to harness its capabilities. For flexibility, I use the terms *IT System* and *system* interchangeably.

The Business Context Versus System Context Conundrum

A common discussion point arises around the scope of what should constitute a System Context definition. Finding it difficult to decide where to draw the boundary is quite common: should only the entities within the enterprise be considered, or can entities in other participating organizations also be considered? This is a classic problem that manifests itself in an inconsistent representation of the application's System Context.

Any entity that resides outside the enterprise perimeter falls, to begin with, under the purview of what is termed as the "Business Context" of a system under construction. The Business Context provides a big picture understanding of interenterprise relationships in relation to interaction between user communities and information exchange. The Business Context consists of one or more diagrams that depict the boundary of the enterprise. Typical examples of Business Context entities are consumers, suppliers, clearinghouses, regulatory bodies, external service providers such as credit card merchandisers, and so on.

Let's look at another explanation for the Business Context. The Business Context provides an organizational-level view of how enterprises and organizations are related to each other, supplemented by the type of information exchange, between the organizations, that may be required. IT System designs benefit from leveraging the Business Context diagrams to determine an initial understanding of the percentage split between intersystem communication that lies within the enterprise and the communication that lies outside the enterprise. This understanding is particularly important while building systems that have a substantial amount of dependency on external organizations. The Business Context does not differentiate between the various users and roles but depicts them as a "user community" that interacts with the business. Say you are building particular software for a university. In this case, the Business Context may depict the university as a central entity and represent dependencies on the government, to request for funding and to obtain and perform regulatory conformance checks; on the IT industry, to request for research projects and educational services; on the user community, to which the university will provide hardware and software support; and on other universities in the consortium to obtain student history and records. Figure 4.1 gives a diagrammatic representation of the example.

Although understanding the Business Context may be essential to developing a system that is properly positioned to support the business, it is important to realize and remember that the Business Context diagram does not represent the application or system that is under consideration. Moreover, a Business Context diagram is not necessarily an IT artifact.

Within the System Context, on the other hand, the IT System is brought into focus and relevance. The System Context leverages the Business Context to identify the external organizations. Once the organizational dependencies to build the IT System are identified, the System Context focuses on identifying the specific IT Systems and applications within each of the dependent organizations with which the IT System needs to interact and communicate. Upon its completion, a system-level view can be formed that represents the relevant external systems that need to be brought in scope of the overall solution. Hence, the System Context not only provides a breakdown of the Business Context but a traceability between Business Context constructs (for example, user community and organizations) and the System Context constructs (for example, user roles and systems within organizations) with the business context information. It is important to recognize that "external" does not necessarily imply systems that are outside the enterprise perimeter. Any entity (system or user) inside or outside the organization perimeter is considered external to the system under construction.

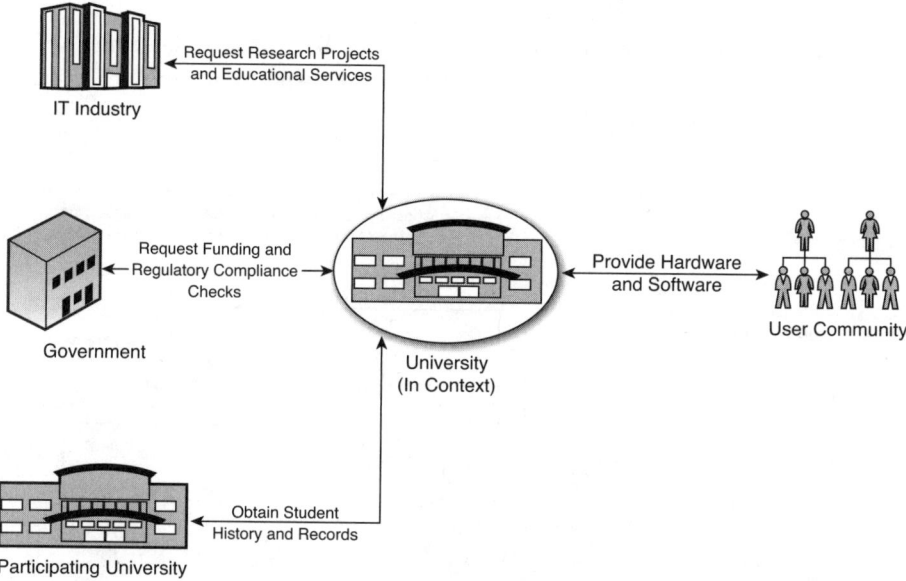

Figure 4.1   A sample Business Context diagram.

Capturing the System Context

As a practical software architect, you must focus on the work at hand. You must agree on, identify, and then analyze the essential artifacts that need to be captured for the System Context. Documenting your understanding of the System Context becomes your top priority.

The first and foremost task in capturing the System Context is to come up with a System Context diagram. The System Context diagram represents the system to be built as a black box (that is, its internal structure and design is hidden), depicts its interaction with external entities (systems and end users), and identifies the information and control flows between the system and the external entities. Keep in mind that external entities need not necessarily be systems that are outside the enterprise perimeter; an existing enterprise application or a database can very well be represented as an external entity in the System Context.

Two essential aspects of the system should be captured:

- The System Context diagram
- The information flows

You may certainly come up with a few more related aspects to capture, but then again, remember that as a practical software architect, you are focusing on *just enough*!

The following sections focus on artifacts to document and how much of them is enough to be captured; any artifact of relevance when documented may also be called a "work product."

The System Context Diagram

The best way to understand a System Context diagram is to take a look at an example. Figure 4.2 shows a sample System Context diagram for a fictitious banking solution; I chose banking because it is a commonly known entity.

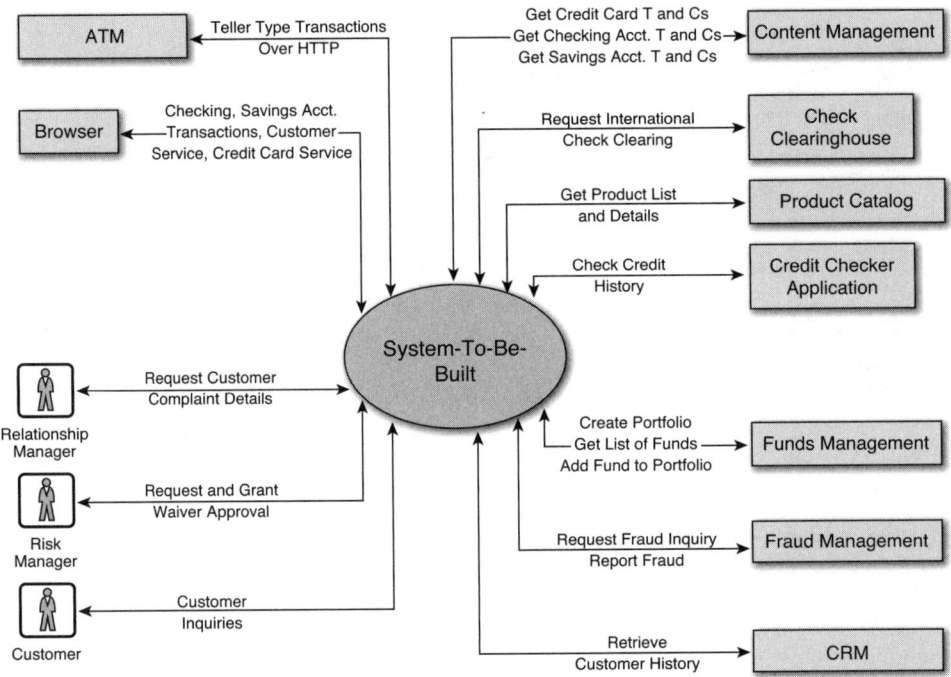

Figure 4.2   A sample System Context diagram.

The first category of artifacts is the users (or user profiles) that interact with the system through a set of delivery channels (end-user devices or applications through which users access the IT System). Although there is no hard and fast rule, a common practice in IT is to depict the users, roles, and channels on the left of the diagram. While you are documenting the System Context work product, the recommendation is to create a subsection, under the main section, where the details of the user roles or profiles and the delivery channels may be captured.

Users are usually categorized by the various roles they play in an organization; a set of characteristics and attributes defines their profile. In the real world, however, you may find that user roles and profiles are used interchangeably. In Figure 4.2, the Relationship Manager, Risk

Manager, and the Customer are three user roles. The documentation for each of the roles or profiles should have the following information:

- A description of the role and the context in which the users access the system
- A description of the various types of information that the users may request from the system
- The volume of transactions that a typical user, in a given role, would be performing in a given unit of time

The second category of artifacts is the different channels that are used for interaction between the users and the system. Similar to the user profiles, capturing the details of the delivery channels in a separate subsection is recommended. In Figure 4.2, the Browser and the ATM are two delivery channels. The minimum set of artifacts for the delivery channels may include

- A description of the channel along with the types of users who typically use it to interact with the system; for example, browsers, mobile devices, and so on
- The network and bandwidth supported by the channels; for example, T1 line, 802.11a/b/g, modems, and so on
- The access protocol used to send data to and receive it from the system; for example, HTTP, sockets, and so on

The third category of artifacts that must be documented is the external systems with which the IT System needs to interact to fulfill some of its functionality. Typically, a significant amount of analysis of requirements occurs, leading up to the identification of the external systems that need to be brought into the scope of the solution. The results of such analysis warrant sufficient documentation. Following a similar pattern, it is best to dedicate a separate subsection to the documentation of external systems. In Figure 4.2, Content Management, Check Clearinghouse, and all the other systems down to the CRM (that is, the "systems represented" side of the figure—to the right of the System-To-Be-Built) are the external systems. The documentation should minimally capture the following information:

- A descriptive overview of the external system, along with information regarding its proximity to the system to be built. For example, the external system may be inside the enterprise intranet, in the extranet as defined by the business, on the public Internet, or in a different organization's network.
- The access protocol required to interface with the external system; for example, secure HTTP, sockets, some proprietary access mechanism, and so on.
- The data formats supported or expected by the external system to facilitate integration.
- Any specific compliance requirements that need to be followed to interact with the external system.

- Nonfunctional specifications of the external system; for example, security, availability, information throughput, and so on. Note that you may not need to document all nonfunctional requirements of the external system. Document only those that may influence the architecture and design of the system that needs to be built.

When documented in a commensurate manner, the user profiles, the delivery channels, and the external system details should provide a good illustration of the System Context diagram. However, the information captured so far provides only a static view of the System Context: the user roles and profiles, the information delivery channels, and the external systems. To depict a complete view, the architect would need to understand both the static as well as a dynamic view of the System Context. Identifying and capturing the information that gets exchanged between the system and each of the external systems provides a dynamic view of the System Context. The next section on information flows focuses on addressing the dynamic view.

The Information Flows

Information is everything. Can we ever live without it? If we cannot, why would we deprive our System Context from it? One of the essential tenets of system characterization is defined by the information exchanged between the IT System and the external systems, users, and delivery channels. Information flow can be in batch mode (for example, bulk data transferred in periodic intervals) or in real time (for example, operational and process data as they are generated) or near real time (for example, transactions at a point of sales terminal [POST] in a popular grocery store). Documenting the information and its characteristics, as a part of the System Context, assumes paramount importance when you are defining the overall software architecture.

The information flow is typically represented by a short phrase that can take either a noun or a verb form. Choosing a noun or a verb form is a matter of preference, but whichever you choose, stick with it! I happen to choose the verb form (for example, the Request International Check Clearing information flow between the System-To-Be-Built and the Check Clearinghouse external system in Figure 4.2), but then again, that is a matter of personal choice. Exercise your free will, and choose what you want!

For each information flow, the following minimal set of artifacts may be captured:

- A description of the information that is flowing between the system and the users, the delivery channels, and the external systems
- Classifying the information flow as either batch, real time, or near real time
- The number of transactions that need to be supported per unit of time
- The type of data that constitutes a typical information flow
- The volume of data transferred in each information flow
- The frequency in which each information flow is executed

The artifacts mentioned here do not address the sequence of the interactions between the system and the external entities. When a chain of information flows between two systems, the information flow may also need to document such sequence of interactions.

It's important to capture the information flow. The reasons that naturally come to mind and are worth noting are as follows:

- The information flow identifies a set of important information entities that will influence the final information model for the software that is going to be built.

- The data formats supported by the external system can be understood by analyzing the information elements. For example, for systems outside the enterprise perimeter, the data format is, more often than not, different from the format that is prescribed to be supported by the IT System. This leads to the identification of data transformation requirements between the two interacting systems.

- The access protocol (network and data) that is used and supported by the external system may be different from the protocol that is agreed upon to be supported by the IT System. The protocol disparity raises technology requirements for application integration. The requirements are usually addressed by the choice of technology adapters. A technology adapter usually normalizes the data format and access protocol differences between the external systems and the IT System. The choice of technology adapters is an important facet of an integration architecture that supports the system that is envisioned to be architected, designed, built, and rolled out.

- The data, protocol, and network adapters are essential recipes that go in the definition of the architecture overview of the system or application. In effect, the heterogeneity of the external systems influences multiple layers of the architecture. (Architecture Overview is covered in the next chapter.)

Business process modeling is a top-down approach to requirements gathering; it is used to analyze and understand the business processes that are in the scope of the business or IT transformation initiative. Process breakdown identifies a set of subprocesses, activities, or tasks that constitute a larger business process. Some of the activities or tasks require interaction or integration with external systems, typically in the form of data dependencies between one system and the other. Such activities can be traced back to one or more information flow definitions that are defined as a part of the portfolio of information flows. This provides a key traceability between the system requirements and their implementation dependency on external systems; such traceability is a fundamental tenet of an efficient and well-organized software development life cycle.

The System Context diagram and its associated information flows, when appropriately captured, provide *just enough* information for the software architect to start formulating the application architecture.

Case Study: System Context for Elixir

Having developed a good understanding of the areas to address and the artifacts to generate, you should have a template in your head to start capturing the System Context for any system that you are tasked to build.

For our case study, we are trying to architect, design, and build a system for Best West Manufacturers, Inc. The IT System is code-named Elixir. Using the artifacts described in the preceding sections, let's develop the System Context for Elixir.

Elixir: System Context Diagram

Figure 4.3 depicts the System Context diagram for Elixir. It follows the guidelines stated earlier in this chapter and dedicates separate subsections describing the user profiles, delivery channels, and external systems.

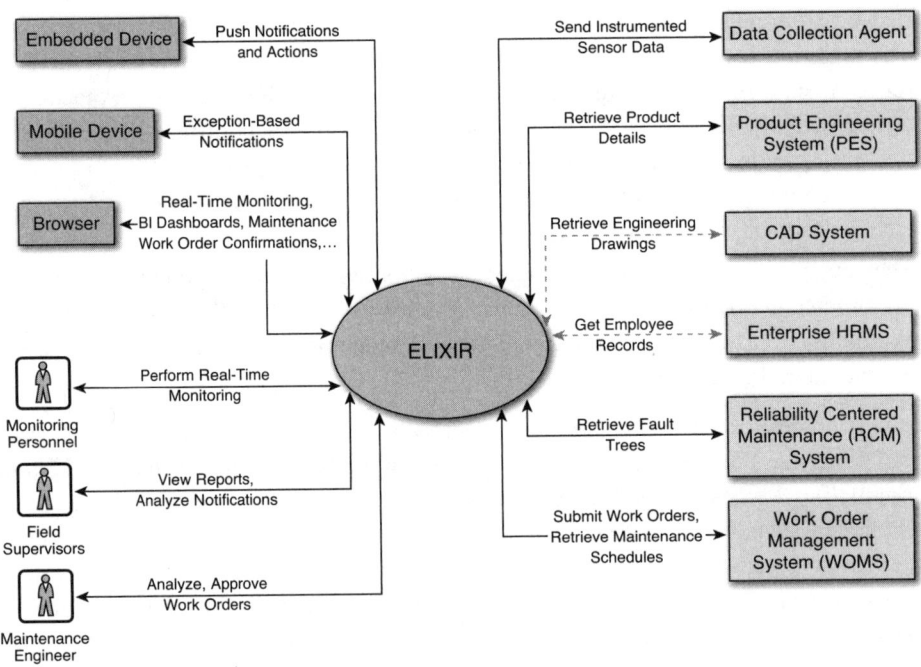

Figure 4.3   The System Context diagram for Elixir.

Elixir: User Profiles

Table 4.1 captures the details for a subset of the user profiles for Elixir. The table has four columns: the name of the user profile or role, a description of the role played by the user profile and how the user accesses the system (Elixir, in this case), the information requested by the user profile from the system, and the frequency (along with the volume of information in each request) in which such information requests are made.

Table 4.1   User Profile Details for the System Context Diagram of the Elixir System

User Profile	Description and Context	Requested Information	Frequency and Volume
Monitoring Personnel	Responsible for monitoring the performance of the machines. Has the ability to identify potential problems, diagnose and analyze the root cause, and take appropriate actions. This user role typically uses either a mobile device while in the field or a browser to access the system from any designated monitoring center.	View one or more of the visual dashboards that contain information around the real-time data for each machine and the performance of the machines against the predefined key performance indicators (KPI).	Information update every second for any machine of interest. Request may span multiple simultaneous machines up to five at one time. Up to 50 concurrent users accessing the system.

For the sake of readability, I have purposefully refrained from continuing with the table format to capture the complete set of user profile information. In the real world, Table 4.1, appropriately filled in, reads perfectly well in a document format such as Microsoft Word.

The rest of the user profile details for the System Context diagram for Elixir are as follows:

User Profile Name—Field Supervisor

Description and Context—Responsible for analyzing the system's output related to machine-related exception conditions. The user will get a set of notifications based on exceptions; that is, possible machine conditions that may require attention.

Requested Information—The user requests the system to display the list of machine-related exceptions along with any supporting data (for example, KPI) that she may use to gain more insights into the machine conditions before taking subsequent action.

Frequency and Volume—There could be up to 20 concurrent field supervisors at any given time. The typical user would request to view up to 5 key performance indicators (KPI) at any time. Each KPI data packet may vary anywhere between 250KB to 500KB.

User Profile Name—Maintenance Engineer

Description and Context—Responsible for analyzing maintenance recommendations suggested by the Elixir system. The user is usually notified of outstanding maintenance recommendations in the form of action items in his workbasket. The user analyzes each recommendation in relation to its criticality and the machine's upcoming maintenance schedule before eventually deciding whether a maintenance order may be dispatched right away or to defer taking action on the system-generated recommendation to the next scheduled maintenance window.

Requested Information—The user requests the system to provide (that is, display) further details regarding the exception conditions that led to the recommendation. The exception details are displayed in the form of a single or composite KPI against which the appropriate business rules were triggered. From the KPI charts, the user can request further details by drilling down to the raw machine data (for example, current, voltage, pressure, temperature, and any relevant values that enable the maintenance engineer to perform additional diagnosis). If, however, the notification was based on a prediction of a future event, instead of an actual occurrence, the user requests the details behind the reason a prediction was made. For example, output of a predictive model stated, with a confidence level of 80 percent, that a specific machine part is predicted to fail in the next 12 hours.

Frequency and Volume—There could be at most 15 concurrent maintenance engineers accessing the system at any given time. The typical user would request to view up to 10 key performance indicators (KPI) at any time. Each KPI data packet may vary anywhere between 250KB to 500KB.

Elixir: Delivery Channels

Table 4.2 captures the details of the delivery channels for Elixir. The delivery channel information, as described earlier in the chapter, focuses on capturing the name of the channel, a brief description of the channel, the type of network used by the delivery channel, and the access protocol used by the network.

Elixir: External Systems

The Elixir system interfaces and exchanges data with six external systems: the Data Collection Agent, Product Engineering System, CAD System, Enterprise HRMS, Reliability Centered Maintenance System, and Work Order Management System. Table 4.3 captures the details of these external systems; specifically the name of the system, a brief description of the system, details about information exchange, and the nonfunctional requirements that are supported by the system.

Table 4.2 Details of Delivery Channels for the System Context Diagram of the Elixir System

Channel	Description	Network	Access Protocol
Browser	A thin client on the user's laptop or desktop machine. Supports Firefox V25.x and above, Internet Explorer V8.x and above, and Google Chrome V30.x and above.	Dedicated quarter T1 leased line. Supports up to 2Gbps of download speed.	HTTPS
Mobile Device	Any thin client on the user's mobile device. Supports iPad V1.x and V2.x, Android tablets version 4.2.x, and Windows 8 tablets.	Wi-Fi network 802.11 a/b/g. Supports up to 100Mbps of download speed.	HTTP
Embedded Device	A touchscreen display on the machine.		HTTP

Table 4.3 Details of the External Systems for the System Context Diagram of the Elixir System

System Name	Description	Data Format and Access Protocol	Nonfunctional Requirements
Data Collection Agent	A software system that is colocated or located in close proximity to the actual instrumented machines. The system collects the data from the sensors on the machine and packages them into a data format expected by the Elixir system before dispatching the data for consumption. The data is encrypted based on the proprietary encryption algorithm.	Each data packet transferred to Elixir contains a string of name-value pairs, with each pair encapsulating the last captured value for a named sensor data variable. Can send data through HTTP, HTTPS, sockets, secure sockets, and MQ protocols.	Security—Supports HTTPS and secure sockets. Availability—The system is available 99.5 percent of the time. For the time it is unavailable, it caches or buffers the captured data. Throughput—Capable of capturing data in subsecond intervals and also dispatching data every second at a rate not exceeding 1Mbps per machine and up to 10 machines concurrently.
Product Engineering System (PES)	An enterprise system that stores all engineering details and information regarding every product that is manufactured.	Data is stored in relational form. Supports standard SQL interfaces to access the data.	Security—Only systems behind the corporate firewall have access. Availability—The system is not available for four hours in every two weeks. The downtime is planned in advance.

System Name	Description	Data Format and Access Protocol	Nonfunctional Requirements
CAD System	A software package that stores the various engineering (CAD) drawings for the as-designed heavy equipment machines.	Data, which is primarily engineering drawings, are stored in a file-based vector format. Data is accessed through a standards-based data exchange format. *Note*: The current implementation of Elixir does not involve any integration with the CAD system and hence further analysis and details are deferred.	Security—Only systems behind the corporate firewall have access. Availability—The system has a planned monthly outage that lasts anywhere between four to eight hours.
Enterprise HRMS	An enterprise system, based on a packaged application, that supports the company's human resource management. It provides detailed information about each employee—personal details, professional development details, among other relevant HR-related information.	Published API provides access to the data. The APIs can be programmatically accessed through the Java™ programming language. *Note*: The current implementation of Elixir does not involve any integration with the CAD system and hence further analysis and details are deferred.	Security—The system is accessible by any user who has enterprise single sign-on credentials. Throughput—All published APIs are guaranteed to return responses within one second for invocations from within the same WLAN or VLAN.
Reliability Centered Maintenance (RCM) System	An enterprise system that stores the maintenance strategy and the assets (in this case, the heavy equipment). It also stores various failure risk analysis techniques for each family of assets.	Although RCM contains a multitude of data types, the only data that is of interest to the solution is failure model analysis (a.k.a. FMEA) data. This data is available as FMEA records and can be extracted using SQL queries.	Security—Only systems behind the corporate firewall have access. Availability—The system has a planned monthly outage. The data will be initially bulk loaded into the system and then periodically updated once a month.

System Name	Description	Data Format and Access Protocol	Nonfunctional Requirements
Work Order Management System (WOMS)	An enterprise system, based on a packaged application, that tracks, manages, and optimizes asset performance, maintenance schedules, and work orders.	Published API provides access to the data. The APIs are compliant to the MIMOSA (n.d.) industry standard.	Security—The system is accessible to any user who has enterprise single sign-on credentials. Availability—99.5 percent uptime. Throughput—Same as that of the RCM System.

Elixir: Information Flows

For the sake of brevity, I have consciously captured only those information flows that occur between Elixir and the four (out of the six) external systems (see Figure 4.3). This is because neither the Enterprise HRMS System nor the CAD System was in the scope of the first release of Elixir. The intent, however, is to capture as much detail of all the information flows as is available at this phase of the architecture definition process (see Table 4.4).

Table 4.4 Details of the Information Flows for the System Context Diagram of the Elixir System

Information Flow	Description	Type	Transaction Details
Send Instrumented Data	Dispatch the formatted and consolidated instrumented data to any data consumer. The Elixir system is the subscribed consumer.	Real time	Up to 50 transactions per second. Each transaction can carry up to 50KB of data.
Retrieve Product Details	Invoked by the Elixir system on the PES System. Retrieves the details of a given class of equipment or machines by using the unique equipment class identifier.	Request-Response	Infrequent usage. Mainly invoked when new machine types are on-boarded on to Elixir. Each transaction can carry up to 500KB of data.
Retrieve Fault Trees	Invoked by the Elixir system on the RCM System. Retrieves the various failure conditions and their related root causes; that is, the fault trees associated with failures.	Batch	Retrieved in a batch mode. After initial load, it is refreshed once a month. Each transaction can carry up to 10Mb of data.

Information Flow	Description	Type	Transaction Details
Submit Work Orders	Invoked by the Elixir system on the WOMS System. Submit Work Orders is invoked whenever Elixir determines that a maintenance work order is required on any equipment.	Request-Response (for Submit Work Orders)	Submit Work Orders is invoked between 10–50 times in a month.
Retrieve Maintenance Schedules	Retrieve Maintenance Schedules is invoked to periodically refresh the equipment-specific maintenance schedules that it may require for optimizing its recommendations.	Batch (for Retrieve Maintenance Schedules)	Retrieve Maintenance Schedules is invoked once a month for every equipment that is on-boarded into Elixir.

Note that the information flows between Elixir and the Enterprise HRMS System and the CAD System are not shown in Table 4.4. This is because neither of the two external systems is in the scope of the first release of Elixir.

Elixir now has a System Context. The complete artifact documentation may be much more elaborate than what we captured, however.

Summary

This chapter focused on our first real software architecture artifact—the System Context. I articulated the distinction between the Business Context and the System Context and also provided some clues on how they may be related.

The primary emphasis of this chapter was on the System Context artifact and the elements that define and characterize it. The System Context diagram is the first of the two main artifacts of the System Context that I recommend to be captured. The *System Context diagram* is composed of the user profiles, the delivery channels, and the external systems with which the IT System interacts and interfaces. The second main artifact is the *information flows* between the external systems and the IT System.

An appropriate level of analysis must be conducted to determine the *just enough* amount of details, which is commensurate in providing a firm contextual setting based on which the software architecture will be defined.

As an exercise, you can now develop a documentation template to capture the essential artifacts of the System Context. Elixir has a System Context that will form the basis of defining its software architecture. The stage is now set for you to define the software architecture!

References

MIMOSA. (n.d.). The MIMOSA specifications. Retrieved from http://www.mimosa.org/.

Mitra, Tilak. (2008, May 13). Documenting the software architecture, Part 2: Develop the system context. Retrieved from http://www.ibm.com/developerworks/library/ar-archdoc2/.

CHAPTER 5

The Architecture Overview

The building is a marvel—its architecture immortal!

The preceding chapter covered the essence of the system context. The system to be built—that is, the IT System—has been a black box until now, and we have been carefully walking around its edges. In this chapter, we take our first bold step in opening up the black box and peek into it for a good look! Specifically, we will put on our view lens to glimpse a set of complementary views of the system's architecture.

The architecture of any system can be rendered through multiple viewpoints, or views. Although each view has a specific value statement, my intent is to focus only on those views of the architecture that are just enough for the solution architect to effectively communicate the solution architecture with the intended stakeholders. (I use the terms "solution architect," "software architect," and "enterprise architect" interchangeably in this book; they refer to the same general role, that of the overall architect for a complex system.)

This chapter introduces three essential views of the systems architecture under consideration: namely, the Enterprise view, the Layered view, and the IT System view. These three views collectively provide a high level overview of the system's architecture. It is important to note that the architecture overview is the first step into the internals of the system. As such, the first treatment of it is conceptual in nature—that is, a technology agnostic overview—for all three views. A technology agnostic view implies that the architecture artifacts, at this stage, are not influenced by the software and middleware products.

The chapter concludes by instantiating the architecture overview for the case study of the Elixir system.

What It Is

The architecture overview is represented by a set of schematic diagrams through which a set of governing ideas and candidate building blocks of an IT System's architecture are described.

It provides an overview of the main conceptual elements (for example, candidate subsystems, components, nodes, connections, data stores, users, external systems among others) and their interrelationships in the architecture. Because the building blocks are conceptual in nature, they are technology agnostic; this is the reason the collection of views is also sometimes called the conceptual architecture of the IT System.

If we go back to first principles and acknowledge the essence of simplicity in support of effective communication, it is more important for the architecture overview diagram to be simple, brief, clear, and understandable than comprehensive or explicit in all its details. Consequently, such diagrams typically use an informal free-form diagrammatic notation, although a current breed of architecture tools provides annotated widgets in an effort to standardize and formalize. Regardless, the schematic diagrams are typically elaborated through supporting text that explains the main concepts of the architecture.

The three types of architecture diagrams are

- The Enterprise view
- The Layered view
- The IT System view

When alternative architectural solutions are being explored, an architecture overview diagram may be produced for each option to enable various stakeholders to discuss the trade-offs between the options.

The Enterprise view of the architecture is often produced as part of an overall IT strategy. It may be used to describe the IT capabilities required by the organization in support of its business objectives vis-a-vis the system or application under consideration that is to be built. It provides an overview of the main conceptual elements (a.k.a. ABBs): components, nodes, connections, data stores, users, external systems, and a definition of the key characteristics and requirements that each of them are expected to meet. The diagram also provides an early view of the placement of the ABBs into conceptual architecture layers. The view is fairly static in nature, which is to say that the interrelationships between the ABBs are not highlighted.

The Layered view focuses on developing a set of architecture layers; each layer is defined by a set of characteristics that determine the placement of the ABBs in one of the many layers. A layered architecture follows a set of guidelines for communication and information exchange between the ABBs. Adherence to the guidelines fosters a good integration strategy prescribing interdependencies, linkages, and communication paths between the ABBs.

The IT System view introduces dynamism into the system by further elaborating (in the form of data flow) on the interrelationships between the ABBs. As such, it influences the inception of the functional and operational models (the topics of Chapter 7, "The Functional Model," and Chapter 8, "The Operational Model").

The architecture overview establishes a big picture view of the system in which the architecture components play the role of the foundational building blocks, the ABBs. It helps formulate some architecture principles and guidelines around how the components may collectively coexist and cooperate to realize architecturally significant use cases. Although some architectural decisions (the topic of the next chapter) may start getting identified as challenges that need to be addressed, the architecture overview is not the step in which I suggest design commitments are formalized. Such commitments are timelier after the functional and operational models (see Chapters 7 and 8) are established.

It is important to understand and acknowledge that the development of the architecture of any system is an iterative process. Recognize that the functional model and the operational model are the primary models. Also, be aware that their establishment and formalization may require you to revisit and revise the architecture overview diagrams if changes are made to the main concepts and relationships.

ARCHITECTURE DOMAINS: THE TOGAF WAY

The Open Group Architecture Framework (TOGAF) (The Open Group n.d.) recognizes that the scope and concerns that architecture has to deal with in any software system are broad. Therefore, it categorizes the architecture definition into the following four domains:

- **Business Architecture**—A description of the structure and interaction between the business strategy, organizations, functions, business processes, and information needs.

- **Application Architecture**—A description of the structure and interaction of applications as groups of capabilities that provide key business functions and manage the data assets.

- **Data/Information Architecture**—A description of the structure and interaction of the enterprise's major types and sources of data, logical data assets, physical data assets, and data management resources.

- **Technical Architecture**—A description of the structure and interaction of the platform services, and logical and physical technology components.

Why We Need It

The architecture overview, primarily represented as a set of diagrams each with a specific focus, is an important artifact (a.k.a. work product). The importance of capturing the architecture overview can be attributed to, but not limited to, the following reasons:

- It serves as a foundation aspect of the system's architecture and is used as a guide for the more elaborate and detailed functional and operational architectures of the solution.

- It is used to communicate a conceptual understanding of the architecture of the evolving solution to the stakeholders.

- It is leveraged as a mechanism to evaluate different architecture options to solving a particular class of problems.

- It is used to capture the Enterprise and the System views of the architecture in a single consolidated artifact.

- It supports the orientation of new technical team members joining the project.

Put simply, the absence of this construct deprives the software development team of envisioning the "big picture." The overview is often used not only to identify and remediate architecture problems early on but also to take a step back, when stuck with a problem, and recognize the guiding principles and patterns that may assist in a constraint-based problem solving process.

The key takeaway for you is to acknowledge the importance of the architecture overview construct so that you are convinced to apportion commensurate time and effort in its development and documentation.

The Enterprise View

Before elaborating on the enterprise architecture view, let's discuss why this view is important to capture.

The target operating model for any organization or enterprise can be categorized into one of these three: operational excellence, product leadership, or customer intimacy. Businesses typically focus on one of the three models to differentiate itself from the competition. An operating model, in turn, is made up of operating (a.k.a. business) processes, business structure, management structure, and culture, all of which are synchronized to foster value generation. From an IT standpoint, the three business operating models can be broadly mapped to four IT-level operating models:

- **Diversification**—With low standardization and low integration requirements

- **Coordination**—With low standardization but high integration focus

- **Replication**—With high standardization but low integration focus

- **Unification**—With high standardization and high integration imperatives

For more information on IT operating models, see Weill and Ross (2004) and Treacy and Wiersema (1997).

The discussion on business and IT operating models here may seem to be a bit out of context when actually it is not. I have found this knowledge to be helpful when interrogating an architect on the rationale for an enterprise-level architecture view and how it is related to the organizational imperatives per se. To be able to talk the talk on business-to-IT alignment is certainly a skill an architect should seek to have in her repertoire.

Enterprise architecture provides a mechanism to identify and represent—in a single unified view—the business processes, data and information sources, technologies, customer-facing user interfaces, and delivery channels that take the operating model from vision to reality. The Enterprise view, which is the enterprise architecture viewpoint, is the single architecture diagram that communicates the enterprise's core business processes along with the application and infrastructure building blocks that foster their realization. The diagram is typically and intentionally represented at a high level and does not drill down into detailed elaborations of the application, data, technology, or business process architectures. However, this single view becomes the starting point, in subsequent treatments, for further detailed elaboration of the artifacts.

Now let's look at a real-world Enterprise view diagram so that we can understand each artifact and how to appropriately capture them. Figure 5.1 depicts a simple one-page diagram of the high-level business processes, technology enablers, data and information, delivery channels, and types of users. Collectively, they represent the Enterprise architecture view of a typical banking system. (I again chose a banking system for illustration, owing to our familiarity with money matters.)

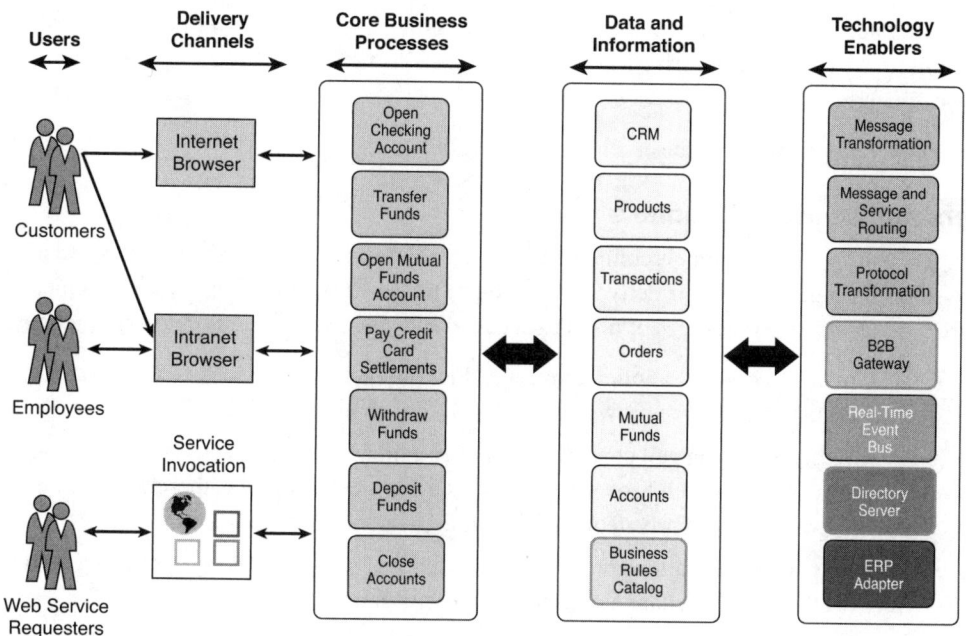

Figure 5.1   Sample Enterprise view diagram from an illustrative banking example.

It is important to justify the rationale for the inclusion of each conceptual element in the Enterprise view. The justification is typically illustrated in textual form. The rest of the section elaborates a systematic approach to capturing the architecture components, using the Enterprise view in Figure 5.1 as an example.

While taking the elevator up to the company cafeteria, for instance, you may get questioned by a colleague: "So how do you read and interpret the enterprise-level view of the systems architecture?" You have to keep your explanation simple lest you lose his attention due to the smell of hot food getting stronger and stronger. So here is a one-minute elevator speech that you may use:

> The Enterprise view categorizes the systems and functions required to build the IT System while depicting the general direction of information flow. Various types of *users* interact with the IT System through a variety of *delivery channels* through which the system functions are made accessible. The system functions are typically implemented as a set of *core business processes. Data and information* are critical to the realization of the business processes; they typically reside in either one or more enterprise information systems or in some system that is external to the enterprise; some of the data is required as inputs to the process steps, while some information is generated by some of the process steps. A set of *technology enablers* is required to interface with the enterprise information systems to facilitate data and information exchange.

Let's now focus on capturing the essential information.

Users and Delivery Channels

The Users and Delivery Channels component artifacts represent the different user roles that access the system through a variety of delivery channels. The illustrative banking system, depicted in Figure 5.1, allows different types of users to access the system over various delivery channels:

- Customers access the applications over the Internet (and in some special cases, the intranet) using their web browsers as the delivery channel.
- Employees, including call center personnel or administrators, access the system over the intranet using their web browsers. These users could also access these applications via their corporate virtual private network (not depicted in the figure).
- External partners are allowed to access a functional subset of the system using web services (as the delivery channel) based service invocations.

Users access a certain subset of functions through one or more delivery channels. The available feature functions may vary between the delivery channels and may also be delivered through different presentation styles that are appropriate for the delivery channel. As an example, employees may be able to access additional functions that customers cannot. Customers may be able to access all functions on both their desktops as well as their mobile devices, whereas employees may have to access the more mundane administrative functions only via the desktop version of the application.

Core Business Processes

The Core Business Process component artifacts represent the set of core business processes that are supported (that is, implemented) by the IT System. The business processes may be traced back to the operating processes of the business operating model. The *core* highlights those operating processes that are identified either for enhancements or for increased automation and are hence significant from an architectural standpoint. Figure 5.1 highlights the critical business processes supported by the representative banking system:

- **Open Checking Account**—Provides the ability to open a checking account for the customer; the process is expected to be completed in less than 10 minutes. The process can be invoked not only at the branch office through a teller counter but also through a self-service online banking portal.

- **Transfer Funds**—Provides the ability to transfer funds from one account type to another within the bank. It also provides the ability to transfer funds between international bank accounts requiring a transaction fee; the process is expected to complete in no more than one business day.

- **Open Mutual Funds Account**—Provides customers and employees (henceforth called *account holders*) the ability to open a mutual fund account with the bank, thereby allowing the account holders to access the bank's most trusted and highest performing funds. The feature also allows the account holders to seamlessly link the account with a checking account and provides up to 40 free transactions per month.

- **Pay Credit Cards Settlement**—Provides customers with the ability to settle credit card payments online. The process is made simpler by providing direct debit from a checking account with overdraft protection to facilitate seamless and hassle-free credit card payments.

The rest of the business processes should also be similarly described and captured at a high level, thereby providing an overview of how the core processes assist the bank in excelling in the operating model that it has chosen for competitive differentiation.

For the sake of brevity, I will not describe all the business processes in Figure 5.1; I will exercise the same liberty while describing the rest of the Enterprise view artifacts.

Data and Information

The Data and Information component artifacts represent the core conceptual data entities and information sources that are required to realize the core set of business processes. For the illustrative banking system, the following data entities and information sources realize and support the core business processes:

- **CRM**—In the customer relationship management system, the customer entity, her demographic information, the number of subscribed banking products, and her account standing, are key business entities that are required to realize the core set of business processes.

- **Products**—This represents the various products that the bank offers to its customers and employees. Examples of products are checking accounts, savings accounts, mutual funds, credit cards, and so on.

- **Orders**—This represents the orders that bank customers place. Orders can be payments, mutual fund transactions, funds transfers, and so on.

- **Business Rules Catalog**—A collection of business rules is used to realize the various implementations of the business processes. Each business rule uses information elements and enforces certain conditional logic upon them. The rules can be represented in natural language and can be modified by business users. Listing 5.1 gives an example of a rule.

Listing 5.1 Business Rule Example

```
If mutual_fund_transaction_number is <= 40 then transaction_fee_flag =
"false"
```

The rest of the information and data entities should be similarly documented.

Technology Enablers

The Technology Enablers component artifacts represent, conceptually, a set of integration components that facilitate data retrieval and storage (a.k.a. persistence) required to implement the core set of business processes. These components provide technology adapters to interface with the systems or record so as to facilitate information exchange through protocol transformation, mediation, and efficient routing of information. For the illustrative banking system, the following technology enablers were identified:

- **Message Transformation**—Facilitates information exchange between heterogeneous systems. This enabler transforms message packets, which are units of information exchange, from one data format (for example, supported by the system of record) to another (for example, as expected by the business process step). It is typically used to standardize on a message format that may be used to implement the core business processes of the IT System. Optionally, it may also help in transforming messages from a standard format to one that an invoking client system may expect or support.

- **Message and Service Routing**—Supports basic and advanced message and service routing capabilities. Also supports the intelligence to find the correct service provider for a given service request and appropriately route the service request.

- **Real-Time Event Bus**—Provides basic and advanced capabilities supporting simple and complex event processing. This enabler facilitates the processing of asynchronous business and system events and may also optionally leverage the message transformation and routing capabilities for event dispatch and processing.

- **Directory Server**—Stores and manages the user profiles that are needed to validate user credentials to perform authentication and authorization for role-based access to the IT System.

- **B2B Gateway**—Facilitates the receipt of requests from third-party external systems, typically through service invocations. The role of the gateway is to provide a focal point for handling both incoming and outgoing requests. For incoming requests, originating from external entities, it determines the right supporting service before invoking the service and generating the response. For outgoing requests, the gateway is responsible for locating the external service, creating the service request, and subsequently invoking the service.

The remaining middleware components should also be captured at least at a similar level of elaboration.

UPGRADING THE ENTERPRISE VIEW

Service-oriented architecture (SOA) has been around long enough and with enough merits to be accepted as a well-proven architecture paradigm. As such, it is quite common to see some of the SOA constructs, specifically the enterprise business services, in the Enterprise view of the architecture. Enterprises that have embraced SOA and have mature SOA-based enterprise architecture have now started exposing and offering their enterprise service portfolio as a part of their enterprise architecture. Hence, you may see that a set of enterprise services has been represented along with a list of core business processes.

In general, as and when enterprise architecture, as a discipline, matures over time, you may see different architecture artifacts making their way into the Enterprise architecture view. In its current state, the reusable architecture constructs (for example, Message Transformation, Message and Service Routing, Protocol Transformation, B2B Gateway, Real-Time Event Bus, Directory Server, Business Rules Catalog) represented in Figure 5.1 are basic, foundational, and common enough to constitute an enterprise-level view of the architecture.

The Layered View

The Layered view of the systems architecture focuses on the placement of the architecture building blocks into a set of architecture layers. Layers are stacked vertically with a notion of layers *above* and *below*. A layer is a logical construct that is characterized by a specific type of capability and characteristic and hence is expected to host similar types of architecture components or building blocks. For example, a presentation layer supports the visualization and user interface features and functions of a given system or application. It contains a set of architecture components that collectively realize the system's user interface and also define how the components in the layer interact with components in other layers to fulfill the desired functionality.

A standard and well-accepted guiding principle determines the placement of components in layers: components in any given layer may interact only with components that are in lower layers in the Layered view of the architecture. A layered architecture fosters modular design; the interlayer dependencies minimize tight coupling in the architecture.

I want to highlight some of the advantages of a Layered view, while making no claim that they are exhaustive. Let me remind you of the recurring theme of this book: *understand just enough to convince yourself of its importance and capture just enough to allow effective communication to all involved stakeholders!* So here are a few reasons for developing a Layered view:

- **Provides an exposition mechanism**—Other applications and systems can use the functionality exposed by the various layers of the IT System.

- **Fosters modular testing of the system**—Test cases can be developed and executed on a per layer basis with normative guidance on the nonfunctional requirements (NFR) that are expected to be met.

- **Fosters best design practices**—Through the enforcement of low coupling (between layers) and high functional cohesion (within the components in each layer), optimal designs can be achieved.

- **Streamlines systems development**—Design and implementation skill sets can be aligned to the technology requirements of each layer.

- **Enforces interlayer communication**—Components, other than communicating with other components in the same layer, can only communicate with components that are in lower layers.

- **Supports nonfunctional requirements**—Components in a layer that are susceptible to high workloads can be distributed into multiple physical servers (tiers), driving standardization of the operational topology of the deployed IT System. (For more details on operational modeling, see Chapter 8.)

Figure 5.2 shows a typical Layered architecture view. I leave it as an exercise for you to determine the placement of the architecture components from the Enterprise view (Figure 5.1) into the Layered architecture view. This section provides a good overview of the various layers in a layered architecture model...just about! You may need to consult a dedicated book on SOA if you are serious about the homework assignment. In that case, see *Executing SOA: A Practical Guide for the Service-Oriented Architect* (Bieberstein, Laird, Jones, & Mitra 2008).

The Layered architecture view in Figure 5.2 introduces a set of commonly used architecture layers of any non-trivial IT System. I recommend this view because it addresses any architecture regardless of whether it is SOA based or non-SOA based. If it is the latter, the Services layer would not be required, whereas the Service Components layer may be replaced by a Components layer. Voilà, you get two in one!

In the following sections, I share definitions of each layer. The intent is not only to provide an understanding and appreciation for each of the layers but also to assist in determining the placement of the architecture components, or architecture building blocks (ABB), into the appropriate layers. Henceforth, I use the terms *architecture components* and *ABBs* interchangeably as they mean the same construct.

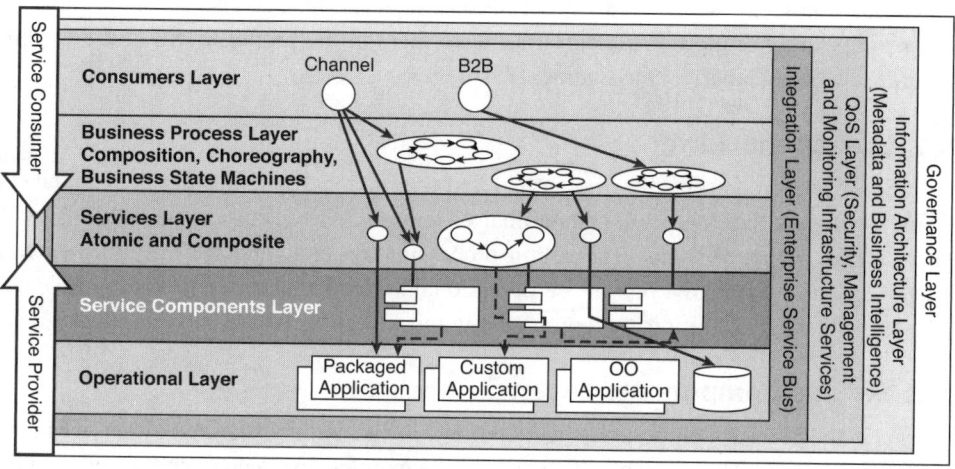

Figure 5.2   A Layered view of an architecture.

Figure 5.2 depicts a nine-layered architecture with five horizontal layers and four vertical layers. The horizontal layers—Operational, Service Components, Services, Business Processes, and Consumers—follow the basic principle of a layered architecture model in which ABBs from layers above can only access ABBs from layers below, and not vice versa. The vertical layers—Integration, QoS, Information Architecture, and Governance—usually contain ABBs that are cross-cutting in nature; cross-cutting implies that the ABBs in this layer may be applicable to and used by ABBs in one or more of the horizontal layers. Some architecture schools may look at the Layered view and opine that it is a partial layered architecture, their rationale being that any layer above does not need to strictly interact with elements from its immediate lower layer. For example, a specific access channel may directly access a service rather than needing to go through a business process. So if you come across students from such a school of thought, relax, take a deep breath, and accept them as your friends, because they are also correct! Just remember that the access constraints between components in layers are dictated by the architectural style, guidelines, and principles that are applicable for a solution.

SOA Reference Architecture (View)

This view of the SOA reference architecture, shown in Figure 5.2, was originally developed by IBM. It is independent of any specific technology, and hence, it is a conceptual, or logical, view. Instances of this logical architecture can be developed for a specific platform and technology.

The following sections provide short definitions for each of the layers. The definitions will help you identify architecture components and place them in the proper layers in the Layered architecture view. Remember your assignment?

Layer 1: Operational Layer

The Operational layer represents the operational and transactional systems that exist in the current IT environment of the enterprise. Operational systems include all custom applications, packaged applications, legacy systems, transaction processing systems, and various other external databases or systems. Typically, only those operational systems that are required to implement the IT System under consideration are represented in this layer.

Layer 2: Service Components Layer

Components in the Service Components layer conform to the contracts defined by services in the Services layer (Layer 3). There is typically a one-to-one mapping between a service and a service component. A service component provides an implementation facade that aggregates functionality from multiple, possibly disparate, operational systems while hiding the integration and access complexities from the service that is exposed to the consumer of the service.

Layer 3: Services Layer

The Services layer includes all the services that are defined in the enterprise service portfolio. The definition of each service (which is both its syntactic and semantic information) is defined in this layer. The syntactic information is essentially the description and definition of the operations on each service, its input and output messages, along with the service faults. The semantic information describes the service policies, service management decisions, service access requirements, service-level agreements, terms of service usage, service availability constraints, and other related and relevant details.

Layer 4: Business Process Layer

Business processes depict how the business operates. A business process is an IT representation of the various activities that are coordinated and collaborated in an enterprise to perform a specific high-level business function. The Business Process layer represents the processes as an orchestration or a composition of loosely coupled services that are available in the Services layer. This layer is also responsible for the entire life-cycle management of the process orchestration and choreography. Processes represented in this layer represent the physical realization of the business processes facilitated by the orchestration of ABBs from other horizontal and vertical layers in the architecture stack. Components in the Consumers layer typically invoke the ABBs in this layer to consume application functionality.

Layer 5: Consumers Layer

The Consumers layer depicts the various delivery channels through which the system functions are delivered to the different user personas. Mobile devices, desktop client applications, and thin browser clients are some of the delivery channels through which user interface applications such as native mobile applications and portals are delivered.

Layer 6: Integration Layer

The Integration layer provides the capability for service consumers to locate business, IT, and data service providers and initiate service invocations. Through the three basic capabilities of mediation, routing, and data and protocol transformation, this layer helps foster a service eco-system in which services can communicate and collaborate with each other to realize (that is, implement) business processes or a subset (that is, a step in a process) thereof. Components in this layer need to consider the key nonfunctional requirements such as security, latency, and quality of service as they try to integrate heterogeneous, disparate, and distributed systems. The functions of this layer are increasingly being collectively defined and referred to as the Enterprise Service Bus (ESB).

Layer 7: QoS Layer

The Quality of Service (QoS) layer focuses on implementing, monitoring, and managing the nonfunctional requirements that the services and components need to support, thereby providing the infrastructure capabilities to realize the NFRs. It also captures the data elements that provide the information around noncompliance to NFRs, primarily at each of the horizontal layers. The most common NFRs that it monitors for compliance are security, availability, performance, scalability, and reliability.

Layer 8: Information Architecture Layer

The Information Architecture layer ensures a proper representation of the data and information that is required to support the services and business processes of the IT System. The data architecture and the information architecture representations, along with key considerations and guidelines for their design and their usage by the components in the rest of the horizontal layers, are the responsibilities of this layer.

Standard industry models like ACORD and MIMOSA are typically leveraged and adopted to define the information architecture and the business protocols used to exchange business data. (ACORD is an insurance industry standard that has a data and information model; see https://www.acord.org/Pages/default.aspx. MIMOSA is an open information standard for operations and maintenance in manufacturing, fleet, and facility environments; see http://www.mimosa.org.) The layer also stores the metadata required for data mining and business intelligence (BI).

Components in this layer ensure the adherence to and the implementation of any data or information standards (industry level or enterprise specific) that are either mandated (legal, corporate policies, IT standards, and so on) or adopted by the IT System.

Note: I have seen layered architectures that have this layer placed either as a vertical or a horizontal layer (just below the service components layer). You can adopt either one of the representations.

Layer 9: Governance Layer

The Governance layer ensures the proper management of the entire life cycle of the business processes and services. It is responsible for prioritizing the implementation of the high-value business processes and services and their supporting components in other layers in the architecture. Enforcing both design-time and runtime policies for the business processes and services is also one of the key responsibilities of this layer.

Further Tips on Using the Layered View

If you are interested in further details, I recommend the book *Executing SOA: A Practical Guide for the Service Oriented Architect* (Bieberstein, et al., 2008) for a detailed treatment of a layered architecture and the characteristics of each one of them.

My expectation is that, based on the definitions provided here, you will be able to identify architecture components and place them in one of the nine layers. You are empowered to leverage the definition of the layers, while you embark on architecting, designing, and documenting your own solution architecture.

Once all the architecture components are placed in one of the nine layers, they need to be appropriately documented such that their description communicates their role, responsibility, and intended usage in the overall solution architecture. You may also notice my use of "components" and "ABB" interchangeably; they refer to the same construct and are used to keep the terminologies a bit flexible.

And lastly, the nine-layered view is meant to be a guideline. You can always refine the Layered view by adding or merging layers as you see relevant; just keep in mind that layers are supposed to be characterized by low coupling (between components *across layers*) and high cohesion (between components *inside layers*). Speaking of guidelines and relevant refinements, in Chapter 11, "Analytics: An Architecture Introduction," I develop a refined Layered view of an analytics reference architecture!

The IT System View

The IT System view provides an additional level of detail, identifying the main nodes of the architecture. A node, at a conceptual level, is a deployment-level component with a clearly defined functional role to play in the architecture. Connections facilitating communications between nodes require a well-defined application programming interface (API) and supporting protocols. The conceptual nature of the nodes, at this point in the architecture construction, does not correspond directly to physical servers.

The IT System view needs to be captured and documented so as to provide enough information, at a conceptual level, for the subsequent development of other more detailed architecture artifacts. The IT System view serves as the starting point for the development of the functional and operational models (topics of Chapters 7 and 8, respectively). This view may be extended or refined during the definition of the functional and operational models. As an example, the conceptual nodes in this view not only serve as key inputs to the identification of physical servers but also help in identifying the right technologies to implement the functionality of each of the nodes. More concretely, the operational model may map the conceptual nodes in the IT System view to actual physical servers. Each physical server may potentially support multiple conceptual nodes, and similarly, any given conceptual node may be deployed on multiple servers. The final deployment topology design is influenced by the system NFRs and constraints.

Figure 5.3 depicts an IT System view for the illustrative banking system. I will not describe each node in Figure 5.3 in great detail. Time and space are more optimally spent by looking at a template that I recommend you follow while documenting each node. I do, however, provide a brief description of each of the numbered nodes in the diagram before discussing the documentation template. I also describe one of the nodes and provide an example of how to fill up the template with the relevant information.

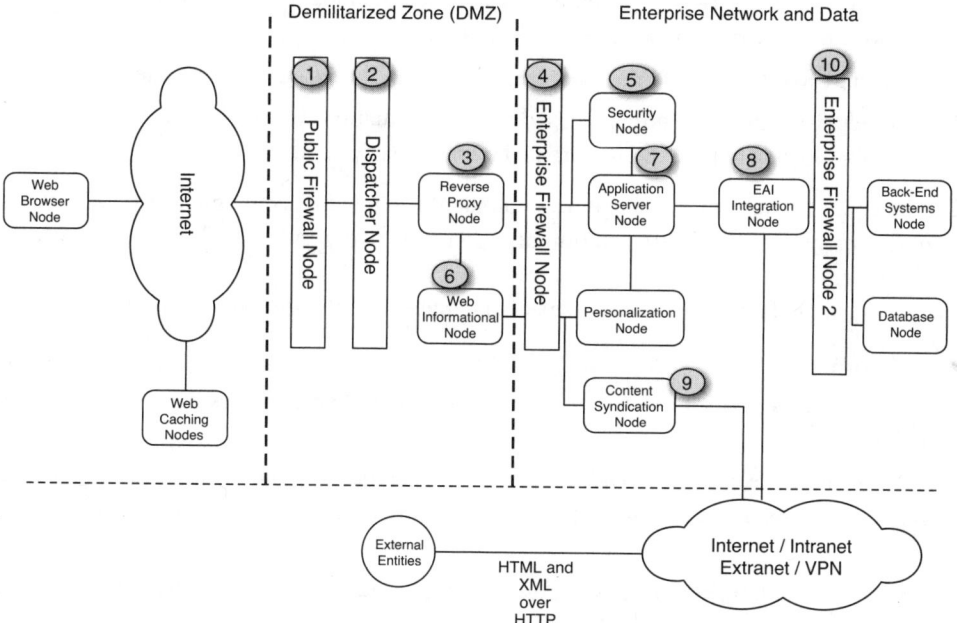

Figure 5.3   An IT System view for the illustrative banking example.

Let's look briefly at the nodes first:

1. **Public Firewall Node**—Resides in the demilitarized zone (DMZ) and allows only HTTP traffic to enter into the enterprise network.

2. **Dispatcher Node**—Used for load balancing of multiple requests across a cluster of Web Informational Nodes and Application Server Nodes.

3. **Reverse Proxy Node**—Is a hardened (that is, has tightened access restrictions, following security guidelines) web server used as an interceptor of any requests from external clients granting access to only authenticated and authorized users and to authorized systems.

4. **Enterprise Firewall Node**—Opens only some selected and secure ports into the secured enterprise network, thereby protecting critical enterprise applications and data through a double door mechanism.

5. **Security Node**—Provides authentication and authorization for some of the enterprise applications, databases, mainframe systems, or packaged applications.

6. **Web Informational Node**—Serves only static content and enhances performance for web-based applications.

7. **Application Server Node**—Hosts the application components that implement the business logic.

8. **EAI Integration Node**—Provides capabilities to integrate with back-end systems. (EAI stands for Enterprise Application Integration.)

9. **Content Syndication Node** —Aggregates and publishes enterprise content.

10. **Enterprise Firewall Node 2** —Used in hosted situations in which a part of the IT System topology is hosted and maintained by third-party vendors.

The preceding documentation becomes redundant when there is enough information available to provide more detailed documentation of each of the nodes in the IT System topology. In the rest of the section, I provide such an example.

Each node in the IT System view is expected to have the following information:

- **Node Name**—Specifies the name of the node.

- **Description**—Provides a detailed description of the characteristics and features of the node.

- **Services or Components**—Describes the services or components that are running on the node; for example, Relational Database, Transaction Manager, State Management, and so on.

- **Nonfunctional Characteristics**—Describes the list of nonfunctional characteristics that the node must support and fulfill.

- **Connections to Other Nodes**—Enlists the other nodes that are connected with this particular node in the topology.

- **Hardware Description and Operating System**—Describes the hardware architecture of the physical server on which the node is deployed and the type of operating system along with its software version.

Let's look at the Application Server Node, labeled number 7 in Figure 5.3, as an example in context, to provide guidance on how to capture the detailed artifacts for each of the nodes in the IT System view.

For the Application Server Node, the following documentation is an example:

- **Node Name**—Application Server

- **Description**—The Application Server Node is responsible for processing the transactions and providing web users access to back-end systems and databases. It supports web transactions and provides many of the operational characteristics identified by the operational requirements of the application; these include multithreaded servers to support multiple client connections, redundant services to handle additional loads, dynamic load-balancing capabilities, a pool of database connections, automatic failover, and recoverability. The node may be deployed in clustered mode and hosted either on multiple virtual machines (on a single physical machine) or on multiple physical servers. Above and beyond providing the technology and operational capabilities, this component also hosts the deployed application components that implement the system's business logic.

- **Services or Components**—The Web Application Server Node, which is an instance of the Application Server Node, will host the following components:

  - The application components that encapsulate the business logic for all the deployed applications.

  - Application Server software.

  - The supported version of the Java Virtual Machine.

  - Software for monitoring web site usage and gathering statistics around usage, threats, and so on.

  - Systems management software to detect, diagnose, and automatically correct failures and configurations to notify system administrators of critical server conditions.

- **Nonfunctional Characteristics**

  - *Response time*—Indicates time to respond to a user request at peak operating hours under maximum workload. As an example, the response time must not exceed 5 seconds at least 90 percent of the time.

- *Availability*—Provides metrics regarding the percentage of operating time that the node must be operational. As an example, the node must have an uptime of 99.95 percent on an annual basis. Availability of the applications running on this node must follow the same uptime metrics.

- *Scalability*—Provides guidance on how to scale the node to support the agreed-upon performance metrics. As an example, guidance on how vertical and horizontal scalability (more on different types of scalability in Chapter 10) may be necessary based on specific type of workload conditions.

- *Workload monitoring*—Statistics must be available on the following:

  - The average and peak load profile of user and system requests during an entire day.

  - The average and peak number of active concurrent database connections during an entire day.

- **Connections to Other Nodes**—The node is directly connected to four nodes:

  - Enterprise Firewall Node provides security at the network protocol level.

  - Personalization Node provides targeted application features and capabilities.

  - Security Node propagates security credentials to the applications.

  - EAI Integration Node provides integration logic facilitating the required integration with database systems, packaged applications, and legacy systems supporting the business processes.

The preceding information may also be represented in a tabular format, which may render it more conducive to the reader (see Figure 5.4). Adopt whichever format is more acceptable for easier communication. Each of the nodes in the IT System view should ideally have the level of documentation illustrated here for the Application Server Node.

This marks the end of the illustration of the three complementary views of a system architecture. As you iterate and refine the development of the views and the ABBs, you will see some patterns emerge not only on how the various ABBs are characterized but also on how they interface and communicate with each other. Fowler (2002) provides a very good reference for enterprise architecture patterns.

Take a moment now to pause and recollect what you read and, more importantly what you understood and consumed so far in this chapter. Before you read further, I recommend you open a document and create your own template for the architecture overview, not to emulate the content described so far but to ensure that your understanding is clear. There is no hard and fast rule that the template has to follow exactly as described. Make it support enough artifacts to adequately communicate the architecture overview as you see pertinent and applicable to your IT System and its intended stakeholders.

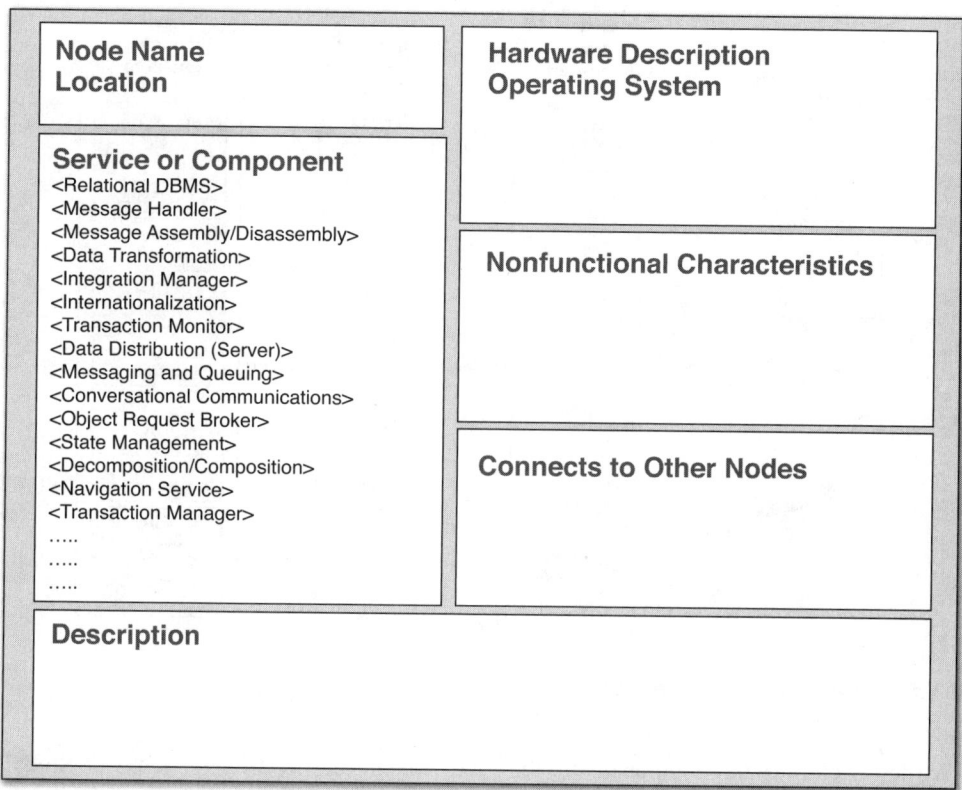

Figure 5.4 A sample tabular format to capture the node descriptions.

Case Study: Architecture Overview of Elixir

Now that you've learned about the various facets of the architecture overview artifact, it's time to get back to the case study of the Elixir system. Although the following sections provide the various views of the architecture, it may not be worthwhile to go through a detailed explanation of every single artifact in each of the views. A better approach may be to use your understanding from this chapter as a baseline, adopt what you consider pertinent, and use it to guide the development of the architecture overview for one of your projects.

Elixir: Enterprise View

Figure 5.5 provides a diagrammatic representation of the Enterprise view of the Elixir system. It uses the same schematic form as in Figure 5.1 to depict an instantiated view of the Elixir system.

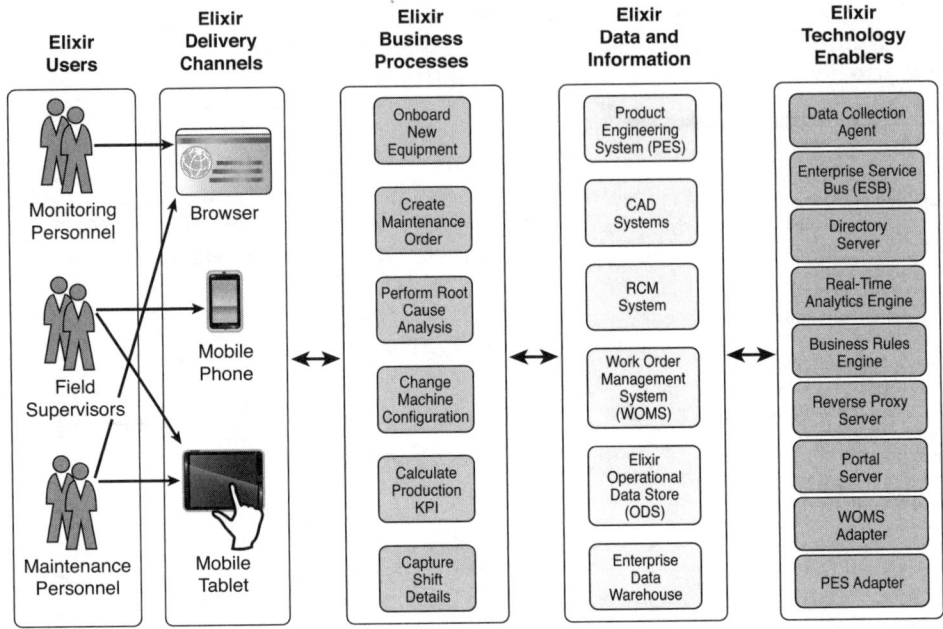

Figure 5.5 Enterprise view of the Elixir system.

While the entities and components in the Elixir Users (refer to Chapter 1, "Case Study") and the Elixir Delivery Channels are self-explanatory, the following sections provide just a brief description of each of the other components or ABBs. The actual definition would certainly be more detailed. The idea is to give you a starting point from where you can develop and document the architecture facets of the IT System you are in charge of architecting.

And before you look at the components, it is important to understand the definition of a middleware component and an adapter. Many of the Elixir Technology Enablers components are categorized as middleware or adapters. Middleware refers to any component that resides between the operating system (OS) and the IT System, in a typically distributed system. An adapter is a component that converts data formats and communication protocols between two heterogeneous systems so that the two systems can seamlessly communicate and exchange information.

Elixir Business Processes

This section provides a brief description of the ABBs in the Business Process category of the Enterprise view of Elixir (refer to Figure 5.5).

> **Onboard New Equipment**—This business process supports the entire process of adding a new machine (for example, SHV_007) or a new machine family (for example, Shovel) to the Elixir system.

Create Maintenance Order—This business process triggers a new maintenance work order in the Elixir Work Order Management System (WOMS).

Perform Root Cause Analysis—This business process kicks off the process of determining the root cause of a machine or parts failure, from initiation to final analysis outcome.

Change Machine Configuration—This business process modifies any change in the configuration of an already operational machine (for example, replacing two engines with one larger and more powerful engine).

Calculate Production KPI—This business process performs the various key performance indicator (KPI) calculations related to key production business metrics (for example, machine availability for operations).

Capture Shift Details—This business process captures all shift-related details (for example, production, machine downtime, operator downtime, and machine faults).

Elixir Data and Information

This section provides a brief description of the ABBs in the Data and Information category of the Enterprise view of Elixir (refer to Figure 5.5).

Product Engineering System (PES)—The system of record that stores the engineering structures for all machine types. It exposes a set of APIs through which the engineering structures may be retrieved.

CAD System—Stores all the digitized engineering drawings for each class of equipment.

RCM System—Stores all the process data around reliability and maintenance of equipment. The failure modes and their probable causes for specific faults and fault types that are stored in this system are used to facilitate root cause analysis of machine or parts failures.

Work Order Management System (WOMS)—Manages the scheduling of maintenance work orders and also capturing the details of finished work orders.

Elixir Operational Data Store (ODS)—Stores all the analytical output and related data attributes that are generated by the Elixir system through successful execution of the business processes.

Enterprise Data Warehouse (EDW)—A corporate data warehouse that stores the historical data for all business-critical data entities and transactions in a way that is amenable to efficient business intelligence reporting.

Note: The Enterprise HRMS System is purposefully omitted; this system is not in the scope of the first phase of the implementation of Elixir.

Elixir Technology Enablers

This section provides a brief description of the ABBs in the Technology Enablers category of the Enterprise view of Elixir (refer to Figure 5.5).

Data Collection Agent (DCA)—A software application that interfaces with the control systems on the machines and collects the data from the machine sensors.

Enterprise Service Bus (ESB)—A middleware component responsible for any protocol conversion (between client data and transport protocols to the protocol used inside the Elixir system), mediation, and routing of data and information to the subscribed consumers.

Directory Server (DS)—A middleware component used to provision the users and their association to one or more application roles along with their access rights to the subset of physical assets that each user is eligible to view, monitor, and take action on.

Real-Time Analytics Engine (RTAE)—A middleware component that ingests real-time data and performs analytical processing in real time—that is, on the streaming data, before it is persisted into a persistent store (for example, a database).

Business Rules Engine (BRE)—A middleware component that supports the hosting and invocation of business rules required in any business process or computation. The component is used to externalize a subset of the business rules in anticipation of their dynamic nature; that is, the rules may need to be changed frequently without affecting the system operations.

Reverse Proxy Server (RPS)—A middleware component used for hardening the web servers in relation to security considerations; it is used as an interceptor of any requests from external clients and provides authentication and authorization to user requests.

Portal Server (PS)—A middleware component used as a container for all presentation layer components and user interface widgets; it aims at providing a consistent and consolidated user experience for all users interacting with Elixir.

WOMS Adapter—An adapter component that provides an industry standard connection to the Work Order Management System.

PES Adapter—An adapter component that provides a unidirectional connection from the Elixir system to the client's Product Engineering System.

Keep in mind that the description of the components here may not be adequate. Use your judgment to ascertain the right level of component description that is effective.

Elixir: Layered View

Rather than cram all the architecture components into the Layered view diagram, I took an alternate approach for the sake of legibility: using a table format to capture how the components are associated with the layers. However, I encourage you to create the Layered view diagram as a template (that is, a version of Figure 5.2) and keep it handy. You can reuse it across your projects. Keep in mind that, for an architecture that does not need to follow a full-blown SOA-based model, Service Components and Services layers can be merged into a single layer; I recommend calling it Components.

Note that the Real-Time Analytics Engine and the Business Rules Engine components are not placed into any of the layers in the Layered view shown in Figure 5.2. With the recent focus on analytics, newer versions of the Layered architecture views are increasingly dedicating a complete layer (with a set of domain-specific pillars) specifically to analytics. The Real-Time Analytics Engine and the Business Rules Engine ABBs will find their natural place in an analytics-centric architecture (refer to Chapter 11).

I encourage you to convert the tabular data in Table 5.1 into a Layered architecture view for Elixir. Have fun with diagrams and component placements—an exercise that often takes up a significant amount of an architect's time!

Table 5.1   Component Placements in Architecture Layers for the Elixir System

Architecture Layer	Components
Operational	PES, CAD System, RCM System, WOMS
Components	Data Collection Agent
Business Process	Onboard New Equipment, Create Maintenance Order, Perform Root Cause Analysis, Change Machine Configuration, Calculate Production KPI, Capture Shift Details
Consumers	Portal Server, Monitoring Personnel, Field Supervisors, Maintenance Personnel, Browser, Mobile Phone, Mobile Tablet
Integration	WOMS Adapter, PES Adapter, ESB, Directory Server
Information Architecture	Elixir Operational Data Store, Enterprise Data Warehouse

I hope that you are beginning to understand the Layered architecture view by now.

Elixir: IT System View

The IT System view for Elixir is shown in Figure 5.6.

At a conceptual level, the Elixir system is an analytical solution with elements of integration with enterprise systems and a user interface front end that interfaces with users through a set of delivery channels.

The IT System view shown in Figure 5.6 is a variation of the sample IT System view depicted in Figure 5.3. Here, I share the characteristics of only the nodes that are specific to Elixir. For the rest of the nodes, refer back to the example in Figure 5.3.

Portal Server Node—Provisions the static and dynamic user interface screens that users use to interface with the system through a set of delivery channels.

Analytics Node—Performs various analytical processing functions—for example, real-time analytics, business intelligence (BI) reporting, and predictive analytics. (Refer to Chapter 11 for a detailed discussion of analytics.)

EDW Node—Consolidates and provisions the data for fast and efficient access, supporting the multitude of queries required for business reporting and ad hoc data analysis.

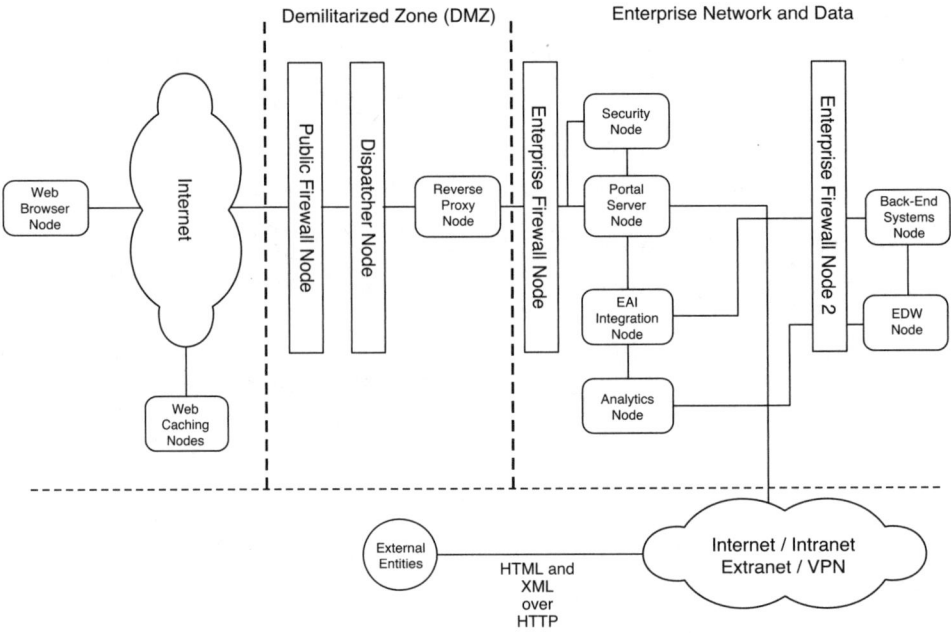

Figure 5.6   The IT System view for Elixir.

As with the Layered view, I suggest that you develop a diagrammatic representation as shown in Figure 5.3 and use it as a template for your projects. You can always repurpose and enhance it to support any IT System views. This exercise will be a good investment of your time.

My intention has not, by any means, been to provide a complete representation of the Elixir system components. I have tried to provide enough detail to give you an idea of *what* needs to be captured, *why*, and *how*. In a real-world implementation of Elixir or a similar system, there could be a few more details. My omission is conscious and is for the sake of brevity.

Summary

This chapter focused on the second software architecture artifact—the architecture overview. It provided a first look of what goes under the hood of any system that you must build. Because it is the first look, the architecture overview, as an artifact, captures some high-level architecture tenets in the form of architecture views from different viewpoints. Although they use different lenses to look into the system, these viewpoints can collectively provide a holistic overview of the system to be developed.

The architecture overview is typically captured as a separate documented artifact. It contains the Enterprise view, Layered architecture view, and IT System view. Although other views may be introduced (you can always add a few), these three views are often adequate to appropriately represent the system under construction. The chapter demonstrated how to document the artifacts—a critical element to effectively communicate the architecture of the system with the stakeholders.

Developing templates for each view would be a good investment of time; once developed, these templates can be reused when you move from one system's development to another. The basic constructs are the same, so they should come in handy.

The chapter also included an architecture overview for the Elixir case study. It demonstrated how most of the artifacts from the template-driven views may be reused and repurposed.

As a parting note from this chapter, I strongly recommend that you pause and try to understand the essence, importance, and value of this artifact as it pertains to the overall system's architecture. If you believe in its importance, you will be committed to apportion commensurate time to its development and documentation.

The stage is set for you to define the software architecture. And you are in the driver's seat already!

References

Bieberstein, N., Laird, R. G., Jones, K., & Mitra, T. (2008) *Executing SOA: A practical guide for the service-oriented architect*. Upper Saddle River, NJ: IBM Press.

Fowler, M. (2002*). Patterns of enterprise application architecture*. New York: Addison-Wesley Professional.

The Open Group. (n.d.) TOGAF specifications. Retrieved from http://www.opengroup.org/togaf/

Treacy, M. & Wiersema, F. (1997). *The discipline of market leaders: Choose your customers, narrow your focus, dominate your market*. New York, NY: Basic Books.

Weill, P., & Ross, J. (2004). *IT governance: How top performers manage IT decision rights for superior results*. Cambridge, MA: HBR Press.

CHAPTER 6

Architecture Decisions

Lead by the power of conviction in your decision.

In the preceding chapter, you gained a comprehensive understanding of the architecture overview. Among other aspects, that chapter illustrated three different architecture views that collectively depicted the IT System's high-level architecture. From the high-level architectural overview, you have to progressively dive into the details of the solution. However, certain decisions that must be made at this point will guide and influence the subsequent detailed design artifacts of the IT System. Such decisions are called architecture decisions. These architecture decisions influence, shape, and guide the framework of the solution.

This chapter discusses the importance of architecture decisions and provides guidance on how to appropriately capture them. It also gives a few examples for the Elixir case study.

Throughout, I use the terms *architecture building block*, its abbreviation *ABB*, *architecture component,* and *building block* interchangeably. Doing so will help you to accept not only any of the four terms that your team chooses to adopt but also any other term that may stick with your team; in the latter case, just ensure that the meaning and intent are the same.

Why We Need It

The importance of the architecture decisions cannot be stressed enough. The collection of architecture decision topics is a direct reflection of the architect's thought process. They indicate how she tackles the most significant problems that are architectural in nature, affecting the solution architecture either in part or in whole. The architect typically decides the set of problems that are architecturally significant in nature and, for each one of the chosen problems, undertakes a structured and systematic process of evaluating various alternatives before arriving at the most acceptable and justifiable solution.

Documenting the architecture decisions is of paramount importance. It is important to highlight the significance of appropriately capturing them. Such a document

- Consolidates all architecture decisions in one single structured and cataloged artifact.

- Articulates the rationale and justifications that underpin each architecture decision.

- Provides a compendium of architectural guidelines for system design.

- Provides a reference to team members to understand and be aware of the decisions that have been made already and how they influence the solution architecture.

- Ensures that the architecture is extensible and can support an evolving system.

- Avoids unnecessary reconsideration of the same issues.

- Ensures a common language to communicate the key architecture decisions with different stakeholders.

- Provides a basis for revisiting the architecture decisions as and when the system evolves and matures, maintaining traceability between newly evolved decisions and the originally approved one.

I cannot emphasize enough the need to formalize architecture decisions in order to substantiate and support a well-defined solution architecture. A multitude of experiences in building systems architecture has taught me that paying adequate attention to architecture decisions is key to developing a useful and productive architecture.

How to Get Started

To get started and as you formalize each of the architecture decisions, you ought to consider certain critical aspects to ensure that all the bases of systems development are commensurately covered. Many factors influence the outcome of architecture decisions. For each decision that is proposed, thoroughly assessing its effect on system cost, performance, maintainability, resource utilization, and development timelines is critical.

Compliance is a very important factor that influences any architecture decision. Paying due attention to the compliance factors is also very important. Following are some of the compliance checks that most architecture decisions need to consider:

- IT policies around system startup and shutdown, error handling, and logging, along with rollback and recovery from indeterminate system conditions

- IT guidelines around the adherence to standards-based interfaces; for example, JDBC/ODBC for database access, Spring framework for Model View Controller (MVC) implementation, information/data exchange standards such as ACORD (for insurance), and so on

- Ability of the relevant architecture components to support the security and privacy requirements and mandates of the enterprise

- Data management policies around data retention, archiving, transaction management, and security, among others

While compliance considerations address policy adherence, I think every decision should factor in some more pure architectural considerations. Think of them as a set of acid tests applied to any consideration before it gets finalized. I call them a Decision Litmus Test (DLT). Here is a starter kit of DLTs that you may find useful while working through each of the architecture decisions for your solution architecture:

- **Integrity**—The introduction and characterization of an architecture component should maintain the integrity of the overall architecture; that is, it does not break or compromise other aspects of the architecture.

- **Completeness**—All characterizations of each of the architecture building blocks (ABB) must be described and defined.

- **Containment**—Each architecture component should be prescribed to be placed in only one architecture layer.

- **Validity**—The ABB should be verified to perform what it is expected to do; that is, what its characterization entails.

- **Reliability**—Each architecture component should be able to work in multiple usage contexts and do so in a consistent manner.

- **Independence**—Each architecture component must be standalone or independent (a.k.a. orthogonal).

- **Flexibility**—The ability of an ABB to be integrated with other components and used in different contexts.

It is important to understand and acknowledge that the application of the DLTs requires prior judgment: apply only those DLTs that are applicable to the specific architecture consideration. The subset of DLTs may vary between one problem and another. Moreover, I do not claim the preceding DLT list to be exhaustive; these examples are available to help you go about developing and finalizing architecture decisions.

Creating an Architecture Decision

Architects from different schools of thought go about developing architecture decisions in various ways. Although I do not intend to perform a comparative analysis of the various techniques, I want to share some prescriptive guidance that could help you develop a systematic thought process on how to go about developing architecture decisions. I have chosen a technique that I have personally used for more than two decades now; I have found it to be *just enough* to capture the essence of this important artifact.

When you want to develop an architecture decision, it is good practice to use a template-driven approach that provides a consistent set of qualitative attributions to help guide the decision-making process. In the rest of this section, I focus on each of the qualitative attributes, what they mean, and how to address them.

Subject Area—Describes a specific domain of the IT System. The domains, also called subject areas, help classify the problems and challenges, which are architectural in nature. Examples of such subject areas could be Systems Management, Security, User Interface, and so on. One way to make things easy is to align the nomenclature of the subject areas with that of the architecture layers (refer to Chapter 5, "The Architecture Overview"). You can always refine them as and when they start to take shape and form.

ID (abbreviated form of **identification**)—Represents a unique number for each of the architecture decisions; for example, AD04, AD16, or AD23. Numbering helps in traceability between related architecture decisions and also may work as shorthand to refer to a particular architecture decision. Program teams often get used to referring to architecture decisions by their ID; team members know all about the decision by just referring to their ID, and when that happens, you are assured of its adoption.

Topic of Interest—Defines a topic of interest within the subject area. Although there is no hard and fast rule on a rigid set of topics, architects typically use topic elements such as efficiency, reliability, scalability, resilience, extensibility, and usability, as good starting points for categorizing the topics of interest.

Architecture Decision—Provides a descriptive name to the architecture decision under consideration. The intent is to be able to identify the architecture decision by its short descriptive name. A combination of the subject area, topic, and name typically serves to provide a quick overview of the problem at hand. As an example, the Security subject area may have a topic on Federated Identity Management with a brief problem statement entitled "Supporting user authentication in a distributed deployment topology."

Problem Statement—Provides a detailed description of the problem statement; it expands on the descriptive name captured earlier. This statement can be as descriptive as is pertinent but usually is kept to a couple of paragraphs.

Assumptions—Describe the constraints and boundary conditions that the resolution to the problem needs to adhere to. The pre-conditions and post-conditions (describing the state of the system before the problem is encountered and the state of the system after the problem is addressed, respectively) may also be stated as a measure of the architectural integrity of the overall solution that needs to be maintained with the problem resolution.

Motivations—Describe one or more incentives to address the specific problem at hand. Examples of motivations may be *to reduce complexity*, *to avoid an inordinate increase in compute with increasing workload*, *to reduce system redundancy*, and so on.

Alternatives—Illustrate the various resolution alternatives that have been considered with the objective of solving the problem under consideration. (They are possibly the most important aspect of any architecture decision.) Each alternative is described in detail along with its pros and cons, or advantages and disadvantages, in addressing the problem. The pros and cons could be in the form of technical ease or complexity, process ease or complexity, cost and time implications, among other factors. Keep in mind that it is not mandatory for all decisions to have multiple alternatives. It is okay if some architecture problems have only one alternative and that is the one chosen as the solution! The advice, though, is to consider multiple alternatives, if applicable.

Decision—Finalizes the decision by choosing the best possible solution, among the alternatives, as the resolution to the problem statement.

Justification—Describes the rationale behind choosing the solution among the various alternatives, substantiated by a list of architecture principles that the solution complies with, along with a potential list of principles that may be in noncompliance (substantiated by an explanation for the deviations).

Implications—Illustrate the consequences that the decision may have on the overall program. An implication can be limited only to the technical aspects if the decision has ramifications on the choice of tool, technology, or platform. The implication may also have consequences on program cost and timelines based on the solution characteristics; for example, implementation complexity, need for different tools or technology or platform, and so on. This element of the architecture decision template can be made optional if the decision does not have too many implications and keeps the solution well within the known constraints, boundaries, and scope.

Derived Requirements—Itemize additional requirements that may be generated by the chosen solution for problem resolution. An example of such a requirement may be the *need to add a second firewall* if the decision is to avoid placing enterprise systems in the demilitarized zone (DMZ). Similar to the implications element, this entity is also optional if no additional requirements are derived from the architecture decision. (*Note:* You don't need to rattle your brain if no additional requirements can be identified; if they exist, they would naturally surface.)

Related Decisions—Describes the set of additional architecture decisions that may be related. Including this attribute helps in decision traceability and linkage.

While looking at the attributes of an architecture decision, I have often felt that either I may miss a few of them or fail to correlate them to get a holistic view. To address this issue, I have always found that having a tabular view of the attributes provides me a more compact representation of the various characterizations of the architecture decision. To that effect, I am sharing the tabular format in Table 6.1, which you may find useful.

Table 6.1   A Tabular Format to Capture Architecture Decisions

Subject Area		ID	Topic of Interest
Architecture Decision			
Issue or Problem			
Assumptions			
Motivations			
Alternatives			
Decision			
Justification			
Implications			
Derived Requirements			
Related Decisions			

Often, I have seen that consultants have a tendency to tinker around with any template they are handed and declare, "I customized it to fit my needs!" I'm sure you have either experienced the same or have done it yourself. Now let me play the role of such a consultant.

Table 6.2 shows a customized version of the template I shared in Table 6.1 and have used in some instances. Remember: a template is only a guideline; fit it to your needs!

Table 6.2   An Example of an Architecture Decision (with a Customized Version of the Suggested Template)

Subject Area	Service Design	ID	Topic of Interest
Architecture Decision	Messaging Style for Web Services	AD007	
Issue or Problem	The impact of using RPC versus document-style encoding to the Web Services architecture of the XYZ system.		
Guiding Principles	• Maximize delivery of business capability within time and money constraints. • Minimize impact of change to Reservation System and existing Point of Sale (POS). • Minimize technology churn, system integration, and host development risk. • Need to support OTA XML.		
Motivation	Minimize performance overhead.		

Subject Area	Service Design	ID	Topic of Interest
Alternatives	*Option 1:* Use Remote Procedure Calls (RPC). RPCs using SOAP messages interact with the back-end service in an RPC-like fashion. The interaction is a simple request/response, where the client sends a SOAP message that contains a call to a method. The application server receiving this request can then translate this request into the back-end object. XML is used for data format and data interchange. *Pros:* This would require very little development effort since all the mapping of messages to the back-end object has already been implemented. *Cons:* RPC is typically static, requiring changes to the client when the method signature changes, resulting in tight coupling between the client and the service provider. In addition, it cannot support OTA XML messages. *Option 2:* Use Document Style. Document-style XML "business documents" are complete and self-contained. When the service receives an XML document, it might perform some data preprocessing, execute some business logic, and construct the response. There is no direct mapping to a back-end object. It is used in conjunction with asynchronous protocols to provide reliable, loosely coupled architectures. *Pros:* • Utilizes full capabilities of XML to describe and validate a business document. • Does not require a tight contract between the client and the service provider. Rules can be less rigid. • Is better suited for asynchronous processing because it is self-contained. • OTA XML messages, because they are document-style oriented, can be supported easily. *Cons:* It is typically more difficult to implement than RPC. The developer has to do much of the work in processing and mapping XML data received, and new tools need to be learned to implement the payload transformation.
Decision	Use both RPC and Document Style.
Justification	A decision was made to go with both the RPC and Document Style messaging options. Document Style will be used for transactions that lend themselves to a document-style approach (for example, OTA XML messages), and RPC based for transactions that lend themselves to an RPC-based approach. It was decided that eventually RPC messaging will be replaced by Document Style messaging because the flexibility gains outweigh the implementation costs.

Subject Area	Service Design	ID	Topic of Interest
Implications	Need to maintain two messaging styles at the onset; that is, in the first phase of the implementation. Potential rework if and when switchover to Document Style messaging is planned.		
Derived Requirements	N/A		
Related Decisions			

The purpose of this section was to give a good glimpse and guidance on how you can develop architecture decisions. Now let's move on to the case study.

Case Study: Architecture Decisions for Elixir

Now that you've learned about the various facets of the architecture decision artifact, it's time to get back to the case study of the Elixir system. The final work product for Elixir had 10 architecture decisions. For the sake of brevity, I share two of the architecture decisions to provide a sneak peak at how it is done in real-world engagements. The two that I share (see Tables 6.3 and 6.4) are also related to each other.

Table 6.3   An Architecture Decision (AD004) for Elixir

Subject Area	Recommendations Management	ID	Topic Area
Architecture Decision	The message format of the generated recommendations from the Elixir system.	AD004	Information Architecture
Issue or Problem	One of the key outputs of Elixir is a recommendation for a possible maintenance job on any equipment. Although the currently used maintenance system is SAP Plant Maintenance (SAP PM), there is a possible migration to IBM Maximo® as the system of record for equipment maintenance and work orders. The challenge is to develop the information exchange between Elixir and the maintenance system in the most optimal manner.		
Assumptions	The current SAP PM interface supports an XML-based message format for work order submissions.		
Motivation	Lessen impact to Elixir when the maintenance system of record is migrated from SAP PM to IBM Maximo.		

Subject Area	Recommendations Management	ID	Topic Area
Alternatives	*Option 1:* Use the exposed SAP PM API to submit a requisition for a work order from Elixir. *Pros:* • Well documented and easy to use. Development team already well acquainted with the API and its usage. • Quick development time frame. *Cons:* • Implementation of the Recommendations Management subsystem will be tightly coupled to the SAP PM specific work order API. • Makes Elixir less resilient to changes when the enterprise migration to IBM Maximo is planned for implementation. *Option 2:* Leverage the MIMOSA Open O&M industry standard. Create an XML message structure that is MIMOSA compliant, and leverage the MIMOSA EAM adapter to SAP PM to pass the MIMOSA-compliant XML structure for work order creation. *Pros:* • Elixir is designed to be resilient to external changes, specifically a future migration from SAP PM to IBM Maximo. • The MIMOSA EAM adapter for IBM Maximo will accept the same MIMOSA-compliant XML message structure for work order creation. This implies that the imminent change would not affect the Elixir system too much. • Adherence to industry standard for data exchange. *Cons:* • MIMOSA-based data exchange format has a steeper learning curve for the development team. • Change from the recently concluded proof of concept where the direct SAP PM API was used. • Additional time and cost for the project.		
Decision	Go with Option 2.		
Justification	Both SAP PM and IBM Maximo products are MIMOSA compliant, and hence the message structure and format for a work order would be very similar, if not identical. This change from SAP PM to IBM Maximo would introduce minimal change to Elixir. Although there is an initial learning curve, analysis reveals that the extra time taken would be much less than it may take to revamp the Recommendations Management subsystem if Option 1 was implemented.		

Subject Area	Recommendations Management	ID	Topic Area
Implications	Plan for additional upfront time in the project plan.		
Derived Requirements	N/A		
Related Decisions	AD007		

Table 6.4 captures another architecture decision that is related to the one in Table 6.3.

Table 6.4   An Architecture Decision (AD007) for Elixir

Subject Area	Recommendations Management	ID	Topic Area
Architecture Decision	Enabling guaranteed delivery of the work order requests to the maintenance system of record.	AD007	Integration Architecture
Issue or Problem	Triggering a work order, based on predictive models, is one of the most important actionable insights and recommendations generated by Elixir. As such, it is critical to ensure that the insights are being acted upon instead of being lost owing to any unanticipated glitch in the enterprise application or in the network. A solution needs to be devised that ensures no loss of the recommendations.		
Assumptions	The MIMOSA-compliant server in both SAP PM as well as in IBM Maximo has an optional feature to support asynchronous delivery of work order requests through a queue-based technique.		
Motivation	Avoid any loss of the work order requests (a.k.a. recommendations).		
Alternatives	*Option 1:* Use the exposed MIMOSA API in SAP PM to submit a requisition for a work order from Elixir. *Pros:* • Quick development time frame. • No additional infrastructure required. *Cons:* • The work order requests may be lost if either the MIMOSA server is down or Elixir has a temporary system glitch. • The work order request may be lost if there is a problem in the network connectivity between Elixir and the maintenance system of record (SAP PM or IBM Maximo).		

Subject Area	Recommendations Management	ID	Topic Area
Alternatives	*Option 2:* Leverage a queue-based mechanism as a mediator between the work order request submission and its actual registration into SAP PM. *Pros:* • The queue-based mediation ensures guaranteed delivery; specifically, any work order request is guaranteed to be delivered regardless of whether the MIMOSA server is down or the SAP PM system is not available or if the network connectivity between Elixir and the MIMOSA server is down. • Work order requests are guaranteed to be delivered even if some components of Elixir go down after the request has been initiated. *Cons:* • A separate messaging system and infrastructure are required. • Queue manager and queue configurations need to be implemented and hence accounted for in the project plan as additional work items and commensurate effort.		
Decision	Go with Option 2.		
Justification	Guaranteed delivery of analytical insights; in this case, the proactive determination of work orders is critical to avoid loss of costly machine parts. A messaging system is already a part of the overall systems architecture. The same may be leveraged for this scenario. As such, the additional cost is not prohibitively high and is more than compensated by the business value of early detection of machine faults and its proactive mitigation.		
Implications	Plan for additional up-front time in the project plan.		
Derived Requirements	N/A		
Related Decisions	AD004		

Summary

This chapter focused on the third software architecture artifact—the architecture decision. This is perhaps the most sought-after living and breathing document in the architecture definition process. Architecture decisions become the foundational pillars and the prescriptive guidance on how to design and implement a complex system. These decisions provide an audit mechanism to trace back the genealogy of the decision-making process. The chief architect or the solution architect of the project leverages the architecture decisions to ensure that the detailed design and the implementation of the system adhere to the overarching architecture decisions.

The chapter provided the rationale for the intent, purpose, and significance of capturing and documenting the architecture decisions. It also provided some key elements that influence the decision-making process. A template, for formally capturing the architecture decisions, was proposed with the intent of maintaining consistency in capturing architecture decisions. The chapter concluded by providing examples of two architecture decisions that were captured for the case study of the Elixir system.

As a parting note from this chapter, and similar to the one in the preceding chapter, I strongly recommend that you pause and try to understand the essence, importance, and value of this artifact as it pertains to the development of the overall systems architecture. If you are currently working on a project as an architect, it may be worthwhile to revisit the decisions that you have either made or are forthcoming and leverage what you learned from this chapter to refine them, if applicable.

At this point, you are all set, with appropriate coverage and support of the decisions, to drive the downstream design and implementation. Did you walk away with something valuable from this chapter? I hope you did!

CHAPTER 7

The Functional Model

I function; therefore, I exist.

There was once a clan of architects who strongly believed that their job, as architects, was complete when they provided a comprehensive treatment of the *system context*, the *architecture overview*, and the *architecture decisions*. The rest of the stuff they considered mere design work to be performed by lesser mortals. Take my word for it that times are much harder, my friends, and we need to work much harder and smarter not only to earn our bread but also, if we are passionate enough, to extend the value and reach of architecture and engrain it into much deeper pockets of the software development process.

This chapter demonstrates how to develop and document the macro-level design artifacts of the functional aspects of a system; that is, how the architecture building blocks (ABBs) are deconstructed into design-level constructs that collectively realize the functional requirements of an IT System. Each ABB describes, at a high level, the capabilities of an architecture component in the context of the entire solution. The components not only help in defining the architecture blueprint but also broadly categorize each to be either functional or operational in nature.

This chapter focuses on the functional ABBs of the system and provides guidance and recommendations on how to transform them into macro-level design artifacts—illustrating the various levels of a functional design models through their iterative evolution from higher to lower levels of specificity. It provides prescriptive instruction on how to best articulate and optimally capture the various steps of the functional deconstruction process. And the chapter concludes by instantiating a subset of the functional model for the case study; that is, the Elixir system.

Why We Need It

The functional model is the step that follows the initiation of the architecture decisions in the realization of the system's architecture. The functional model helps in identifying and defining the following:

- The structure of the IT System

- The dependencies and interactions between a particular set of components of the IT System

- Components that are either specific to the IT System or to a set of technical components that may be leveraged by the IT System

The set of components in the functional model serve a wide variety of purposes. Let's take a closer look at some of important ones:

Managing system complexity—The functional model follows a process of iterative deconstruction of the ABBs. The technique breaks down a larger system into a set of smaller, more manageable blocks. Each block has a clear set of responsibilities with a well-defined set of interfaces through which it not only realizes its responsibilities but also communicates (that is, collaborates) with other manageable blocks. The manageable blocks are called *IT subsystems* or just *subsystems*. You can independently design and implement each subsystem without worrying too much about the rest of the system, thereby managing the complexity of the system design and implementation process. (The book by Jacobson et al. [1999] provides a detailed treatment of UML-based systems design.) The overall functionality of the IT System, supporting the functional use cases, is realized by integrating the subsystems through their well-defined interfaces. The mantra is to divide and conquer (that is, decompose into subsystems) and then integrate back the 'conquered' pieces (that is, orchestrating subsystem functionality through their published interfaces in support of all the required use cases) to build your empire!

Establishing the link with the operational model—The functional model evolves by starting from a logical high-level definition to a physical instantiation, following a series of iterative steps. During this iterative process, the physical components are attributed with the nonfunctional parameters that they are expected to honor and support. The component characteristics (defined by their attributions) typically influence and determine the type of deployment units or nodes on which they would be running; that is, operational. The detailed-level specification of the functional model (a.k.a. physical model) enables the integration with the physical operational model. (You learn more about this later in the chapter; I won't leave you high and dry, I promise!)

Establishing traceability between architecture and design activities and artifacts— The functional model identifies a set of components. The components are a direct derivative of and traceable to the ABBs; as such, they are directly traceable to the system architecture. Moreover, the components are specified at a level of detail that serves as the building blocks that may subsequently be designed and documented for implementation activities. The functional model thus serves as the glue between the system's architecture and implementation artifacts.

Establishing traceability between requirements and architecture—The functional model explicitly specifies both the functional and nonfunctional capabilities for each of the components. As such, there is a direct traceability to the system requirements.

It is important to acknowledge the value of the functional model as it relates to the overall architecture discipline. My intent is to illustrate the various aspects of the functional model and the techniques to develop and capture the relevant artifacts. Once you acknowledge the value of functional modeling and understand the techniques to develop it, you will be in a position to not only direct the implementation team but also assist the project manager to apportion commensurate time to the design and implementation aspects of the project.

A Few Words on Traceability

It is paramount that any IT construct or artifact must, directly or indirectly, be traceable to some business construct. Being able to trace IT architecture constructs to the business domain assumes paramount importance; ensuring that architecture artifacts (a.k.a. work products) are coherent with and align to the business drivers, goals, and problems that are to be solved. Business analysts analyze the business domain and capture business requirements in a technology-neutral format. They try to capture *what* needs to be built while leaving *how* it should be implemented to the IT architects, designers, and implementation team.

Business domain analysis falls under the larger discipline of business architecture, the construction of which involves distinctive techniques and methods that are beyond the current scope of this discussion. However, let me offer a simple example. Component Business Modeling (CBM) is a mechanism used to define business architectures. The CBM matrix (see the "CBM Matrix" sidebar) is defined by a set of business competencies as columns, and accountability levels are rows. The elements in the matrix cell are individual business components that play a specific role within the enterprise ecosystem, collaborating and integrating seamlessly within each other to define and realize the enterprise business processes. (See IBM [2005] for more information on IBM's CBM method and technique.)

Figure 7.1 shows an example of a typical Component Business Model (CBM) map. This figure is just a diagrammatic reference; if you come across something similar, you will know you are looking at something like a CBM!

CBM MATRIX

Business Competencies—These competencies provide a high-level description of the activities conducted. You can think of them as organizational units within an enterprise. As an example, a set of business competencies in a CBM can be Customers, Products & Services, Channels, Logistics, and Business Administration.

Accountability Levels—The business components are assigned to one of the following three accountability levels:

- **Direct** —Components at this level provide strategic direction and corporate policies to other components.
- **Control** —Components at this level monitor performance, manage exceptions, and act as gatekeepers of enterprise assets and information.
- **Execute** —Components at this level drive value creation in the enterprise.

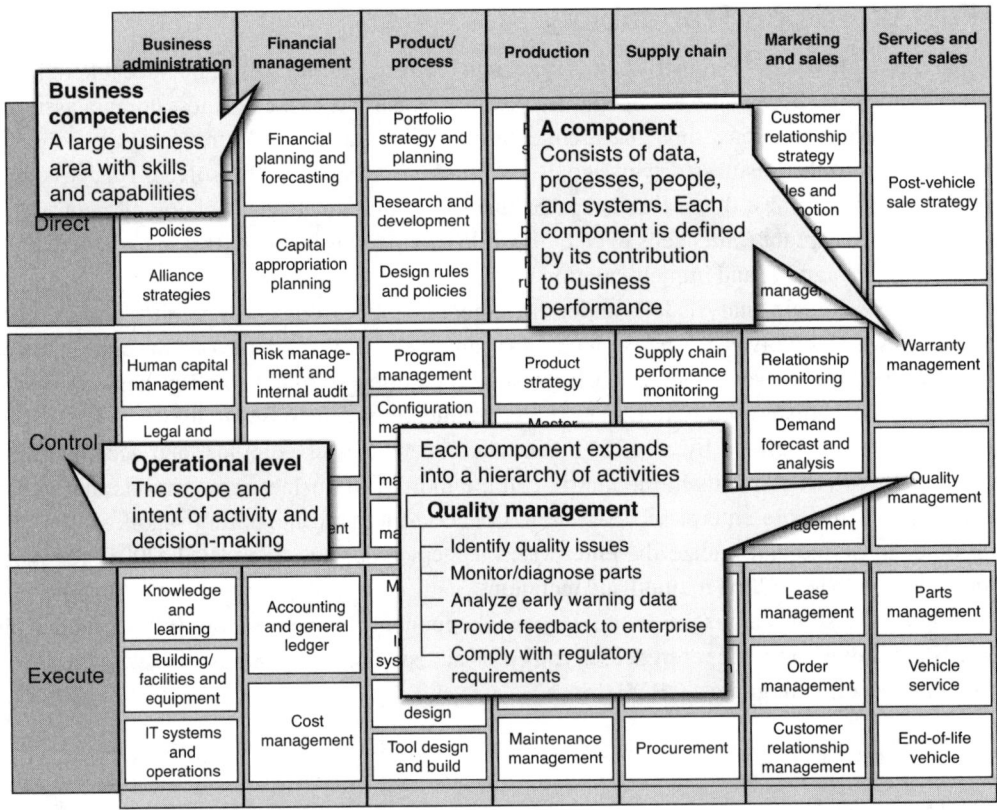

Figure 7.1   An example of a CBM map. This example is from the automotive industry.

Source: IBM Business Consulting Services and IBM Institute for Business Value.

While moving from the business architecture to the IT architecture of an IT System (supporting a whole or part of the business architecture), the business competencies in the CBM model may be used to define a core set of business domains. A business domain may be deconstructed into a set of functional areas. A functional area encapsulates the business processes, subprocesses, and business use cases of a business domain, each one of them being logically cohesive functional units. The functional areas provide a modular view of the business and form the basis of IT subsystem identification, nomenclature, and design. IT subsystem identification and design form the initiation of the functional model. There you go—the traceability is right here!

Developing the Functional Model

The functional model is developed in an iterative manner, enhancing the level of specificity in subsequent iterations, moving from higher levels of abstraction to more specific design and implementation artifacts. The intent is to close the gaps between high-level ABBs and implementation. The three iteration phases I focus on here are the logical-level, specification-level, and physical-level designs. I have found that using these three levels of iterative design is not only the most commonly used but also the most effective technique in developing a functional model for the overall architecture of the system. For the sake of completeness, I'd like to point out a fourth construct that is commonly termed the conceptual-level design; it describes the highest level of abstraction in an evolving functional model.

The four different semantic levels can be briefly summarized as follows:

Conceptual—Described through models that represent the concepts in the domain under consideration. The model elements are technology agnostic (that is, they are not specific to any technology) and deal with real-world entities such as people, processes, and objects, along with their associated attributes.

Logical—Described through a set of artifacts that define a structure of the software system through a set of functionally cohesive constructs called subsystems, each of which encapsulates one or more named components.

Specified—Described through models representing software components (with a detailed level of attribution) that collectively define the specification of the IT System through the interfaces and their externally visible behavior.

Physical—Described through a technology-specific realization of the specified components.

This chapter focuses only on the logical, specified, and physical levels of design because I feel that, from a practical standpoint, they drive more value, and hence focusing on them optimizes the time and effort spent in developing a functional model artifact.

Logical-Level Design

There are two main steps in developing the logical-level view of the functional model. The first step is to identify a set of subsystems (along with a set of identified interfaces for each subsystem) that are typically standalone in nature and collectively depict the behavior of the IT System through a set of well-defined interdependencies between one or more subsystems. The second step is to define the detailed specifications of the each of the components within the subsystems, focusing on their behavior through exposed interfaces and collaborations.

In this chapter, I use a banking scenario for illustrative purposes, choosing banking again because money matters are close to our hearts!

Subsystem Identification

A subsystem is a first-class IT construct and is a direct rendition of the functional areas. The capabilities of a functional area can be represented and realized by one or more IT subsystems. What business functions are to functional areas, IT functions are to IT subsystems: functional areas support business functions, while IT subsystems encapsulate IT functions. Just like functional areas are mapped to and deconstructed into IT subsystems, the business functions are realized by one or more IT functions. These IT functions are logically grouped, encapsulated by, and implemented as a single unit. That unit is the IT subsystem. IT functions are implemented using a collection (that is, one or more) of software components. Hence, a subsystem is a grouping of software components. The IT functions are exposed by a set of interfaces at the subsystem level; each such interface is implemented by a software component inside the subsystem. The subsystem groups the components that are functionally cohesive in nature; changes in the form of enhancements or fixes are hence controlled and their effects localized within a subsystem boundary. The modularization of an IT System into its constituent subsystems fosters parallel development: implementation teams can separately develop the internals of the subsystem while adhering to the external interface contracts.

Identifying the subsystems is typically the first task. Subsystems need to be identified and their definition and characteristics captured. For each subsystem, each of its high-level interfaces also needs to be identified and declared. Adhering to the principles of capturing *just enough* architecture artifacts, I recommend using a template, like the one shown in Table 7.1, to capture the necessary artifacts for each subsystem.

Table 7.1   Capturing a Necessary Set of Details About an IT Subsystem

Subsystem ID:	SUBSYS-01
Subsystem Name:	My Subsystem
Function(s):	F1, F2
Interface(s):	I11, I12, I21

Subsystem ID—Provides a unique ID for each subsystem so that it is easy to identify and also to cross-reference between subsystems.

Subsystem Name —Indicates the name given to a subsystem; for example, Accounts Management, Transaction Management.

Function(s)—Provides a list of IT functions that the subsystem exposes as its behavior. The recommended technique to identify this set is to analyze the system use cases, group them logically, and assign them to the most functionally aligned subsystem.

Interface(s)—Enlists all the interfaces that the subsystem supports or exposes. For example, in an Accounts Management subsystem, an interface may be Withdrawal. At this level, only a textual description of the interface would suffice.

A Unified Modeling Language (UML) representation of the subsystems and their interdependencies may be produced as a part of capturing the design artifacts at the logical level. Figure 7.2 shows an example.

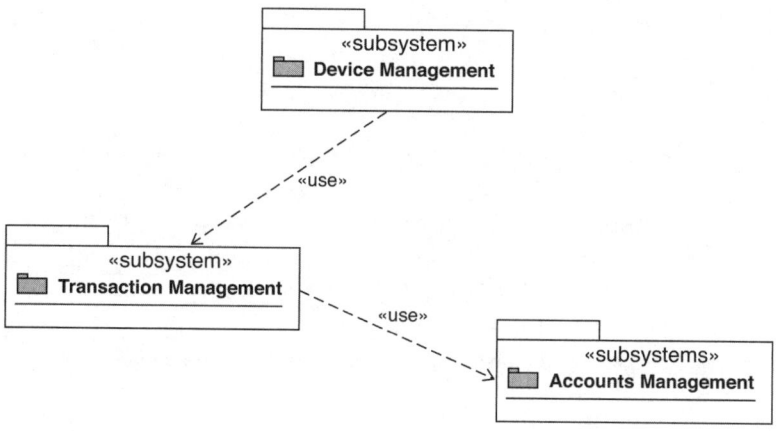

Figure 7.2   Depiction of a subsystem relationship.

For more details on UML, refer to the UML specifications maintained by the Object Management Group (2011) .

Component Identification

Once the subsystems are identified and their responsibilities captured, the next logical step is to identify a set of high-level software components, which collectively realize the interfaces that are exposed by the subsystem. An IT subsystem, as mentioned previously, is a first-class IT manifestation of a functional model. As such, the IT functions within a subsystem can be aligned according to their affinity with a set of core business entities. For example, for the Accounts

Management subsystem in Figure 7.2, there might be a couple of software components, one addressing the savings account while the other focuses on implementing the features of the checking account.

So, in this example, there could be two components: namely, Savings Account Manager and Checking Account Manager. The identification of components is not an exact science, and it depends on the designer's approach toward component granularity. As an example, some designers may choose to identify a single component called Accounts Manager (instead of two; that is, Savings Account Manager and Checking Account Manager) for the Accounts Management subsystem. There is no right or wrong between the two approaches; just keep in mind that the identified components should ideally be intuitive and relevant.

It is important to capture some of the essential details about each of the identified components. Table 7.2 provides a minimal set of details that I recommend capturing.

Table 7.2   High-Level Component Responsibilities—An Illustrative Example

Subsystem ID:	SUBSYS-01
Component ID:	COMP-01-01
Component Name:	Accounts Manager
Component Responsibilities:	The responsibilities include • Identifying the savings and checking accounts for an identified customer • Managing all the activities on the savings account of a given customer • Managing all the activities on the checking account of a given customer • Managing the linkages to the customer's profile information

Subsystem ID—Denotes the unique identifier of the subsystem containing the component.

Component ID—Assigns a unique identifier (ID) to the component.

Component Name—Indicates the name given to the component. Ideally, the name should be intuitive based on the business entities that the component may typically manage.

Component Responsibilities—Provides a textual description for the set of responsibilities that are assigned to and are expected (to be implemented) of the component.

Component Interactions

Once the components are identified at a logical level, the next step is to identify the architecturally significant business use cases. The use cases are analyzed, and subsets of them that are significant from an architectural standpoint are chosen. For each of the architecturally significant use cases, component interaction diagrams are used to elaborate how the use case may be realized through a collaborating set of components. A collaboration diagram illustrates how components interact by creating links between the components and by attaching messages to these links. The name of the message denotes the intent of invoking a specific behavior (a.k.a. function) of the invoked component to fulfill a part of the overall use case. Think of the messages as pseudo operations on the components. These pseudo operations manifest themselves as the responsibilities of the component.

ON BUSINESS AND SYSTEM USE CASES

A *business use case* describes a business process. The business process is realized through one or more system functions. Each such system function can be considered to be a *system use case*.

While depicting the high-level realization of a business use case through component collaborations, the message denoting a component invocation may be either associated to a system use case or the system use case itself. So, in essence, you can think of a system use case to be directly aligned with a subset of a component's responsibility. This responsibility is often encoded in the form of an interface or an operation on an interface. The granularity of the system use case typically dictates how the system use case maps to an interface or an operation on an interface.

Figure 7.3 illustrates a component interaction diagram. The Accounts Manager component and a couple of other components depict how a *Withdraw from ATM* business use case can be realized at a high level.

To summarize, the three steps—Subsystem Identification, Component Identification, and Component Interaction—are usually adequate to capture the logical-level design of the functional model.

Specified-Level Design

The specified-level design of the functional model focuses on elaborating the detailed behavior of each of the identified components. The logical definitions of the components are used as a starting point and are subsequently expanded to a point that ensures the following:

- The component interfaces are well defined.
- The data elements or entities owned by each subsystem are identified and detailed. (Data entities are aligned with the core business entities of an enterprise, the subset of which is applicable to the IT System being considered.)
- The responsibilities of each component are flushed out in more detail.

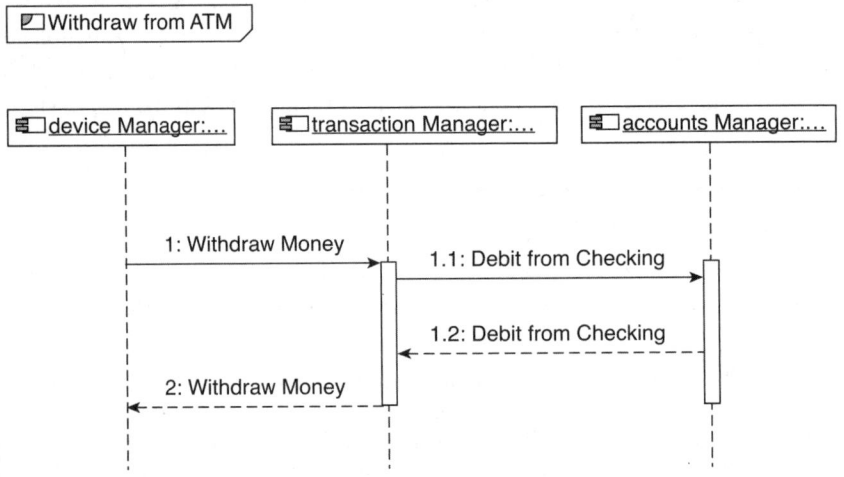

Figure 7.3   A high-level component interaction diagram for a business use case.

I typically recommend following a five-step process for developing the specified-level design for the functional model. The steps could be as follows:

- Component responsibility matrix (detailed)
- Interface specification for components
- Identification and association of data to subsystems
- Component interaction diagram (detailed)
- Assignment of components to layers

Component Responsibility Matrix

This step builds on the initial matrix (see Table 7.1) that was developed during the logical-level design. The existing matrix is enhanced with a more detailed and refined set of component responsibilities.

The existing responsibilities were identified based only on the functional specifications obtained through the analysis of the use cases; the nonfunctional requirements (NFR) of the application were not considered. The nonfunctional requirements are usually captured separately as a part of the requirements-gathering process. Each NFR is analyzed to determine which component or components may need to implement them. The component specification is thus assigned the set of NFRs it will support.

Like NFRs, business rules are typically captured separately in a business rules catalog. Each business rule is analyzed in relation to the functional responsibilities of the components. The outcome of this analysis results in the addition of one or more business rules to the responsibility set of the components. During the implementation phase, a business rules engine is typically selected to implement the collective set of business rules.

For purposes of this example, I assume that you realize how the high-level component responsibilities in the logical-level design are being expanded and elaborated during the specified level of component design.

A snippet of an updated component responsibility matrix is shown in Table 7.3.

Table 7.3 Updated Component Responsibility Matrix—An Illustrative Example

Subsystem ID:	SUBSYS-01
Component ID:	COMP-01-01
Component Name:	Accounts Manager
Component Responsibilities:	<<Existing Responsibilities; see Table 7.2>>
	NFR-01—Support more than 500 concurrent invocations.
	Complete all invocations in less than 1 second regardless of the number of concurrent invocations. (Refer to NFR-005.)
	Incorporate BRC-001 business rule, which provides added account benefits for a Gold customer.

Note: References to NFR-01 and BRC-001 in Table 7.3 are representative examples of documented nonfunctional requirements and a business rule catalog.

ON BUSINESS RULES

Business rules have always been a critical component of any complex IT System. The abundance of business rules management tools has made the use of business rules automation a pervasive architecture component of most systems and applications.

Business rules are codifications of some of the business operational decisions in the domain of IT programming. In today's world, when business rules and policies change so frequently, enterprises need to sense and respond to changes—for example, to the dynamics of the marketplace—and quickly adapt their IT Systems to maintain competitive and differentiated advantage. To support such dynamism, the business rules cannot be embedded into the core programming logic. Embedding business rules results in applications that are not

> resilient to change; business rules may change frequently based on business metrics and key performance indicators. Hence, business rules need to be externalized so that they can be changed at runtime.

Interface Specification

I introduced the idea of identifying interfaces for subsystems during the logical-level component design. A subsystem is just a logical grouping of components that are functionally cohesive in nature. Hence, the subsystem interfaces, in reality, are interfaces on the components within the subsystem. The components are true physical entities that manifest themselves as executable code.

Now let's focus on the component interfaces—in particular, their definition and design.

An interface is a software construct through which a component exposes its functionality to the outside world. In technical terms, an interface is a contract described through a collection of operations or methods. Developing the specifications for interfaces primarily deals with the art and science of identifying operations or methods and grouping them within interface boundaries.

To begin with, you should analyze each system use case that is owned by a component, keeping the key factors of complexity and cohesiveness in mind. System use cases that are atomic in nature—for example, *Retrieve Customer Profile*—should be categorized as operations (on an interface), whereas, for example, a use case like *Savings Accounts Management* would typically be categorized as an interface. A key point to note here is that many times use cases are documented at various and often inconsistent levels of granularity. As an example, some use cases are captured in such a way that the main flow is to create a particular entity, whereas its alternative flows are to update or delete the entity. Such use cases need to be tackled in either of two ways:

1. Refactor the use case and break it down where the main operations on the entity are in separate use cases; or

2. Consider the implementation of the use case at the level of an interface; an interface is a collection of a set of logically cohesive operations.

Once the operations are all identified through use case analysis, interfaces can be formally defined. The recommended approach is to consider a grouping of operations that exhibit logical cohesiveness, work on the same set of business entities, and are mutually exclusive from the rest of the operation set. Such a logical grouping of operations may be defined as an interface. As such, this exercise identifies a set of interfaces that are exposed by a given component. Figure 7.4 shows an example of mapping system use cases (as method operations) to interfaces.

A friendly disclaimer: the technique I share here is by no means the only mechanism to identify interfaces and their operations. In fact, I'd submit that this is only one of the few techniques that I have used myself and found it to be successful more often than not. It is an effective one!

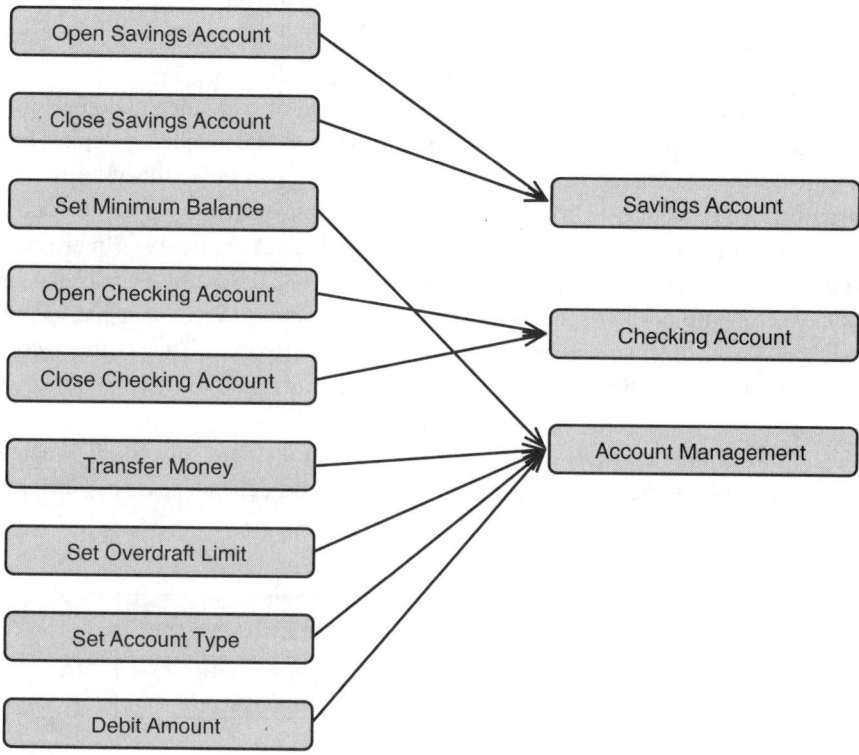

Figure 7.4 Example of associating operations to interfaces.

Capturing the outcomes in a way that fosters effective communication is paramount. The first part of the interface design is to document and model the interfaces and their operations with the proper signature and parameter list. Table 7.4 illustrates a format for capturing the information.

Table 7.4 An Example of Capturing the Interface Details of a Component

Component ID (it belongs to)	COMP-01-01
Interface Name and ID	Name: Savings Account ID: IF-01-01-01
Interface Operations	1. Account openSavingsAccount(custProfile: CustomerProfile) 2. Boolean closeSavingsAccount(account: Account)

At this point, the interfaces are identified and their methods defined. Continuing with this work, the next task at hand is to identify how interfaces are dependent on other interfaces—interface dependency.

There are two types of interface dependency. The first type of dependency depicts how interfaces within a single subsystem are interrelated. The second type of dependency depicts how interfaces in one subsystem are related to or depend upon interfaces in other subsystems. This dependency is usually documented as a UML class diagram, wherein each class is stereotyped as an "interface" and association lines are used to depict the dependencies explicitly. A more complete definition takes this one step further to provide a complete textual description qualifying and elaborating on the exact nature of the dependency; for example, *SavingsAccount::openAccount* has a dependency on *AccountsManagement::setAccountType*, and so on. This is the recommended approach, but often the realities of time and cost constraints limit our freedom to exercise it.

Figure 7.5 shows a simple dependency of interfaces within a single subsystem, whereas Figure 7.6 shows an illustrative example of how interfaces may be dependent across different subsystems.

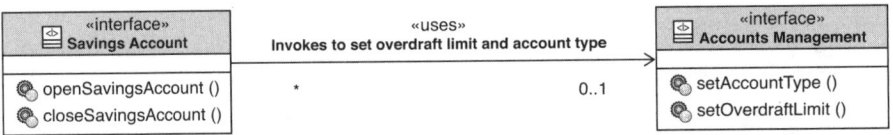

Figure 7.5   Example of interface dependency.

Identification and Association of Data Entries to Subsystems

The first two steps discussed so far focused primarily on component responsibilities. One of the fundamental aspects of component design is to identify the data entities that are owned by a subsystem and are used by the components to realize or implement its functionality.

The logical data model is used as an input to this task. The logical data model identifies the core business entities of the IT System to be built. A subsystem has a set of responsibilities to fulfill. These responsibilities, in turn, are implemented by the components that are encapsulated within the subsystem. The components expose the responsibilities through the interfaces and more specifically through the interface operations. Each of the interface operations requires data to be operated on to realize the functionality. The parameters on the interface operations are indicative of a logical grouping of data entities that are likely to be used and referenced together. Here is a simple set of rules to assist in identifying the data entities and associate them with subsystems:

1. Analyze, collect, and collate the parameter list on an interface.

2. Map the parameters to the closest business entities or data types in the logical data model.

3. Repeat steps 1 and 2 for each of the interfaces on a component.

4. Keep a running list of the data types that are identified.

5. Repeat steps 1 through 4 for each of the components within a subsystem.

6. Consolidate the list of data entities identified through steps 1 through 5.

7. Draw a boundary around the identified data entities from the logical data model and associate the data entities to the subsystem.

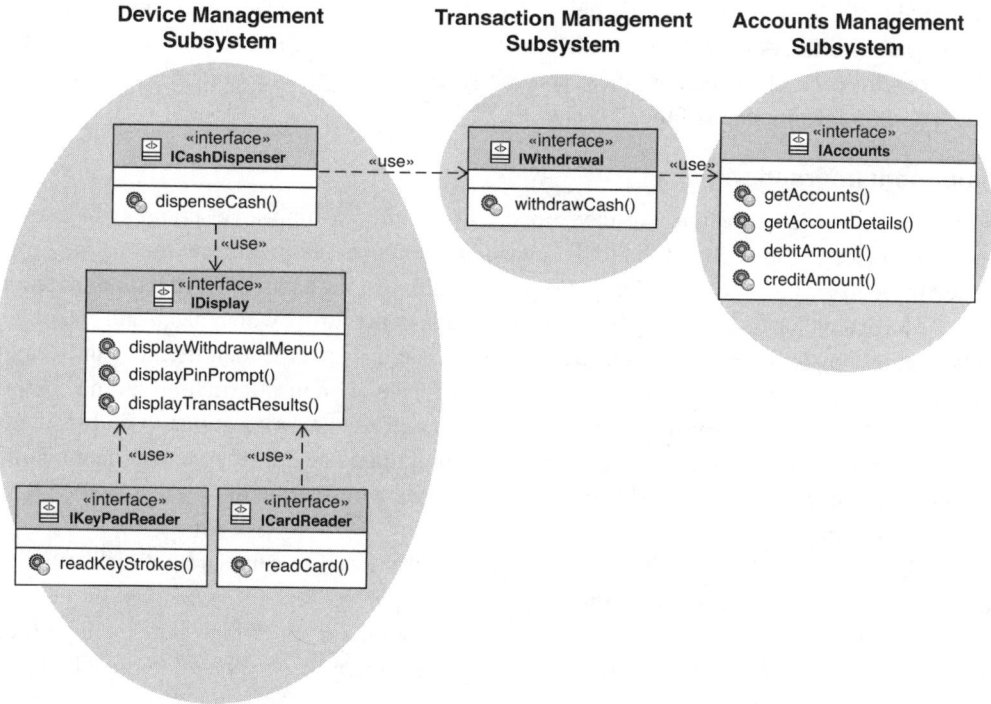

Figure 7.6 Interface dependency inside and in between subsystems.

When you are following these steps, it is common to be faced with a situation in which you identify a few data entities belonging to more than one subsystem. For such entities, put on your architecture rationalization hat to analyze and assess which subsystem performs the primary operations on the data entity and determine the subsystem to be primarily responsible to own the data entity. An example of primary responsibility might be that a subsystem, say SUBSYS-01, may be responsible for the CRUD (Create, Read, Update, Delete) operations on a data entity, whereas another subsystem, say SUBSYS-04, may use the data entity to check the value of an attribute flag; for example, to check whether the customer is a premium or standard customer. In such a situation, your refactoring and rationalization thinking hat should influence you to associate the data entity to SUBSYS-01. Such a refactoring and rationalization activity is required for the data entities that are faced with this dilemma; some are intuitive, whereas some require you to exercise a little more gray matter!

Interface dependency should be captured, ideally using standard UML notations, explicitly identifying the dependencies of interfaces to the data entities. A picture is worth a thousand words, as the adage goes, and I recommend erring on the side of having more (rather than fewer) architecture and design diagrams while capturing the important architecture and design artifacts. You should typically develop UML model artifacts to depict the subsystem and component ownership of data entities. A good UML model, in this case, negates the necessity to provide textual descriptions for each of the data entities; you can refer to the logical data model to obtain such detailed descriptions for each of the data entities.

Component Interaction

During the logical-level design, we developed and captured a high-level component interaction diagram (see Figure 7.3). At the logical level, the components interacted; that is, they were invoked through pseudo operations only. From then until now, as a part of the detailed specifications, we have developed a significant amount of details in the form of an updated and elaborated component responsibility matrix, the interface's specifications, and the identification and assignment of data entities to subsystems. At this stage, we have enough information on the components to update the component interaction diagrams: from pseudo invocations to real methods. The time is ripe and the information content rich enough to update the set of component interaction diagrams for the architecturally significant use cases with real method invocations. Figure 7.7 shows an example.

Referring to Figure 7.7, although the details of all the components are not elaborated for the sake of brevity, you can see how the *Accounts Manager* component is invoked through the *debitAccount* method. When I analyze the artifacts in Figure 7.6 and try to relate them with the component interaction in Figure 7.7, I can see that the *Accounts Management* interface in Figure 7.6 has an exposed *debitAccount* method and can imagine how the *Accounts Management* interface is exposed by the *Accounts Manager* component in Figure 7.7. Now, if I can figure that one out, I am convinced beyond doubt that you had already figured it out!

For each UML sequence diagram, you ideally should capture a textual description of the step-by-step invocation of the operations on the components.

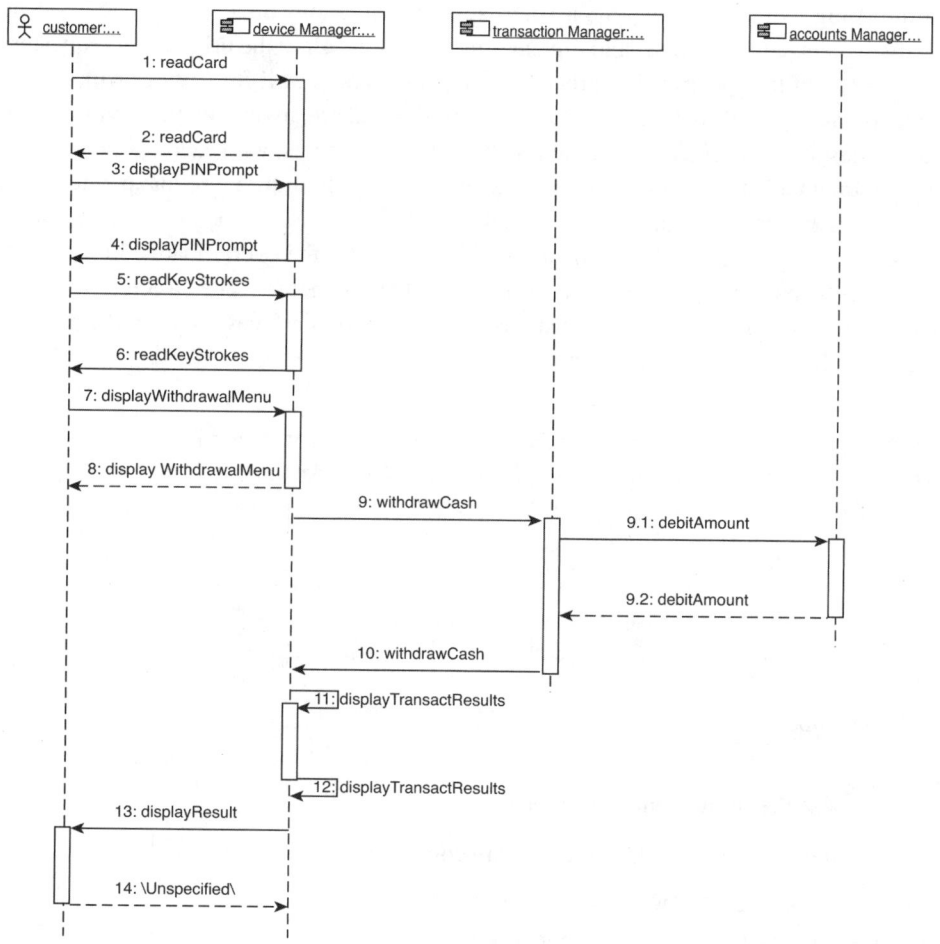

Figure 7.7 Component collaboration diagram (detailed) for Withdraw from ATM use case—an illustrative example.

The level of specificity discussed here should be applied to all the architecturally significant use cases that were elaborated through component interactions during the logical-level design. In fact, as you drill down into more and more details and specificities, I advocate that you augment the list of use cases (that is, above and beyond only the architecturally significant ones). Doing so will not only provide additional overall coverage but also will exercise and validate most, if not all, of the operations on each of the interfaces. For each use case, UML sequence diagrams are used to draw the component interaction diagrams. Each component interaction diagram starts from an originating requestor (an actor), invokes specific operations on a series of components that collectively realize the use case, and typically returns the result to the originating requestor.

By this stage of the specification process, each subsystem is well flushed out with each of its components having a well-defined set of responsibilities that are, in turn, exposed through one or more interfaces; each interface is specified with a set of operations, with each operation being well defined through a list of input and output parameters, which, in turn, are mapped to one or more data entities that may or may not be owned by the subsystem. Sounds like a handful but actually it is quite trivial. Let me show you a little bit extra: even the overly loaded long preceding sentence can be pictorially represented through an object structure. The structure in Figure 7.8 depicts the relationship between subsystems, components, interfaces, and interface operations and is typically called the component meta-model.

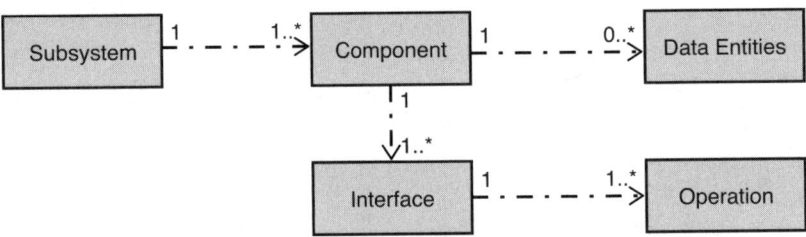

Figure 7.8   A component meta-model.

To summarize the component meta-model:

- A subsystem may encapsulate one or more components.
- A component may expose one or more interfaces.
- An interface may expose one or more operations.
- A component may assume primary responsibility of interacting with one or more data entities.

It is important to highlight that subsystems may also require refinement and refactoring after their initial identification. If a subsystem has grown to take up too much responsibility, it may be too complex to implement; if it looks to be less than optimal in features, it may need to be consolidated and merged with another related subsystem. Also, not all subsystems need to be custom built; some represent existing assets or products (for example, an HR module from an ERP package) .

Component Assignment to Layers

Imagine that you were doing the design of a real-world IT System (for example, a banking application), and you identified and specified a list of system components (or a smaller set thereof), as shown in Table 7.5.

Table 7.5 Components (or a Subset Thereof) for a Simple Banking Application

Subsystem	Components
Accounts Management	Account Manager
	Checking Account (CKA) Manager
	Savings Account (SA) Manager
Security Management	Security Manager
Customer Profile Management	Customer Profile (CP) Manager

Above and beyond the components in Table 7.5, there would be a set of technical components that typically do not belong to any functional subsystem. An illustrative subset of technical components may be the following:

- *DialogControl*—Facilitates communication between the presentation components and the business logic components.

- *Error Logger*—Logs all application-specific errors and warnings into a file to facilitate subsequent diagnostics of application or system errors of failures.

- *Relational DBMS*—Stores the required data entities.

- *ESB*—Middleware component that serves as an information exchange layer facilitating mediation, routing, and transformation of data and protocols.

- *Application Server*—Middleware component in which the application will be deployed.

- *Business Rules Engine (BRE)*—Middleware component in which business rules are developed and hosted.

- *Directory Server*—Middleware component in which the user credentials and their access rights are modeled and stored.

Note the difference between functional components (that is, the ones in Table 7.5) and the technical components. The functional components encapsulate some specific business function or a subset thereof, whereas the technical components represent utility components such as DialogControl and ErrorLogger as well as technology tools and packaged applications such as RDBMS, ESB, BRE and Application Server, which are generally applicable to and leveraged by multiple functional components.

Recall from Chapter 5, "The Architecture Overview," that one of the views of the architecture is the Layered view. Layering is a very important concept and technique in software architecture. Following are two value drivers of layering that I would like to reiterate:

- Enforces key characteristics for each layer that are influenced not only by the interlayer communication constraints and rules but also by the ever-so-important NFRs that are associated to and supported by the different layers

- Helps determine the placement of the components into the appropriate layers

Figure 7.9 depicts a representative allocation of the components, identified earlier, onto a layered view of the architecture.

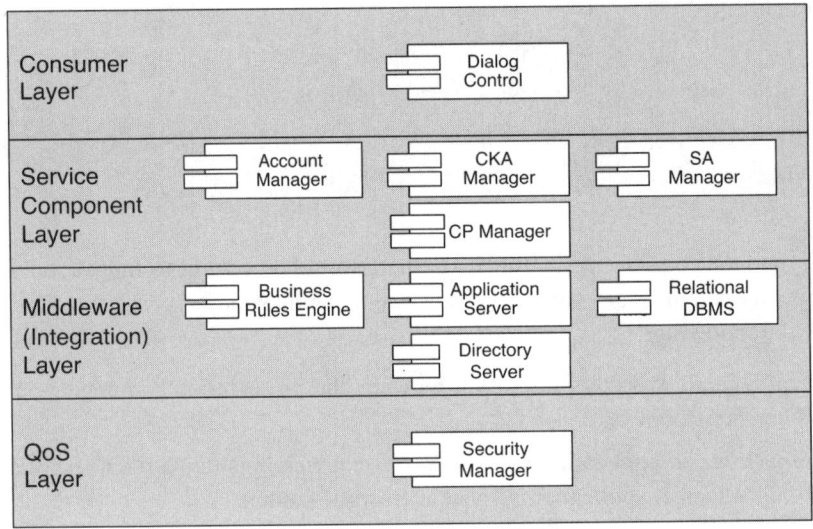

Figure 7.9   Allocation of component to layers—an illustrative example.

Obviously, this example does not show a complete layered view because it is missing quite a few layers from the layered architecture view in Chapter 5 and also a few components, for example, the ESB. Nonetheless, the idea here is to demonstrate the concept of component allocation to layers. (Notice, in Figure 7.9, that the QoS and Integration layers are depicted as horizontal layers, whereas in reality they are cross-cutting vertical layers. This depiction is done here for pictorial simplicity.)

The Layered view of the components and their placements on layers provides key data points on the physical-level design of the functional model—the topic of the next section.

Physical-Level Design

The physical-level design essentially revolves around two key elements:

- The choice of specific technology to implement the functional and technical components. For some technical components, the use of standard tools or products drives their implementation choice.
- The distribution of application components on a preliminary set of nodes so that they can be subsequently installed, configured, and hosted on physical hardware nodes, the latter representing the infrastructure topology of the system.

Hence, component design at the physical level focuses on the determination of the technology choice for implementation as well as the identification of the appropriate deployment components (nodes) on which the functional and technical components may be placed for run-time execution. Figure 7.10 shows a schematic of the nodal distribution of the components; that is, the placement of the components on infrastructure nodes.

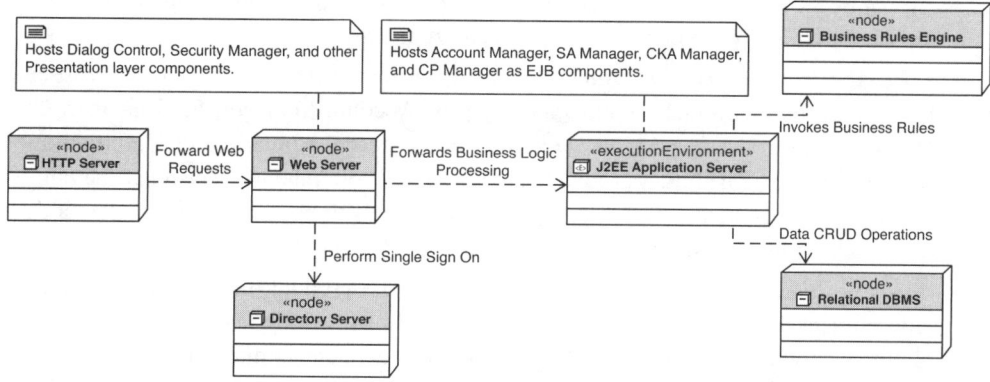

Figure 7.10 A physical-level component design—an illustrative example.

Notice in Figure 7.10 that the HTTP Server, Directory Server, Web Server, Relational DBMS, and Business Rules Engine are placed on dedicated physical machines while the J2EE Application Server is also placed on its own execution environment.

Many factors influence the decision of placing components onto deployment nodes. Specific NFRs and service-level agreements (SLAs) are core—availability, extensibility, latency, throughput, user response times, scalability, portability, and maintainability. The choice of technology is also critical; choosing between J2EE or .NET, choosing between leveraging a Commercial Off The Shelf (COTS) package software for business rules or custom developing them as a part of the embedded business logic, and choosing between a COTS portal technology for user experience or custom-developed user experience application front end, are some examples of decision points (specific to the illustrative banking example used here).

Now let's peek at some of the rationale that may be used to arrive at the physical component design. Focusing on the 10 components in Figure 7.9, the decision (from a real-world implementation) to place the components on the physical infrastructure may be influenced by the following:

- *HTTP Server on its own node*—The application contains a good mix of both static as well as dynamic web content; the static content hosted on a dedicated HTTP server node that has built-in caching and other performance-optimizing techniques for better user experience. Further, based on the user traffic, this node can be mirrored and load-balanced to distribute the load from user requests.

- *Web Server on its own node*—The reasons for this are similar to the reasons for which the HTTP server is placed on a dedicated node. Additionally, horizontal scaling (more on horizontal scaling in Chapter 8, "The Operational Model") of Presentation layer components, supporting peak loads and future projected workloads, is required to support the NFRs around user experience of the IT System. The node also hosts the *DialogControl* and the *SecurityManager* component.

- *Directory Server on its own node*—The COTS product that would implement the user repository typically mandates a dedicated environment.

- *J2EE Application Server on its own execution environment*—The technology chosen to implement the functional components—that is, Account Manager, SA Manager, CKA Manager, and CP Manager—is stateless session Enterprise JavaBeans (EJB) running on a J2EE platform. The NFRs around these functional components, especially the number of concurrent instances of each component that needs to be maintained, dictate a dedicated right-sized environment for execution.

- *Business Rules Engine on its own node*—The COTS product recommends a dedicated environment coupled with the fact that the transactional workload characteristics are different from other functional or technical components in the architecture.

- *Relational DBMS on its own node*—The NFRs around transactional workload metrics, along with concurrency requirements for simultaneous read and writes, mandate a dedicated compute node and environment .

Note that the reasons for your physical component design and placement decisions may be quite different from the ones presented here and would be dictated by the uniqueness of the NFRs, COTS products in the mix, and the choice of the implementation technology. You should use the example provided here as a guide to the thought process and decision-making criteria.

ON PHYSICAL-LEVEL DESIGN AND MICRO DESIGN

There are various schools of thought that try to define and document software architecture in different ways. Physical-level design has different interpretations and use in IT System design.

One school of thought considers physical-level design as more of the micro design of the components. Micro design is the domain in which a component is considered as the highest level of abstraction. Each component is broken down into a set of participating classes that collectively realize the operations that the component exposes through its interfaces. A designer applies well-known and proven design patterns and best practices to solve a specific class of problem. Patterns can be combined to develop composite design patterns that solve a given problem within the component. (The *Design Patterns* book by Gamma et al. [1994], provides one of the best treatments on design patterns.) Detailed sequence diagrams are used to elaborate the dynamic nature of how each operation (on the interface) is implemented through the participating classes in the *class* or *object* model. Such detailed design is performed for each of the components of the application.

The physical level component design should not be confused with the micro design interpretation of physical level design.

As you can see, physical-level component design provides a lot of information to influence the operational model of the system architecture—the topic of the next chapter.

Before closing out this chapter with the functional model for the Elixir case study, let me share some thoughts about functional modeling. Although the evolutionary steps of conceptual-, logical-, specified-, and physical-level design are apt and well thought out, time concerns often encroach upon projects, and frequently, architects must cut short their work activities. In such time-constrained situations, it is often beneficial to consider the specified-level design as the core first step in functional modeling; the artifacts that are typically identified in the conceptual and logical design phases can be built into the specified-level design artifacts . Thus, the practical architect is born!

Case Study: Functional Model for Elixir

Before returning to the case study, refer to the high-level components of Elixir that were identified in Table 5.1 in Chapter 5.

Here, I focus only on capturing the artifacts of the functional model and avoid illustrating the rationale behind each one of them. The technique followed is similar to what is described in the preceding sections on the general formulation of the functional model and its various artifacts.

Logical Level

This section illustrates the logical-level artifacts of the functional model of Elixir.

Subsystem Identification

Four subsystems were identified for Elixir: Asset Onboarding Management, Machine Health Management, Reporting Management, and Reliability Maintenance Management. Figure 7.11 depicts the subsystems and their interrelationships.

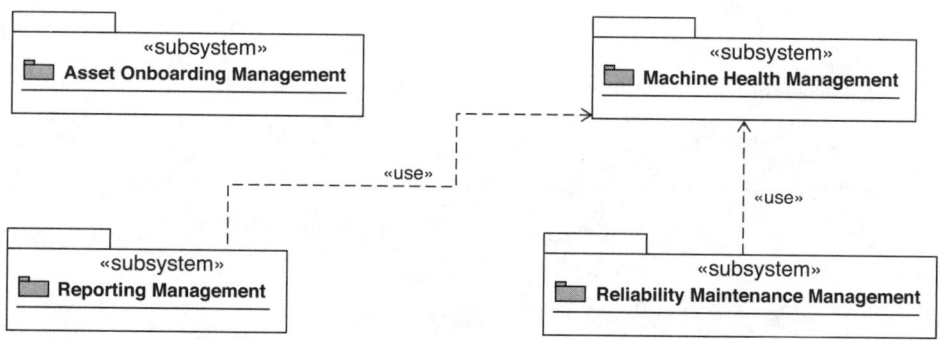

Figure 7.11   Subsystems and their dependencies for the Elixir system.

Tables 7.6 through 7.9 expand on each of the subsystems and their functions.

Table 7.6   Asset Onboarding Management

Subsystem ID:	SUBSYS-01
Subsystem Name:	Asset Onboarding Management
Function(s):	• Manage the addition of a new machine type to the system. • Manage the addition of a new machine of an existing type to the system.
Interface(s):	• Add New Machine Type. • Add New Machine. • Edit Machine Configuration.

Table 7.7   Machine Health Management

Subsystem ID:	SUBSYS-02
Subsystem Name:	Machine Health Management
Function(s):	• Monitor the health of the operating machines in real time. • Perform calculations of key performance indicators (KPI) for operational machines in real time. • Generate alerts on critical machine conditions. • Visualize the machine health metrics (KPI) in real time as and when they are generated.
Interface(s):	• Calculate KPI. • Dispatch Alert.

Table 7.8   Reliability Maintenance Management

Subsystem ID:	SUBSYS-03
Subsystem Name:	Reliability Maintenance Management
Function(s):	• Associate machine failure modes with generated alerts. • Generate recommended action to address faulty or inefficient conditions.
Interface(s):	• Generate Recommended Action.

Table 7.9 Reporting Management

Subsystem ID:	SUBSYS-04
Subsystem Name:	Reporting Management
Function(s):	• Support the creation of predefined reports for the different types (roles) of users using the system. • Formulate and generate productivity reports for each asset rolling up to each geographical region. • Support comparative analysis between cross-asset performance and failures. • Support comparative analysis between cross-geographical regions on productions, maintenance windows, and machine faults.
Interface(s):	• Machine Productivity Report. • Region Productivity Report. • Regional Comparative Analysis Report.

Component Identification

Note that the components covered in this section are the functional components that are identified as a part of the subsystems. There is an additional set of components that are more technical in nature. The later section, on specified level design, has more details.

Tables 7.10 and 7.11 describe the components of the Asset Onboarding Management subsystem of Elixir.

Table 7.10 Responsibilities of the Asset Onboard Manager Component

Subsystem ID:	SUBSYS-01
Component ID:	COMP-01-01
Component Name:	Asset Onboard Manager
Component Responsibilities:	The responsibilities include • Add new machine type. • Add new machine of existing type.

Table 7.11   Responsibilities of the Asset Configuration Manager Component

Subsystem ID:	SUBSYS-01
Component ID:	COMP-01-02
Component Name:	Asset Configuration Manager
Component Responsibilities:	The responsibilities include • Define machine configuration. • Update machine configuration.

Because the preceding tables do not look too impressive or exciting, I have deferred the full details for each subsection of logical, specified, and physical design, wherever applicable, in Appendix B, "Elixir Functional Model (Continued)."

Component Collaboration

The logical level has three main architecturally significant use cases, namely:

• Machine Onboarding

• Generate Machine Alerts

• Recommend Work Orders

Figure 7.12 depicts the component collaboration for the Machine Onboarding use case.

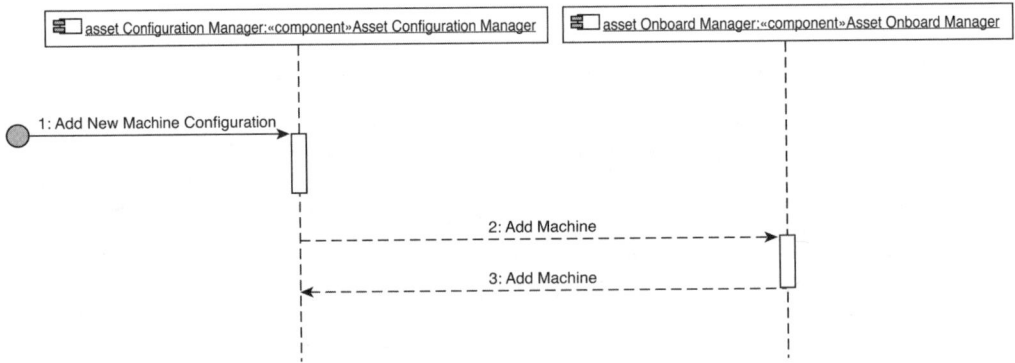

Figure 7.12   Component collaboration for Machine Onboarding use case.

Refer to Appendix B for the other two component collaboration views.

Specified Level

This section illustrates the specified-level artifacts of the functional model of Elixir.

Component Responsibility Matrix

Tables 7.12 and 7.13 expand the component responsibilities of the first subsystem of Elixir, Asset Onboard Manager, to support the NFRs and business rules.

Table 7.12 Component Responsibility for Asset Onboard Manager

Subsystem ID:	SUBSYS-01
Component ID:	COMP-01-01
Component Name:	Asset Onboard Manager
Component Responsibilities:	<<Existing Responsibilities; see Table 7.10>>
	NFR-01—System should support a fleet of around 4,000 machines globally distributed.
	The onboarding process should be automatic and should be completed within the time mandated by NFR-02.
	NFR-02—System should be able to support batch loads of machines of a known and existing type of machine. A batch load of 100 machines must be completed in less than 1 minute. The maximum batch size would be 500 machines and should be completed in less than 3 minutes.

Table 7.13 Component Responsibility for Asset Configuration Manager

Subsystem ID:	SUBSYS-01
Component ID:	COMP-01-02
Component Name:	Asset Configuration Manager
Component Responsibilities:	<<Existing Responsibilities; see Table 7.11>>
	BRC-001—Different versions of a machine have different configurations. The variability should be dynamically used during machine onboarding. (Details of the version to internal machine configuration are omitted for brevity.)

Interface Specification

Two interfaces are identified for the Asset Onboard Manager component of Elixir (see Tables 7.14 and 7.15).

Table 7.14   Specification for Machine Onboarding Interface

Component ID (it belongs to)	COMP-01-01
Interface Name and ID	Name: Machine Onboarding ID: IF-01-01-01
Interface Operations	1. String ID addMachine(mProfile: MachineProfile) 2. Boolean editMachine(mProfile: MachineProfile)

Table 7.15   Specification for Machine Configuration Interface

Component ID (it belongs to)	COMP-01-02
Interface Name and ID	Name: Machine Configuration ID: IF-01-02-01
Interface Operations	1. String ID createConfiguration(cProfile: MachineConfiguration) 2. Boolean editConfiguration(cProfile: Configuration) 3. Boolean changeMachineVersion(mProfile: MachineProfile, cProfile:MachineConfiguration)

Refer to Appendix B for the component interface definitions for the rest of the components.

Associate Data Entities with Subsystems

Figure 7.13 depicts the most important data entities and their association to the subsystems of Elixir. Notice that the Reporting Management subsystem is not shown in the figure. The reason for its absence is that the Reporting Management subsystem uses most of the data entities to support the specific user reports; *uses* is the operative word here. As such, it does not own any specific data entities, only accessing them as appropriate.

Component Assignment to Layers

Figure 7.14 depicts all the identified components (both functional and technical) of Elixir and their allocation to the different layers of a typical layered view of an architecture. Although one such component (that is, the ErrorLogger) is identified to be specific to Elixir, the components in the Consumer, Middleware, and QoS layers in Figure 7.14 are also part of the Elixir system. An additional component in the Consumer layer of Elixir—namely, the Portal Container component—is responsible for managing the interaction between the various user interface widgets and the user inputs.

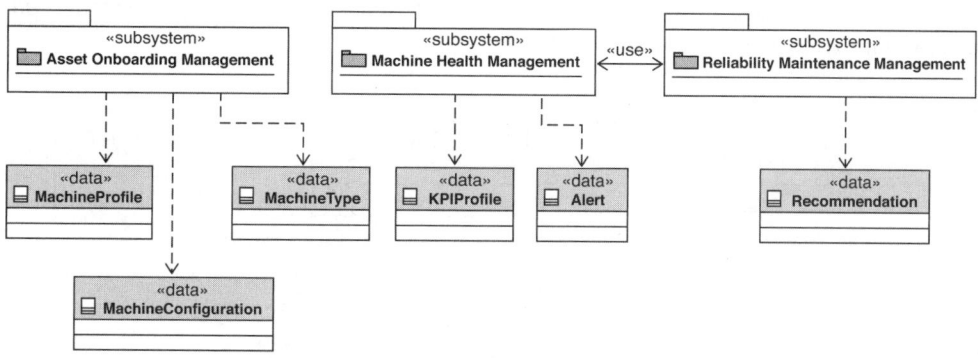

Figure 7.13   Data entity ownership for the subsystems of Elixir.

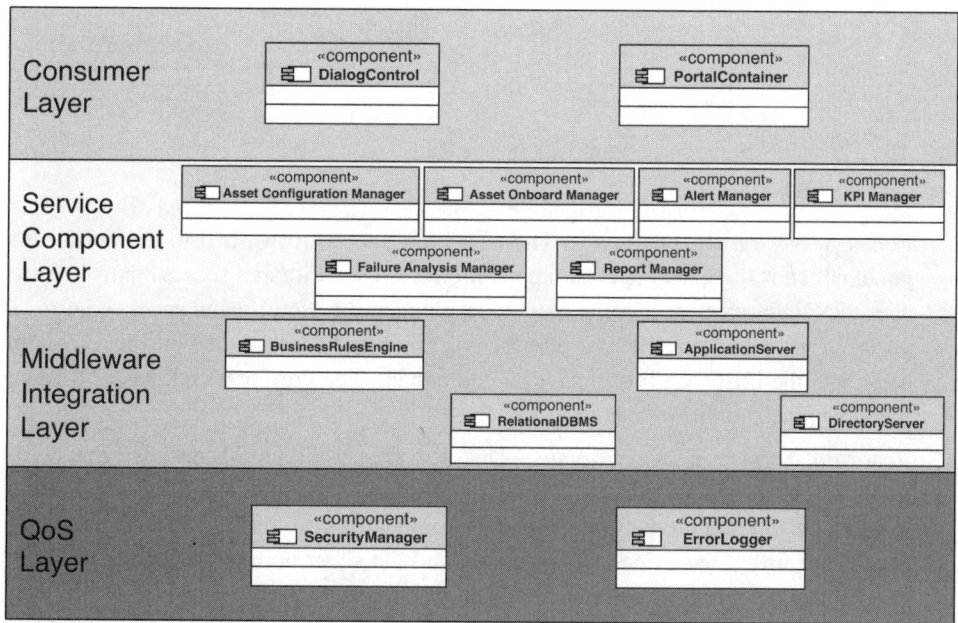

Figure 7.14   Allocation of Elixir components to architecture layers.

Physical Level

The physical component design for Elixir is similar to the example used to illustrate the physical-level component design earlier in this chapter; Figure 7.10 and its associated narrative provide details on the techniques and criteria used to determine the physical-level design.

Figure 7.15 depicts the physical-level component design for Elixir. I explain only the additional (to Figure 7.10) nodes that appear in this diagram.

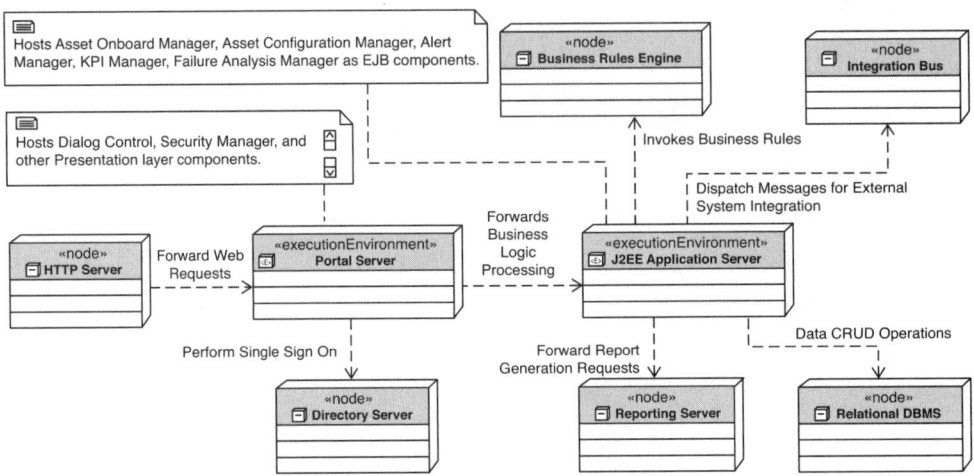

Figure 7.15 Physical-level component design for Elixir.

Portal Server on its own node—The user requests are forwarded to the portal server node, which is the gatekeeper for application-level security and access control. It leverages the Directory Server component to implement the security and access control. The portal server maintains the user interface of Elixir and forwards the business logic processing to the J2EE Application Server component. The Presentation layer NFRs dictate that it be placed on its own node.

Reporting Server on its own node—This node hosts the COTS package that will be used as the reporting engine for Elixir. Support for ad hoc and preconfigured reports on machine health and production metrics are among the core features of Elixir. The number of concurrent users requesting reports and the sheer number of reports necessitate the reporting server be hosted on a dedicated node.

Integration Bus—This is a separate dedicated node for the ESB technical component. The middleware COTS package currently owned by the client is already hosted on its own dedicated infrastructure (a.k.a. node) and hence the choice was simple.

Note: Keep in mind that a lot of software engineering best practices and techniques are employed to determine the rationale for component placement on physical nodes. A detailed study of these practices and techniques is beyond the scope of the current discussion.

Summary

The functional model is one of the most important domains of software architecture. A well-designed functional model is the key to building a robust and functional system architecture. The functional model not only addresses the architectural techniques used to deconstruct the problem domain into a set of architecture artifacts but also illustrates how to progressively build upon them by incrementally moving from the abstract to more detailed architectural constructs. The functional model is iteratively built through the four major phases of conceptual-, logical-, specified-, and physical-level design—a methodical approach that reaps maximum value.

Due to the time-critical nature of almost all IT projects, a four-step rigor may not be a natural fit. As such, it is acceptable to initiate the focus on the logical-level design and then progressively build the detailed functional model. In more time-critical situations, it is okay to take a calculated risk of initiating with the specified-level design. However, compromising on apportioning commensurate time and focus on the specified-level design will certainly defeat the purpose of this architecture and design work effort.

The main focus of this chapter was to provide a bit of a prescriptive guidance on how to go about iteratively and incrementally developing the functional model, focusing on the essential artifacts to capture and the techniques that may be used to rationalize the decision-making process. While the discourse may be quite detailed, the framework is not too hard to grasp:

- Identify the subsystems that could form a natural grouping of capabilities.
- Identify components, for each subsystem, that would work together internally (to the subsystem) to support the subsystem capabilities.
- Identify the subsystems that will hold primary ownership of the core data entities of the system.
- Identify the interfaces, on each of the components, that will collectively expose and implement the component functions.
- Determine the placement of the components onto a layered view of the system architecture and subsequently onto a set of logical infrastructure components.

And that's all there is to it!

The Elixir case study now has a functional model. So as not to extend this chapter beyond what is necessary, the complete details of the functional model artifacts of Elixir are available in Appendix B.

Take a moment now to give yourself a well-deserved pat on the back if you have come this far in the book. I have seen many software architects who only dwell in what has been covered so far in this book, and they still make quite a good name and fan following for themselves!

The physical-level functional component design is a very good segue into the operational model—the topic of the next chapter!

References

Gamma, E., Helm, R., Johnson, R., & Vlissides, J. (1994). *Design patterns: Elements of reusable object-oriented software.* New York: Addison-Wesley Professional.

IBM. (2005). Component business models: Making specialization real. Retrieved from https://www-935.ibm.com/services/us/imc/pdf/g510-6163-component-business-models.pdf.

Jacobson, I, Booch, G., Rambaugh J. (1999). *The unified software development process.* New York: Addison-Wesley Professional.

Object Management Group (OMG) (2011). Documents associated with Unified Modeling Language (UML), v2.4.1. Retrieved from http://www.omg.org/spec/UML/2.4.1/.

CHAPTER 8

The Operational Model

The tires hit the road; let the fun begin!

At this point, if you feel that you've earned your bread, here is some breaking news for you: *The job ain't yet done, my friend. Who will put your functional model into operation? I hear a familiar voice in the background calling out: "I rely on you to put this all into action. Let the tires hit the road!"*

With a well-defined functional model, the components, once implemented, would need a home; that is, each of the components needs to run on a piece of hardware that is commensurate with the workload that the component has to support. While the functional model treated the system in terms of its usage (that is, *who* was using the system, *how* they were interacting with the system, and *which* components were used for the interactions), the operational model views the system in terms of its deployed context (that is, *where* the components are deployed and *when* they are invoked).

This chapter focuses on the operational model (OM) of a system. The OM defines and captures the distribution of the components in the IT System onto geographically distributed nodes, together with the connections necessary to support the required interactions between the components to achieve the IT System's functional and nonfunctional requirements (NFRs); the purpose is to honor time, budget, and technology constraints. The chapter also focuses on how to iteratively build the operational model of an IT System through a three-phased approach starting with the logical operational model (LOM) and subsequently defining more specificities (elaboration) of the OM through two more views—the specification operational model (SOM) and the physical operational model (POM). Elaboration is an act of refinement that establishes increased accuracy and a greater degree of detail or precision.

The discipline of operational modeling is significantly expansive; it can get into the details of hardware architectures, into network topologies and architecture, or into distributed processing architectures. However, keeping to the central theme of this book, which is to focus on the essential ingredients and recipes to be a consistently successful software architect by defining *just enough* architecture artifacts, this chapter focuses on the elements of the OM that are essential for a software architect to understand to either be able to develop the OM on her own or to oversee its development. And yes, the chapter concludes by instantiating a subset of the operational model for the Elixir system case study.

Why We Need It

The goal of the operational model is to provide a blueprint that illustrates the appropriate set of network, server, and computational test beds necessary for the functional components to operate—not only individually but also supporting their intercomponent communications. The operational model helps in identifying and defining the

- Servers on which one or more of the functional components may be placed
- Compute capacity (memory, processors, storage) for each of the servers
- Network topology on which the servers are installed; that is, their locations, along with their intercommunication links

It is important to recognize and acknowledge the value of the operational model artifact of any software architecture; you can dedicate commensurate effort and diligence to its formulation only if you are convinced of its importance. I can only share with you the reasons that compel me to spend adequate time in its formulation:

Component placement and structuring—Functional components need to be placed on nodes (operational) to meet the system's service-level requirements along with other quality requirements of the IT System; serviceability and manageability, among others. As an example, colocated components may be grouped into deployable units to simplify placement. Also, where required, the component's stored data can be placed on a node that is separate from the one where the component itself is hosted. The OM maps the interactions (functional) to the deployable nodes and connections (operational). The operational concerns also typically influence the structuring of the components; technical components may be added and application components restructured to take into account distribution requirements, operational constraints, and the need to achieve service-level requirements.

Functional and nonfunctional requirements coverage—The logical- and specification-level views of the operational model provide details around the functional and nonfunctional characteristics for all elements within the target IT System, while the physical-level view provides a fully detailed, appropriately capacity-sized configuration, suitable for use as a blueprint for the procurement, installation, and subsequent maintenance of the system. The OM provides the functional model an infrastructure to run on; appropriate diligence is required to have a fully operational system.

Enables product selection—The blueprint definition (hardware, network, and software technologies) gets more formalized and consolidated through the incorporation of the proper product and technology selection. Some examples of hardware selection include deciding between Linux® and Windows® OS, between virtual machines and bare metal servers, or between various machine processor families such as the Intel Xeon E series versus X series. The technology architecture then becomes complete.

Enables project metrics—A well-defined operational model contributes to and influences cost estimates of the solution's infrastructure, both for budgeting and as part of the business case for the solution. The choice of technologies also helps influence the types of skills (product specific know-how) required to align with the various implementation and deployment activities.

It is important to realize that the technical components, identified as a part of the operational model, must be integrated with the functional components. The operational model ensures that the technical architecture and the application architecture of a software system converge—that they are related and aligned. As an example, you can think of a business process workflow runtime server as a technical component (part of a middleware software product), yet it contains business process definitions and information about the business organization that are clearly application concepts. This component, therefore, has both application and technical responsibilities.

Just as with the functional model, it is critically important to acknowledge the value of the operational model as it relates to the overall architecture discipline. I intend to carry forward a similar objective from the functional model and into the operational model to illustrate the various aspects of the operational model and the techniques to develop and capture them.

Just take a step back and think about the power you are soon to be bestowed with—a master of both functional modeling and operational modeling!

On Traceability and Service Levels

The operational model is a critical constituent of the systems architecture, which connects many systems notes to form an architectural melody. In a way, the OM brings everything together. It is paramount that the IT constructs or artifacts that are defined must, directly or indirectly, be traceable to some business construct. In the case of the operational model, the business constructs manifest themselves in the form of service levels and quality attributes.

Quality attributes typically do not enhance the functionality of the system. However, they are necessary characteristics that enable end users to use an operational system relative to its performance, accuracy, and the "-ilities," as they are popularly called—availability, security, usability, compatibility, portability, modifiability, reliability and maintainability. An understanding of the typical NFR attributes is in order.

- **Performance**—Defines a set of metrics that concerns the speed of operation of the system relative to its timing characteristics. Performance metrics either can be stated in somewhat vague terms (for example, "the searching capability should be very fast") or can be made more specific through quantification techniques (for example, "searching of a document from a corpus of a 1TB document store should not exceed 750 milliseconds").

- **Accuracy and precision**—Defines the level of accuracy and precision of the results (or outcomes) generated by the system. This is typically measured in terms of the tolerance to the deviation from the technically correct results (for example, "KPI calculations should remain within +/- 1% of the actual engineering values").

- **Availability**—Determines the amount of uptime of the system during which it is operational. The most-talked-about example is when systems are expected to maintain an uptime SLA of five 9s, that is, 99.999 percent.

- **Security**—Defines the requirements for the protection of the system (from unwanted access) and its data (from being exposed to malicious users). Examples may include authentication and authorization of users using single sign-on techniques, support for data encryption across the wires, support for nonrepudiation, and so on.

- **Usability**—Determines the degree of ease of effectively learning, operating, and interacting with the system. The metric is typically qualified in terms of intuitiveness of the system's usage by its users and may be quantified in terms of learning curve time required by users to comfortably and effectively use the system.

- **Compatibility**—Defines the criteria for the system to maintain various types of support levels. Examples may include backward compatibility of software versions, ability to render the user interface on desktops as well as mobile tablets, and so on.

- **Portability**—Specifies the ease with which the system can be deployed on multiple different technology platforms. Examples may include support for both Windows and Linux operating systems.

- **Modifiability**—Determines the effort required to make changes, such as new feature additions or enhancements, to an existing system. The quantification is usually in terms of effort required to add a set of system enhancements.

- **Reliability**—Determines the consistency with which a system maintains its performance metrics, its predictability in the pattern and frequency of failure, and its deterministic resolution techniques.

- **Maintainability**—Determines the ease or complexity measures to rectify system errors and to restore the system to a point of consistency and integrity; essentially adapting the system to different changing environments. The metrics are typically defined in terms of efforts (person weeks) required to recover the system from various categories of faults and also the system's scheduled maintenance-related downtimes, if any.

- **Scalability**—Defines the various capacities (that is, system workload) that may be supported by the system. The capacities are typically supported by increased compute power (processor speeds, storage, memory) required to meet the increased workloads. *Horizontal* scalability (a.k.a. scale out) denotes the nodal growth (that is, adding more compute nodes) for a system to handle the increased workloads. *Vertical* scalability (a.k.a. scale up) denotes the need to add more system resources (that is, compute power) to support the increased workload.

- **Systems Management** —Defines the set of functions that manage and control irregular events, or other "nonapplication" events, whether they are continuous (such as performance monitoring) or intermittent (such as software upgrades—that is, maintainability).

There are definitely many other NFR attributes such as reusability and robustness that may be part of the system's characteristics. However, in the spirit of *just enough*, the preceding ones are the most commonly used.

As a parting remark on service levels, let me add that you need to take SLAs very seriously for any system under construction. The SLAs are notorious for coming to bite you as you try to make the system ready for prime-time usage. SLAs are legal and contractual bindings that have financial implications such as fees and penalties. If you are not sure whether your system can meet the quantified SLAs (for example, 99.999 percent system uptime, available in 20 international languages, and so on), consider thinking in terms of service-level objectives (SLOs), which are statements of intent and individual performance metrics (for example, the system will make a best effort to support 99 percent uptime, pages will refresh at most in 10 seconds, and so on). Unlike SLAs, SLOs leave room for negotiations and some wiggle room; they may or may not be bound by legal and financial implications!

Developing the Operational Model

The operational model is developed in an iterative manner, enhancing the level of specificity between subsequent iterations, moving from higher levels of abstraction to more specific deployment and execution artifacts. The three iteration phases I focus on here are the conceptual operational model (COM), the specification operational model (SOM), and the physical operational model (POM).

The COM is the highest level of abstraction, a high-level overview of the distributed structure of the business solution represented in a completely technology-neutral manner. The SOM focuses on the definition of the technical services that are required to make the solution work. The POM focuses on the products and execution platforms chosen to deliver both the functional and nonfunctional requirements of the solution. The COM–SOM–POM story connotes that they ought to be developed in sequence, which, however, may not be the case. As an example, it may be completely legitimate to start thinking about but not fully develop the POM in the second week of a six-month OM development cycle. COM–SOM–POM deserves a little bit more page space to warrant a formal definition. A brief description follows:

COM —Provides a technology-neutral view of the operational model. COM concerns itself only with application-level components that are identified and represented to communicate directly with one another; the technical components that facilitate the communication are not brought into focus.

SOM—Transforms, or more appropriately augments, the COM view into and with a set of technical components. The technical components are identified and their specifications appropriately defined to support the business functions along with appropriate service-level agreements that each of them need to support.

POM—Provides a blueprint for the procurement, installation, and subsequent maintenance of the system. The functional specifications (from the functional model) influence and dictate the identification of the software products (or components) that are verified to support the relevant NFRs. The software components are executed on the physical servers (nodes). Software components collectively define the functional model; the set of physical servers (nodes) defines the physical operational blueprint.

These levels (or representations) of the OM typically evolve or are "elaborated" together during the development process, in much the same way as the functional model (see Chapter 7, "The Functional Model").

Conceptual Operational Model (COM)

The COM is built out through a series of activities. The development of the COM is based on a few fundamental techniques: identify the zones and locations, identify the conceptual nodes of the system, place the nodes in the zones and locations, and categorize the placement of the nodes into a set of deployable units. The rest of this section elaborates on these techniques and activities.

For example, consider a retail scenario. I purposefully deviate from the banking example used in the earlier chapters; the retail scenario provides opportunities to address more variability as it pertains to the development of the system's OM. The retail scenario, at a high level, is simplistic (on purpose). Users of this retail system can work in either offline or online mode. Users typically view inventories and submit orders at multiple stores. Two back-end systems—Stock Management System (SMS) and Order Management System (OMS)—form the core of the data and systems interface.

The development of the COM may be performed in four major steps:

1. Define the zone and locations.

2. Identify the components.

3. Place the components.

4. Rationalize and validate the COM.

Define the Zones and Locations

The first step is to identify and determine the various locations where system components (external or internal) are going to reside and from where users and other external systems may access the system. Zones are used to designate locations that have common security requirements. They are areas in the system landscape that share a common subset of the NFRs.

The recommendation is to adopt, standardize, and follow some notational scheme to represent OM artifacts. Keeping the notation catalog to a minimum reduces unnecessary ancillary complexities.

At a minimum, adopting a naming scheme to denote actors and system components is always beneficial. Artifacts (actors and components) in one zone may or may not have access to the artifacts in a neighboring zone. Some visual indicators that can assist in depicting interzone communication, or lack thereof, come in very handy; for example, double vertical lines between two zones indicate that interzonal communication is not allowed. The diagrammatic representation in Figure 8.1 depicts the locations and zones for an illustrative retail scenario.

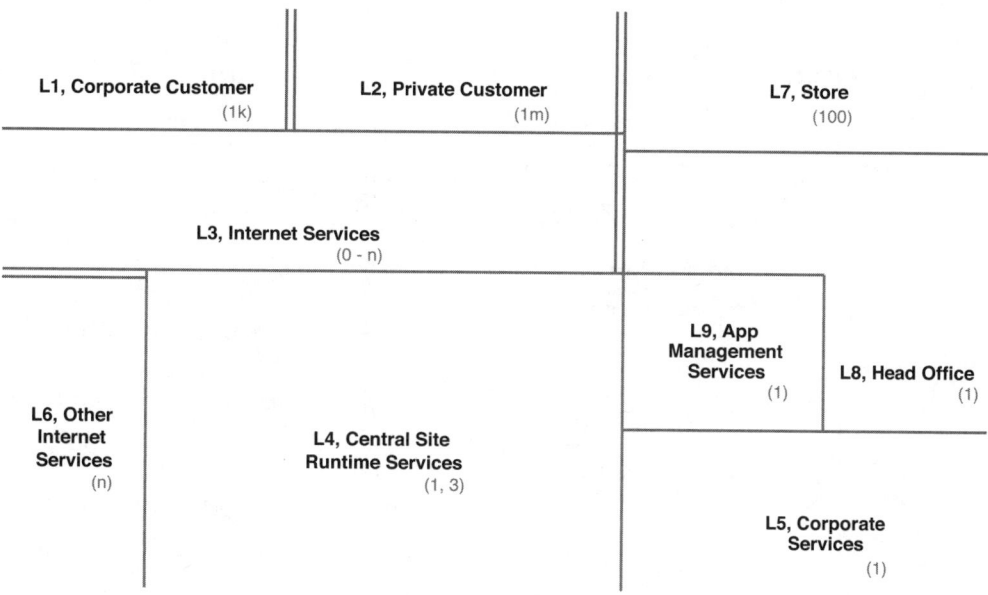

Figure 8.1   Example of locations and zones in a COM.

The figure shows different zones labeled as Lxx, <Zone Name> with a number in parentheses. Lxx refers to the standard abbreviation used to designate a unique location (xx is a unique number). The number in the parentheses denotes the cardinality. For example, L1 has a cardinality of 1,000, which implies that there could be up to 1,000 corporate customers (potentially distributed while similar in nature). A second example is L4, which has a cardinality of 1 or 3; a cardinality of 1 denotes the existence of only one data center instance (which will implicitly require 24/7 support), whereas having 3 instances implies that three data centers would support three geographies (a "chasing the sun" pattern). Notice that there are double lines between L1 and L2, whereas there is a single line between L4 and L6. The double lines provide a visual clue that the boundaries are strict enough to have no connection across the two zones that they demarcate. A single solid line, on the other hand, denotes that connectivity (for example, slow or high speed, and so on) exists across the two zones.

It is safe to state that architects introduce variances or extensions of the zonation depiction. However, the preceding simple principles would be good enough for a solution architect to illustrate the evolving operational model.

Zones can also be colored to denote the various access constraints and security measures that are applied to each one of them. The most commonly used enumeration of zones may be Internet, intranet, DMZ (demilitarized zone), extranet, untrusted zone, and secured zone. Figure 8.2 shows the categorization of these various zones as an illustrative example.

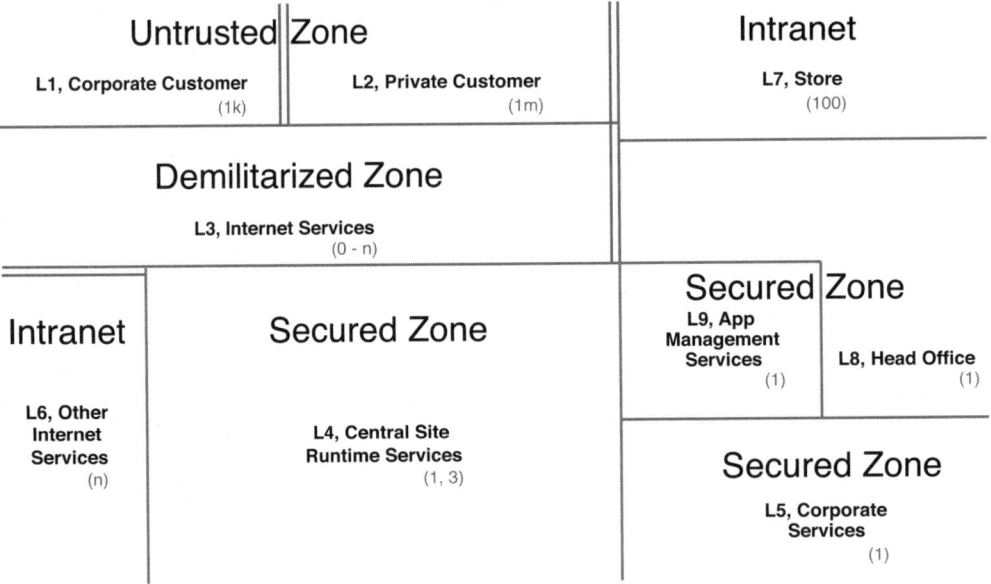

Figure 8.2   Categorization of the zones in a COM.

Identify the Components

A conceptual component node is used to denote a potential infrastructure node, which can host one or more application-level functional components. A conceptual component attributes the appropriate service-level requirements (a.k.a. NFRs) to the functional component (as developed in the functional model; refer to Chapter 7). The conceptual nodes may be identified by performing the following type of analysis:

- How different system actors interface with the system
- How the system interfaces with external systems
- How a node may satisfy one or more nonfunctional requirements
- How different locations may require different types of deployable entities

Networking artifacts—for example, LANs, WANs, routers, and specific hardware devices and components (for example, pSeries, xSeries servers)—do not get identified as conceptual components. In other words, a conceptual component node provides a home for one or more functional components on the deployed system. Figure 8.3 shows a set of conceptual components along with a set of actors and how they are distributed into different zones in the COM.

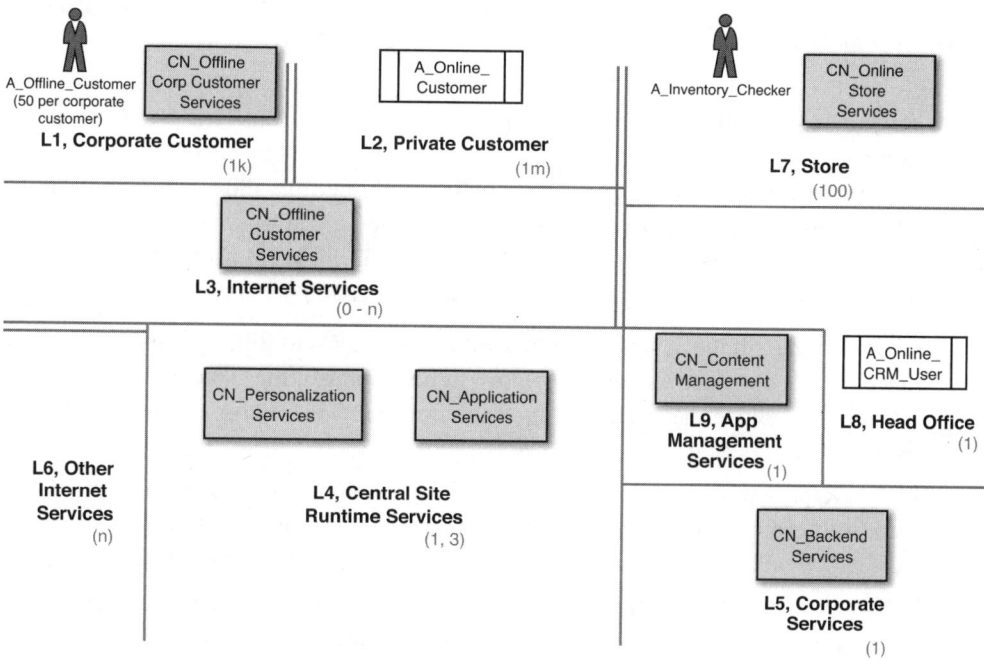

Figure 8.3 Conceptual components distributed across various zones of the COM.

Place the Components

The most significant challenge in bringing the functional model and operational model together is the placement of the functional components on the operational model. While it is technically possible to place the components directly, doing so often is far more difficult. Wouldn't it be good to have some technique to introduce some formalism to bridging the proverbial functional-operational model gap? *Deployable units* could be the answer; see Figure 8.4. (Refer also to the "Deployment Operational Models" [n.d.] article.)

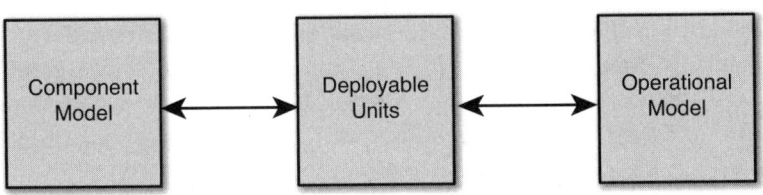

Figure 8.4   Deployable units are typically used to bridge the gap between the functional model and the operational model.

Note: The component model in Figure 8.4 contains the "functions" (refer to Chapter 7 for more details).

And just when you thought that your repertoire might be full, allow me to introduce yet another categorization scheme; this one is for the deployable units! Deployable units (DU) come in four flavors: Data Deployable Units (DDU), Presentation Deployable Units (PDU), Execution Deployable Units (EDU), and Installation Deployable Units (IDU):

- **DDU**—Represent the data that is used by the components to support a given behavior or function; it is the place where data is provisioned. Some of the aspects of the data worth considering include the volume of the data, frequency of data refresh, data archive and retention policies, and so on.

- **PDU**—Represent the various techniques through which access needs to be provided to harness the functionality of a component. It supports the interface of the system to external actors (real users on devices such as laptops and handhelds) and systems.

- **EDU**—Focus on the execution aspects of a component, for example, compute power needs (processor speeds, memory, disk space), frequency of invocation of the component, and so on.

- **IDU**—Focus on the installation aspects of a component. Examples include configuration files required for installation, component upgrade procedures, and so on.

To keep matters simple, it is okay for solution architects to focus on the DDU, PDU, and on some aspects of the EDU. Keep in mind that the complete development of the OM definitely requires a dedicated infrastructure architect, especially for nontrivial systems. The techniques outlined in the following sections allow you to get a good head start on the OM while being able to talk the talk with the infrastructure architect as you validate and verify the operational model for your system.

Let's spend some time on some of the considerations while placing the different types of DUs. Placement starts by assigning xDUs (x could be P, D, or E) to the conceptual component nodes (CNs).

Place the Presentation Deployable Units (PDU)

The types of users (that is, the user personas in a location) provide a good indicator to the type of presentation components required for the user to interface with the system. A rule of thumb here could be to assign a PDU for each system interface. Such a PDU could support an actor either to the system interface or to an intersystem interface.

To provide some examples (refer to Figure 8.3), you can assign a PDU called U_Priv-Browser to the CN_Online_Customer_Services component through which the A_Online_Customer actor can access the system features. Similarly, you can assign U_Inventory to CN_Online_Store_Services, U_SMS and U_OMS to CN_Backend_Services, and so on. Figure 8.6 shows a consolidated diagram with all the PDUs placed on the COM.

Place the Data Deployable Units (DDU)

Having the placement of DDUs follow that of the PDUs makes the job a bit easier; it becomes easy to figure out which PDUs need what data. However, the placement of the DDUs gets a bit more tricky and involved.

In the retail example, it is quite common to have orders submitted both in online as well as in offline mode. Each local store also requires that its inventory records be updated. Not only the inventory needs to be updated locally, but also the central inventory management system requires updating. As you can see, it is important for data to not only be updated locally (inventory) and temporarily stored (submitted orders), but also to be updated in the back office; that is, the back-end services. The DDUs need to support both forms. As such, a data entity may require multiple types and instances of DDUs. For example, an *Inventory* business entity may require a DDU per store (let us give it a name: D_Inventory_Upd_Local) supporting the local update in each store location and also a single DDU (let us give it a name: D_Inventory_Upd_Aggr) that aggregates the updates from each store-level DDU and finally updates the master inventory system in the back office. Submitted orders typically follow the same lineage; that is, they could be stored locally (let us give it a name: D_Order_Upd_Local) before they are staged and updated into the central order management system (let us give it a name: D_Order_Upd) once a day or at any preconfigured frequency. Figure 8.6 shows the consolidated diagram with all the DDUs placed on the COM.

Other variations to the DDU also may be considered. For example, a customer relationship management (CRM) system can have data entities that are not too large in volume and do not change very frequently, so there is a possibility to hold them in an in-memory data cache. In the same CRM, other data entities can be highly volatile and with very high transactional data volumes; they may require frequent and high-volume writes. Data, along with its operational characteristics, dictates its rendition through one of the types of DDUs. To summarize, a catalog of data characteristics may need to be considered while determining the most appropriate DDU. Some of the following characteristics are quite common:

- *Scope* of the location where the data resides; for example, local storage or centralized storage
- *Volatility* of the data; that is, the frequency at which the data needs to be refreshed
- *Volume* of the data being used at any given instance; that is, the amount of data used and exchanged by the application
- *Velocity* of the data; that is, the speed at which data enters the IT System from external sources
- *Lifetime* of the data entity; that is, the time when the data may be archived or backed up

Don't assume that all business or data entities end up with the same fate of being instantiated through multiple deployable units. Some easier ones have a single place where all the CRUD (create, read, update, delete) operations are performed. So do not panic!

Place the Execution Deployable Units (EDU)

The identification of the PDUs and DDUs is a natural step before we turn our attention to the placement of the EDUs. There are a few choices available for placing the EDUs: "close to the data," "close to the interface," or both (which implies that we split the EDU).

Colocating execution and data is clearly the default option, thereby acknowledging the affinity between data and the application code that is the primary owner of the data (see Chapter 7). So, in many circumstances, this will probably be the easiest and apparently the safest choice. If the business function demands highly interactive processing with only occasional light access to data, it may be appropriate to put the execution nearest to the end user even if the data is located elsewhere (perhaps for scope reasons). It is very important to note that the commonality of service-level requirements of multiple components may dictate the consolidation of their respective EDUs into a single EDU.

In the retail example, the EDU E_Submit_Inventory_Upd is placed close to the conceptual component called CN_Online_Store_Services; that is, the local stores from where such updates are triggered. A related EDU called E_Consolidate_Inventory_Upd is placed close to the data; that is, close to the CN_Backend_Services conceptual component that resides at the back office. Similarly, E_Create_Order is placed close to the interface, while E_Consolidate_Order is placed close to the CN_Backend_Services conceptual component. On the other hand, E_Browse is an EDU that is placed close to the PDU where the inventory is browsed by the offline and online customers. Figure 8.6 shows the consolidated diagram with all the EDUs placed on the COM.

It is important to recognize that the intent of illustrating the retail example without providing too many in-depth use cases is to provide guidance on how a typical COM may look; I chose relatively self-descriptive names for the CNs in the example (refer to Figure 8.3) so that you can more easily comprehend their intent. The COM for your project-specific OM may look very different.

Note: The terms *conceptual component* and *conceptual node* are used interchangeably.

Having placed all the deployable units, we can turn our attention to the interactions between the various deployable units. From the PDU <-> EDU & DDU <-> EDU matrices, we can infer the inter DU interactions.

It is important to note that

- Interactions occur between DUs that have been placed on conceptual nodes.

- You are primarily interested in the interactions between DUs that have been placed on different nodes.

- In some situations, you also need to keep track of interactions between DUs placed on different instances of the same conceptual node (for example, if DUs placed on the CN in L3 interact with the same DU placed on the same CN but located in one of the different L3 instances). Note that you can have more than one instance of L3.

Interactions provide great clues on the placement of the EDUs. As a case in point, consider a slight variation of the retail example such that the data needs to be held centrally (in the back office), as shown in Figure 8.5. Also, assume that it was decided (maybe for reasons of scope) to hold the attributes of a component centrally (labeled as HQ in Figure 8.5), represented by the data deployable unit D3. And further, this example also has distributed users who need access to this data (through their appropriate presentation component, U1), via the execution component P3.

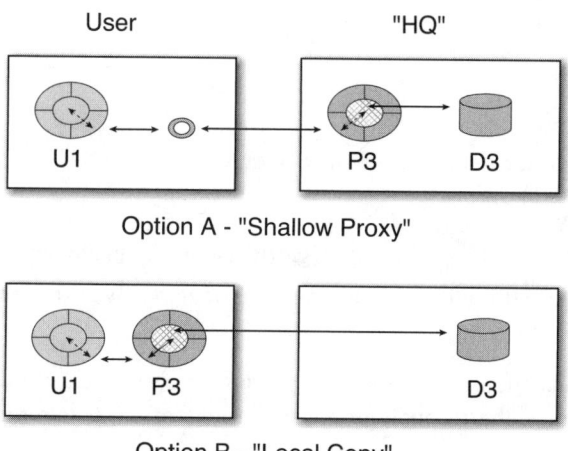

Figure 8.5   Placement options for EDUs.

How do you link these deployable units?

Of the many options, let's consider the following two:

1. In the first option, P3 is colocated with D3 on the HQ component node, and a "shallow proxy" technical component, which is on the User component node, acts as a broker between the components U1 and P3. This is a fairly normal arrangement in architectures in which distributed computing technologies (for example, CORBA or DCOM object brokers) may be used.

2. In the second option, P3 is colocated with U1, and some form of middleware is used to fetch the necessary attributes of the required components from D3 "into" P3. This is also a fairly normal arrangement, although at the time of this writing, it usually relies on bespoke (custom developed) middleware code.

Which of these two options is better? Although you can quickly start with the standard consulting answer "It depends," you may need to qualify and substantiate the classic cliché with the fact that the choice should be informed and influenced by the operational service-level requirements and characteristics that are required to be met. Let's look at some of the strengths and weaknesses of each of the two options.

Option 1 (shallow proxy):
Strengths:

• Response times between U1–P3 interactions should be fairly consistent.

Weaknesses:

• As the requirements placed on the shallow proxy middleware grow, system management may become more complex.

• Response times may be long, particularly if interactions between U1 and P3 need to traverse slower networks or require multiple network hops.

Option 2 (local copy):
Strengths:

• Following the initial fetch of attributes, response times may be quick.

Weaknesses:

• "Roll your own" (custom) middleware code may require significant code management.

• Initial response time, while fetching attributes, may be long, particularly over slower, constrained networks.

As is evident from the preceding descriptions, often multiple placement options exist; the service-level requirements or agreements and the technology considerations often dictate the most appropriate choice.

Getting back to the retail example (a representative COM for the retail scenario example), the COM may look like Figure 8.6.

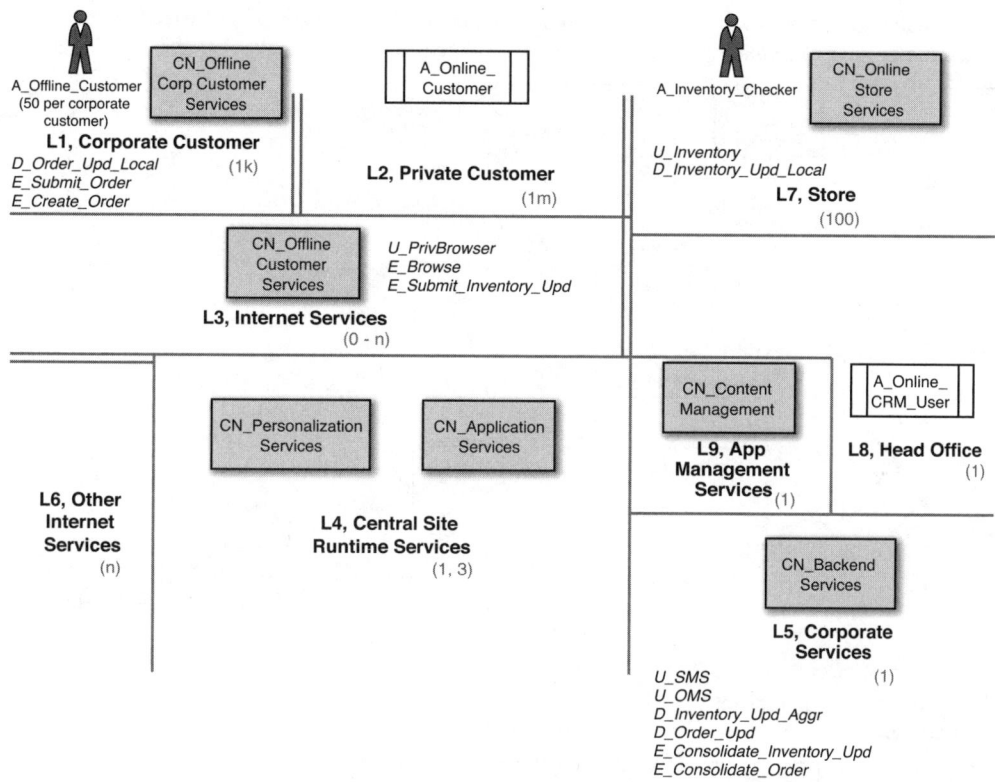

Figure 8.6   PDUs, DDUs, and EDUs placed on the COM (retail example).

Note: The deployable units are shown in italic in Figure 8.6.

Rationalize and Validate the COM

Before you call the COM complete, one suggestion, if not a mandate, would be to validate the COM. First of all, you should have a good feeling of what you have developed so far and for which you can use some sniff-test techniques. For starters, does it have the right shape and feel? For example, some of the litmus test verification questions you should be asking include: *Is the COM implementable using available technology? Is the degree of DU distribution adequate to realize the NFRs? Are the cost implications of meeting the NFRs reasonable (budget, cost benefit analysis)?* And finally, if the COM passes these tests to your degree of satisfaction, I recommend one last step: to walk through some of the carefully selected architecturally significant use case scenarios. Such walkthroughs provide a powerful mechanism of verifying the viability of the operational model. Figures 8.7 and 8.8 provide a pictorial representation of a walkthrough for the retail scenario.

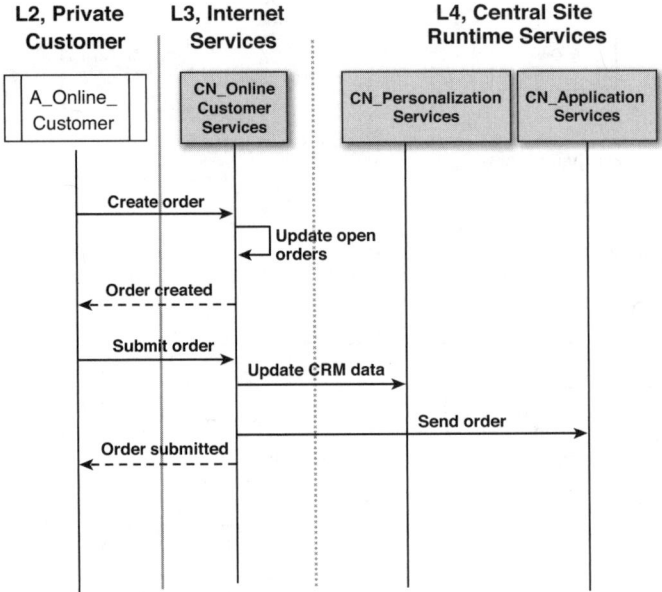

Figure 8.7 Walkthrough diagram for the order creation usage scenario.

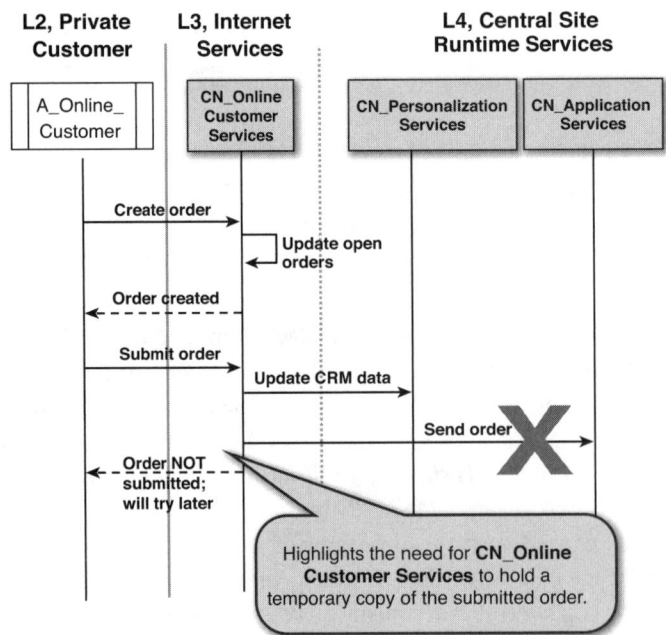

Figure 8.8 Walkthrough diagram highlighting the capability of handling error conditions and also some design decisions.

Although we spent quite a bit more time than usual on one section, the idea is to have a solid understanding and appreciation for the COM such that the SOM and POM will be easier to comprehend. More importantly, as a solution architect, you will be more involved in the COM, and once it is commensurate with what your system needs are, you can delegate the ownership of developing the SOM and POM to your infrastructure architect!

Specification Operational Model (SOM)

The specification operational model (SOM) identifies and defines the technical services and their specifications required to make the solution work with the same key objective: the solution meets all the nonfunctional requirements. So, while the COM gave a shape and feel to the operational model, the SOM enables the COM to put on its shoes and go for a run, so to speak—by identifying and defining a set of technical services that take one step forward toward instantiating the runtime topology. And although this chapter covers the most commonly needed aspects of extended operational modeling, it is important to acknowledge that the activities outlined in this section, for the SOM, provide the basis of many specialized subject areas in operational modeling, namely:

- Developing a security model
- Analyzing and designing the process and technologies for system availability
- Planning for elasticity and system scaling
- Performance modeling and capacity planning

Developing the specifications for the technical services and components is about answering questions: How will the COM be instantiated? What are the IT capabilities of each part of the system that are required to make it work? and so on. The main focus is on the infrastructure components—defining their specifications required to support and instantiate the COM. Although the technical specifications are developed in a product- and vendor-independent manner, their development drives the selection of the infrastructure products and physical platforms. It also defines how the application-level DU placement strategy will be supported technically: how to ensure maintaining distributed copies of data at the right level of currency; how to achieve the required levels of transaction control or workflow management, and so on. And similar to the COM, an infrastructure walkthrough ensures validation and completeness. Collection of the technical services and their associated components provides a view of the runtime architecture of the system—the nodes and connections that have to be defined, designed, developed, and deployed. The SOM is expected to provide the IT operations personnel with valuable insights into how and why the physical system works the way it does.

The development of the SOM may be performed in three major steps:

1. Identify specification nodes.
2. Identify technical components.
3. Rationalize and validate the SOM.

Identify Specification Nodes

The initial focus is to determine the specification nodes (SNs). The determination process starts by examining the catalog of CNs and grouping them by similarity of their service-level requirements. In the process, CNs may undergo splitting such that various types of users, with different service-level needs, may be accommodated. To be explicit, the deployable units (PDU, DDU, EDU) may need to be rearranged; that is, split, consolidated, or refactored. It may be interesting to note here that, although the functional model focuses on identifying subsystems by grouping functionally similar components, the operational model focuses on identifying specification nodes by grouping components by service level requirements.

On one hand, I am saying that the DUs may be split or refactored, while on the other hand, I am suggesting a consolidation of CNs based on their proximity of service-level requirements. Confusing, huh? You bet it is! Let me see if I can clarify this a bit using an example.

In the retail example, consider the requirement that users are split between using mobile devices and workstations; that is, some users use the mobile devices to place orders, whereas some others typically use their workstations for interfacing with the system. To support both user communities, you may split the PDU and EDU components for customer order creation. The PDU is split into two DUs and placed on two separate SNs (SN_Create_Order_Mobile and SN_Create_Order) for mobile device users and desktop users, respectively. The EDU is split between one that accepts user input from the mobile devices (SN_Order_Accept_Mobile), a second that accesses data from the desktop users (SN_Order_Accept), and a third that accesses the data from the back-end systems (SN_Order_Retrieve). You can think of the identified SNs as virtual machines, on each of which various application-level components are placed. Each identified SN may need installation DUs for installing and managing the various application components that it hosts.

In summary, in the process of identifying the SNs, we end up playing around with the catalog of DUs, assessing their commonalities relative to the various NFRs (response time, throughput, availability, reliability, performance, security, manageability, and so on) and end up splitting or merging the DUs to place them on the SNs to ensure that the various NFRs are met.

Identify Technical Components

The focus of this step is to augment the SN catalog with any other required nodes and identify the set of technical components required to satisfy the specified service-level agreements.

The SNs identified in the previous step are primarily derived from the DUs, along with the NFRs that are expected to be met. You need to ensure that the identified SNs can communicate between each other (that is, the virtual machines have established connectivity) and which new SNs (for component interconnections, among other integration needs) may be identified. Subsequently, you need to identify technical components that will support the implementation of the identified SNs and their interconnections. It is important to note that, since any SN may host multiple DUs and components, both the intracommunication between components within an SN and the intercommunication between SNs would require commensurate interconnectivity techniques to meet the service-level requirements. This may necessitate additional SNs to be introduced, for example, to facilitate the interactions.

Let's look at an example. In the retail example, consider intercommunication between components in the store locations and the back office. Some of the data exchange may be synchronous and mission critical in nature to warrant a high-throughput subsecond response communication gateway (identified as SN_Messaging_Mgr). On the other hand, some other usage scenarios can work with a much more relaxed throughput requirement, and hence, asynchronous batch transfer (identified as SN_File_Transfer_Mgr) of data may well be a feasible and cost-effective option. As you can see, a single conceptual line of communication, between the store location and the back-end office, could need two different technical components to support the intercommunication between the SNs. Network gateways, firewalls, and directory services (SN_Access_Control) are some examples of technical components that directly or indirectly support the business functions.

A Personal Note

To my respected readers,

Allow me, if you will, to take a personal pause.

Today is March 5, 2015. And as I just finished writing the preceding paragraph, I got a call from my senior management to let me know that I was honored as an IBM Distinguished Engineer (DE) and formally announced as the CTO role for the Industrial Sector.

My father left us just 45 days ago, on January 19, 2015. I used to call him "baba," which in Bengali means father. It was his (more than my) wish and intense desire to see me become a DE; he had that strong conviction and faith. I know he was waiting for this day, in eager anticipation, for quite some time. It was also my cherished dream to be able to share this significant career achievement of mine with him—to pick up the phone and call him to let him know that his son did indeed become a DE.

And while today, with a very heavy heart, I am unable to pick up the phone and hear his voice, I hope he can hear me: "Baba, I have become a DE. I made it! It is your sheer belief in me that has brought me this significant achievement. You are the first with whom I share this news as I had promised to myself. You are there by my side and I can feel it ever so strongly. Be good and safe where you are, Baba."

Thank you, readers, for allowing me to pause.

Technical components address multiple aspects of the system. Some technical components directly support the DUs (the presentation, data, and execution). Other types of technical components address system aspects such as the operating systems, physical hardware components (for example, network interfaces, processor speed and family, memory, and so on) for each of the SNs, the middleware integration components bridging the various DUs (for example, message queues, file handlers, and so on), some systems management components (for example, performance monitoring, downtime management, and so on), and some application specific components (for example, error logging, diagnostics, and so on). It is noteworthy how different types of technical components address different system characteristics. As examples, the middleware integration components are attributed with protocols and security they support, along with data exchange traffic and throughput metrics; the systems management components determine planned system downtime and systems support, and the hardware components determine the scalability potential of the system and various means to achieve them.

The integration components and the various connection types (connecting the components) carry key attributes and characteristics that address the system NFRs. The following attributes of system interconnects provide key insights:

- **Connection types**—Synchronous or asynchronous modes of data exchange
- **Transaction**—Smallest, largest, and average size of each transaction
- **Latency**—Expected transmission times for smallest, largest, and average size transactions between major system components
- **Bandwidth**—Capacity of the network pipe to sustain the volume and latency expectations for the transactions

The identification of the technical components provides a clearer picture of the hardware, operational, communications, and systems management characteristics of the system—aspects that serve as key inputs to the POM!

Rationalize and Validate the SOM

The proof of the pudding is in the eating, as the adage goes, and SOM activities are no exception to that rule! It is important to pause, take a step back, and assess the viability (technical, cost, resources, timeline) of the SOM as it pertains to the solution's architecture. Here, you use the same technique used while developing the COM to assess the viability: scenario walkthroughs to ensure that the normal and failure conditions can be exercised while meeting the nonfunctional requirements and the desired service levels.

The technical viability assessment of the SOMs may consider, but is not limited to, the following aspects:

- **Characteristics of the included DDUs**—Volume, data types, data integrity, and security
- **Characteristics of the included EDUs**—Response time latency, execution volumes, availability, transaction type (batch, real time)
- **System integrity**—Transaction commits or rollbacks to previous deterministic state of the system
- **Distribution of data across multiple SNs in various zones and locations**—Is it commensurate with required transactional integrity and response times?

The intent of the technical viability assessment is to validate that the SOMs will support the service-level requirements and support the architecture decisions that primarily address the system's NFRs.

Let's take an inventory of some of the SNs that we identified, in our retail example, as we walked through a portion of the system:

- **SN_Create_Order_Mobile**—A virtual machine that encapsulates the presentation-level CNs that orchestrate the collection of order details from a mobile device.

- **SN_Create_Order**—A virtual machine that encapsulates the presentation-level CNs that orchestrate the collection of order details from any desktop machine.

- **SN_Order_Accept_Mobile**—A virtual machine that encapsulates the execution-level CN that triggers and processes the order creation business logic from a mobile device.

- **SN_Order_Accept**—A virtual machine that encapsulates the execution-level CN that triggers and processes the order creation logic from any desktop machine.

- **SN_Order_Retrieve**—A virtual machine that works in conjunction with the SN_Order_Accept_Mobile and SN_Order_Accept nodes to send and retrieve order details from the order management system that resides at the back office.

- **SN_Messaging_Mgr**—A technical component that supports high-speed, low-latency, asynchronous data transfer between the store locations and the back office.

- **SN_File_Transfer_Mgr**—A technical component that supports relatively (to SN_Messaging_Mgr) lower-speed, higher-latency, batch mode of data transfer between the store locations and the back office.

- **SN_Access_Control**—A technical component that enables user authentication and authorization along with other policy-driven security management.

- **SN_Systems_Mgmt_Local**—A technical component that implements systems monitoring and management at each store location, one per store location.

- **SN_Systems_Mgmt_Central**—A technical component that implements systems monitoring and management functions at the back office.

- **SN_Data_Services**—A technical service at the back office that functions as a data adapter, abstracting all access to the system's one or more databases.

- **SN_Order_Management_Services**—A set of technical services that expose the functional features of the order management system.

As a part of the validation activities, a step-by-step walkthrough of a set of sequence diagrams is recommended (see Figure 8.9). It is, however, important to take note of the fact that not all use cases must be illustrated by sequence (walkthrough) diagrams during the SOM elaboration phase; only the architecturally significant use cases should be walked through. This further highlights the fact that, as a practical measure, it is important to focus on the use cases that are architecturally important and foundational to drive the system's overall architecture and blueprint.

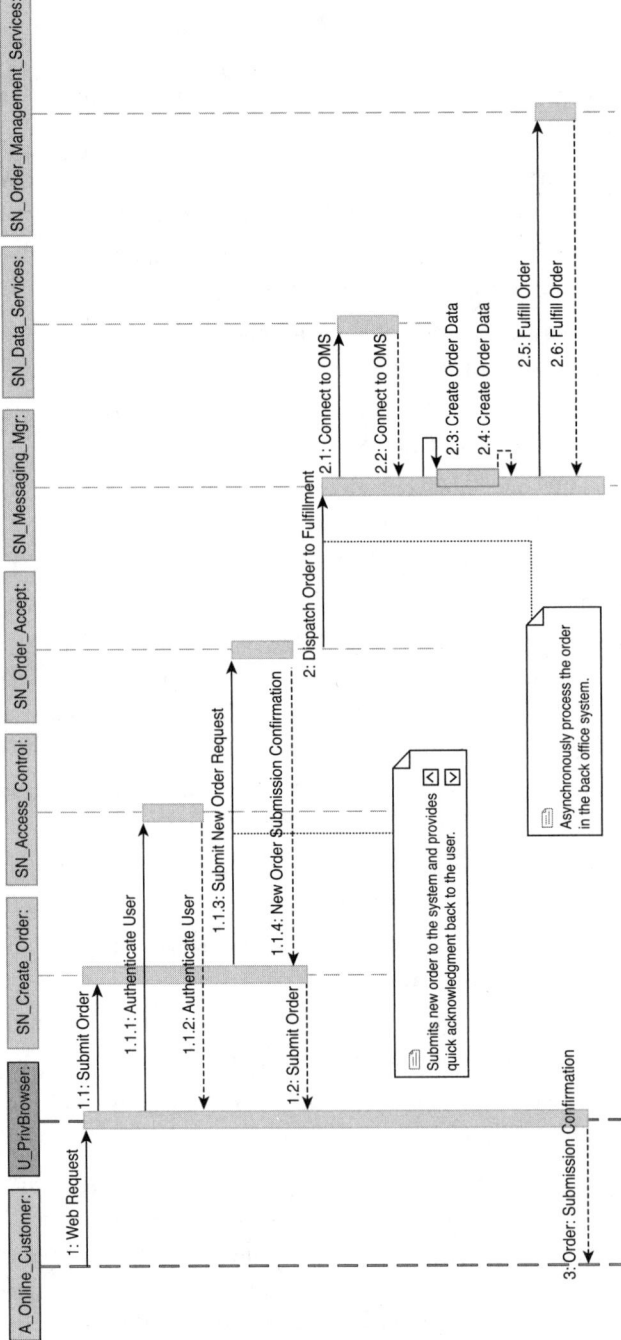

Figure 8.9   Walkthrough diagram for Order Submission usage scenario for the retail example.

To summarize, the activities of the SOM focus on the placement of the solution's application and technical components—that is, the CNs, compute (storage, processor, memory), installation units, middleware and external presentation function, onto specified nodes together with the identification and placement of the communications and interactions between the specified nodes. This is done so that the system can deliver the solution's functional and nonfunctional requirements, including consideration for constraints such as budget, skills, and technical viability.

And just to be clear, unless you are climbing up the infrastructure architect ranks to your newfound high ground as the solution architect, you will typically delegate the elaboration and completion of the SOM to your infrastructure architect while you focus on the bigger picture; that is, the other critical aspects of your overarching solution architecture. This should either give you comfort (if you are an infrastructure architect to begin with) or relief (for being able to establish the foundation and then delegate) to be able to move on!

Physical Operational Model (POM)

The physical operational model (POM) focuses on making the appropriate technology and product choices to instantiate the SOM and hence to deliver the required functionality and expected service levels. It is used as a blueprint for the procurement, installation, and subsequent maintenance of the system. The creation of the POM involves taking decisions that tread a fine balance between three conflicting forces—feasibility, cost, and risk—as they relate to the realization of the requested capabilities. It is not uncommon to see that the outcome of the feasibility-cost-risk triage results in making compromises (postponement or severance) on the functional and nonfunctional capabilities for a less risky or a more cost-effective solution.

The POM may be developed in three major steps:

1. Implement the nodes and connections.
2. Ensure meeting the Quality of Service (QoS).
3. Rationalize and validate the POM.

Implement the Nodes and Connections

The focus of this step is to select the most appropriate hardware, software, and middleware products that collectively meet the functional and nonfunctional requirements of the system.

The selection of the infrastructure components (hardware, software, middleware, and networks) is often nontrivial in nature, primarily owing to the multiple factors that influence the selection process. Let me share my experience with some of the most common questions and considerations that typically influence the selection and decision-making process:

- **The maturity of the product in the marketplace**—Often, however promising a marketing brochure touts a new product, it is wise to avoid adopting early versions of the product. (Let someone else be the guinea pig of something new! We frequently get enamored with the "shiny toy" syndrome.)

- **The extent to which a product meets the required functional specifications**—The product's ability and its proven track record to integrate with other chosen products (for the system) should be considerations.

- **The physical topology required to install and configure the product**—As an example, some products are easy to install and configure, and they can work in both on-premise data centers as well as in cloud data centers. Some others, such as purpose-built hardware appliances, may not be as easily installable on cloud data centers as they are on traditional data centers.

- **The roadmap of the product along with the stability and experience of the product vendor**—Some product vendors may not have adequate regional establishments for product maintenance and support. A vendor's strategic roadmap of maintaining and enhancing the product's vitality and capabilities is also a key consideration (for example, a product may be close to its end of life). We must also assess and validate the track record of the product being productively used in specific industry domains of interest.

- **The enterprise architecture blueprint and the company guidelines**—An existing enterprise architecture blueprint drives a set of guidelines around the usage of some products in the context of the existing enterprise landscape. Vendor relations also drive explicit or implicit company guidelines around vendor preferences. It is quite common to come across situations in which a company, for example, is already vested in an all-IBM product portfolio; in such cases, considering a non-IBM product may be a difficult sell and also may introduce additional technology integration challenges.

- **The hardware infrastructure required to install the product to support the non-functional requirements**—Some products can scale vertically quite easily (adding more memory, using faster processor family and storage), whereas some may require a quicker adoption of horizontal scaling to achieve the required scaling needs (adding more servers and product instances). Cost implications, typically, are heavily influenced by scaling needs.

The selection process, as you can see, may turn out to be quite complex and time consuming. You have to be on a continuous and proactive lookout for opportunities to simplify and accelerate the selection process. My eyes usually light up when I spot opportunities to embrace the theories of natural selection. Following are some opportunities that I have come across:

- Identify the givens, policies, vendor preferences, and rules for qualification in a given enterprise. This certainly reduces the coverage area where you need to cast your net and reduces the frustration of product acquisition and procurement.

- Leverage past experiences where a product has worked great in a similar industry and functional landscape.

- Assess how preselected products may influence the rest of the selection process. For example, stay with one vendor product portfolio to ease integration challenges and vendor support. This way, you can identify the source of any problems.

Think you have enough information for you to oversee the product selection process? As the overall enterprise architect, I certainly would consider myself to be equipped enough at this point. I could ensure that the proper process and techniques are in place to not only assist the infrastructure architect to formalize the product selection but also for me to be able to review and validate the outcome.

And just when you thought that this step was complete, I have to remind you that we have not yet worked on the connections! How would these selected products communicate with each other? How may products need to be connected and in how many locations? Are the connections identical in all locations, or do they vary based on nonfunctional needs or network bandwidth limitations, among other factors?

Let's consider the retail example for a moment. The COM identified a set of zones and locations along with a set of logical nodes that were placed in each of the zones. The functional needs determine the connectivity between the logical nodes to satisfy one or more use case scenarios. The nonfunctional needs drive the nature and mode of data exchange—for example, request-response versus asynchronous batch data delivery.

The realm of connections and their design and implementation squarely fall under the purview of a network architect—one who lives and breathes in the world of LANs, WANs, MPLS, routers, and switches. As the enterprise architect, you need to understand the rationale of the design and buildout of the network topology that supports the connections required for the system to be operational.

A ROAD ANALOGY

While I was attending a course on enterprise architecture many moons ago, the instructor used an elegant means to describe the various nuances to be considered when defining a network topology. He used a traffic and road analogy that stuck with me and that I would like to share.

He stated that the logical connections (between the various system components) are analogous to the sum total of all journeys that motorists need to make between two cities (logical nodes). Some journeys will need to be fast, whereas others can take much longer. Some roads will have large loads from heavy trucks, whereas others may just have drivers in a car. Given the various types of journeys, we need to build an optimal road network. The road network is akin to the physical connections in a system's network topology.

And, continuing with the road analogy, some roads will be motorways, whereas others will be country lanes. Some roads may be constantly used (with 24×7 traffic), whereas others are more heavily used only during rush hour or weekends.

And finally, the instructor reminded us that there may be completely separate networks capable of supporting the required journeys—such as air travel. Thus, amidst the more ubiquitous and conventional LANs and WANs, snail mail may be acceptable in some cases or even telephones (for help desk–to–user interactions).

It is important to empower the network architect with the required NFRs that need to be supported, along with the various architecture alternatives for data exchange between various nodes. The "exchange between various nodes" provides a clue that, in order to come up with a commensurate network topology, it is critical to formalize a node-to-node connectivity matrix. The quest for such a connectivity matrix begins!

I have typically employed some matrix computation techniques to develop the node-to-node connectivity matrix that I elaborate on in the rest of this section. It requires you to have some basic knowledge of linear algebra (specifically of matrix manipulations). You may choose to skip the rest of this math-heavy section. If you take away nothing else from the mathematical treatment, at least understand the following essence:

> You need to understand not only how each node is connected to each other but also the relative strengths of the connections. For example, a node N_1 may be connected to another node N_2 and the relative weight of the connection may be 3. N_1 may also be connected to N_3 with a relative weight of 2 and to N_4 with a relative weight of 5; N_2, on the other hand, may be connected only to N_1. In such a scenario, it is evident that the network that connects N_1 to the rest of the nodes in the operational topology would need to be more robust and support a higher bandwidth than the network that is required to connect N_2 to the rest of the system.
>
> The purpose of the matrix algebra manipulations in this section is to come up with a mathematical technique to aid in such a derivation.

To make matters comprehensible, you might find a little refresher on matrix algebra helpful (see the "Matrix Algebra" sidebar).

MATRIX ALGEBRA

Two matrices can be multiplied if the number of columns of the first matrix is equal to the number of rows in the second matrix. If the first matrix has m rows and n columns and the second matrix has n rows and p columns, the resultant matrix will have m rows and p columns:

$$C_{m,p} = A_{m,n} \times B_{n,p}$$

The transpose of a matrix operates on a single matrix and implies that the resultant matrix has its rows and columns interchanged. For example, if A is a matrix with m rows and n columns, the transpose of A will be a matrix with n rows and m columns:

$$B_{n,m} = (A_{m,n})^{T}$$

So, let's apply a bit of matrix algebra. The goal is to find out how each node is connected to the rest of the nodes and also to get a sense of the relative weight of the connections. A node, in this discussion, represents a physical server that hosts and runs one or more middleware components or software products. From the COM, you get a clear picture of the interconnectivity between the DUs.

Let A denote the *DU accesses DU* matrix. You have already done the hard work of placing DUs on nodes when developing the SOM. Let B denote the *Node hosts DU* matrix (that is, nodes are the rows, and the DUs are the columns). Let's introduce a third matrix that represents *DU belongs to Node*; this is nothing but the transpose of the B matrix (that is, DUs are the rows, and the nodes are the columns). The goal is to find the representation of *Node is connected to Node* matrix in which the value in each cell will provide a good representation of the expected relative strengths for each of the internode connections. To formulate the representation of how nodes are connected to other nodes; that is, the *Node is connected to Node* matrix representation, you need to apply some smart matrix manipulations (see the "Matrix Manipulation for Node-Node Connectivity" sidebar).

MATRIX MANIPULATION FOR NODE-NODE CONNECTIVITY

My IBM colleague Bert Eggen came up with a smart little matrix manipulation trick with which we can derive how the nodes may be connected to other nodes. The number in each of the matrix cells represents the relative strength of the internode connections.

Here, I use the same example that Bert uses when he explains this concept.

Let A be the matrix that represents how 26 DUs are interrelated; that is, *DU accesses DU*. This type of matrix is often called an adjacency matrix:

$A_{26,26}$ (see Figure 8.10).

DU accesses DU	D_1	D_2	D_3	D_4	D_5	D_6	D_7	D_8	D_9	E_1	E_2	E_3	E_4	E_5	E_6	E_7	E_8	E_9	U_1	U_2	U_3	U_4	U_5	U_6	U_7	U_8
D_1	0	0	0	0	0	0	0	0	0	0	0	0	0	0	0	0	0	0	0	0	0	0	0	0	0	0
D_2	1	0	0	0	0	0	0	0	0	0	0	0	0	0	0	0	0	0	0	0	0	0	0	0	0	0
D_3	0	0	0	0	0	0	0	0	0	0	0	0	0	0	0	0	0	0	0	0	0	0	0	0	0	0
D_4	0	0	0	0	0	0	0	0	0	0	0	0	0	0	0	0	0	0	0	0	0	0	0	0	0	0
D_5	0	0	0	0	0	0	0	0	0	0	0	0	0	0	0	0	0	0	0	0	0	0	0	0	0	0
D_6	0	0	0	0	0	0	0	0	0	0	0	0	0	0	0	0	0	0	0	0	0	0	0	0	0	0
D_7	0	0	1	1	1	0	0	0	0	0	0	0	0	0	0	0	0	0	0	0	0	0	0	0	0	0
D_8	0	0	0	0	0	1	0	0	0	0	0	0	0	0	0	0	0	0	0	0	0	0	0	0	0	0
D_9	0	0	0	0	0	1	0	0	0	0	0	0	0	0	0	0	0	0	0	0	0	0	0	0	0	0
E_1	0	0	0	0	0	1	0	0	0	0	0	0	0	0	0	0	0	0	0	0	0	0	0	0	0	0
E_2	0	0	0	0	0	1	0	0	0	0	0	0	0	0	0	0	0	0	0	0	0	0	0	0	0	0
E_3	0	0	0	0	0	0	0	0	0	1	0	0	0	0	0	0	0	0	0	0	0	0	0	0	0	0
E_4	0	0	0	0	0	0	0	0	0	1	0	0	0	0	0	0	0	0	0	0	0	0	0	0	0	0
E_5	0	0	0	0	0	0	0	0	0	1	0	0	0	0	0	0	0	0	0	0	0	0	0	0	0	0
E_6	0	0	0	0	0	0	0	0	0	1	0	0	0	0	0	0	0	0	0	0	0	0	0	0	0	0
E_7	0	0	0	0	0	0	0	0	0	1	0	0	0	0	0	0	0	0	0	0	0	0	0	0	0	0
E_8	0	0	0	0	0	0	0	0	0	0	0	0	0	0	0	0	0	0	0	0	0	0	0	0	0	0
E_9	0	0	0	0	0	0	0	0	0	0	0	0	0	0	0	0	1	0	1	0	0	0	0	0	0	0
U_1	0	0	0	0	0	0	0	0	0	0	0	1	0	0	0	0	0	0	1	0	0	0	0	0	0	0
U_2	0	0	0	0	0	0	0	0	0	0	0	1	0	0	0	0	0	0	0	0	0	0	0	0	0	0
U_3	0	0	0	0	0	0	0	0	0	0	0	1	0	0	0	0	0	0	1	0	0	0	0	0	0	0
U_4	0	0	0	0	0	0	0	0	0	0	0	1	0	0	0	0	0	0	1	0	0	0	0	0	0	0
U_5	0	0	0	0	0	0	0	0	0	0	0	0	0	0	0	0	0	0	1	0	0	0	0	0	0	0
U_6	0	0	0	0	0	0	0	0	0	0	0	0	0	0	0	0	0	0	1	0	0	0	0	0	0	0
U_7	0	0	0	0	0	0	0	0	0	0	0	0	0	0	0	0	0	0	1	0	0	0	0	0	0	0
U_8	0	0	0	0	0	0	0	0	0	0	0	11	0	0	0	0	0	0	0	0	0	0	0	0	0	0

Figure 8.10 Matrix A.

Let B be the matrix that represents how 6 nodes host the 26 DUs, that is; *Node hosts DU*:

$B_{6,26}$ (see Figure 8.11).

Node has DU	U_3	D_3	D_4	E_9	E_5	U_8	U_4	D_6	E_7	E_1	U_6	D_9	E_2	U_5	U_7	D_7	E_8	E_6	U_1	D_1	D_8	D_5	E_3	U_2	D_2	E_4
Customer Relationship Mgmt	1	1	1	1	1	0	0	0	0	0	0	0	0	0	0	0	0	0	0	0	0	0	0	0	0	0
Stock Mgmt	0	0	0	0	0	1	1	1	1	1	0	0	0	0	0	0	0	0	0	0	0	0	0	0	0	0
Order Mgmt	0	0	0	0	0	0	0	0	0	0	1	1	1	0	0	0	0	0	0	0	0	0	0	0	0	0
Order Entry	0	0	0	0	0	0	0	0	0	0	0	0	0	1	1	1	1	1	0	0	0	0	0	0	0	0
Catalog Mgmt	0	0	0	0	0	0	0	0	0	0	0	0	0	0	0	0	0	0	1	1	1	1	1	0	0	0
Content Mgmt	0	0	0	0	0	0	0	0	0	0	0	0	0	0	0	1	0	0	0	0	0	0	0	1	1	1

Figure 8.11   Matrix B.

Let's transpose B to get the matrix that represents *DU belongs to Node*:

$(B_{26,6})^T$ (see Figure 8.12).

DU belongs to Node	Customer Relationship Mgmt	Stock Mgmt	Order Mgmt	Order Entry	Catalog Mgmt	Content Mgmt
U_3	1	0	0	0	0	0
D_3	1	0	0	0	0	0
D_4	1	0	0	0	0	0
E_9	1	0	0	0	0	0
E_5	1	0	0	0	0	0
U_8	0	1	0	0	0	0
U_4	0	1	0	0	0	0
D_6	0	1	0	0	0	0
E_7	0	1	0	0	0	0
E_1	0	1	0	0	0	0
U_6	0	0	1	0	0	0
D_9	0	0	1	0	0	0
E_2	0	0	1	0	0	0
U_5	0	0	0	1	0	0
U_7	0	0	0	1	0	0
D_7	0	0	0	1	0	1
E_8	0	0	0	1	0	0
E_6	0	0	0	1	0	0
U_1	0	0	0	0	1	0
D_1	0	0	0	0	1	0
D_8	0	0	0	0	1	0
D_5	0	0	0	0	1	0
E_3	0	0	0	0	1	0
U_2	0	0	0	0	0	1
D_2	0	0	0	0	0	1
E_4	0	0	0	0	0	1

Figure 8.12   Matrix B^T.

The following matrix multiplication yields the matrix Y:

$$Y_{6,6} = B_{6,26} \times A_{26,26} \times (B_{26,6})^T \text{ (see Figure 8.13).}$$

Node is connected to Node	Customer Relationship Mgmt	Stock Mgmt	Order Mgmt	Order Entry	Catalog Mgmt	Content Mgmt
Customer Relationship Mgmt	1	0	0	0	0	0
Stock Mgmt	3	4	0	0	0	0
Order Mgmt	0	4	0	0	0	0
Order Entry	0	3	0	2	0	0
Catalog Mgmt	0	0	4	3	0	0
Content Mgmt	0	1	12	2	0	0

Figure 8.13   Matrix Y

As you can see, the matrix Y gives us what we are looking for; that is, the *Node is connected to Node* matrix.

Pay particular attention to values in the cells. The values indicate the strength or the weight of the connections between the different nodes.

Referring to the Y matrix in the "Matrix Manipulation for Node-Node Connectivity" sidebar, the values in each cell signify the strength of a specific node-node pair communication or interaction.

The network architect is well positioned to take it from here. The weights of each interconnection, between the nodes, will be a key input in the final determination of the bandwidth requirements. The locations, zones, frequency, and volume of data exchange, along with the physical deployment topology of the products and application components, will also serve as key inputs to determine the network topology and its physical instantiation.

So, although you would, in all possibilities, require a dedicated network architect to finalize the network infrastructure, enough information and guidelines have been developed here to aid the validation of how the connections will be physically implemented and also testify to their adequacy to support the nonfunctional and service-level requirements of the system.

Ensure Meeting the Quality of Service (QoS)

The previous step ensures t hat the physical operating model is defined: the products and technologies chosen, along with the network layout and infrastructure required to connect the products together to support not only the required functionality but also most of the NFRs.

This step focuses on refining the configurations of the products, technologies, and networks so that some key NFRs—for example, performance, capacity planning, fault tolerance, and disaster recovery, among others—may also be addressed. An entire book can be written on QoS; this chapter focuses only on some of the important concepts that a solution architect would need to recognize, understand, and appreciate so that she can better equip herself to work with the infrastructure architect while formalizing the POM.

System performance is a critical metric, the satisfaction of which is imperative for the system's ultimate users to accept and be happy with using it. Performance describes the operating speed of the system; that is, the response of the system to user requests. QoS, in the context of performance, should define, in a deterministic manner, how the system maintains or degrades its ability to keep up with the performance benchmarks in the event of increased system workload. What happens when the load on the system increases?

First of all, what defines increased load? Think about a system that is operational. Each time the system is running, it may generate new transactional data. This data would be stored in the persistent store; the volume of generated data will increase with time. A system's ability to maintain the latency of the same database queries on a 5GB database versus on the same database that increases to, say, 1TB is an example of the system's ability to maintain its performance with increased system workload.

In another example, the number of users who are exposed to using the system may also increase with time; the number of concurrent users accessing the user interface may well be on the rise. The system's ability to maintain latency by generating or refreshing its user interface when 10 concurrent users access the system versus when 125 users access the same user interface is a measure of the system's performance capabilities. In fact, there is a very fine line between a system's performance and its scalability. Scalability defines how a system can keep up with increased workload while either maintaining its performance measures or degrading it in a deterministic manner.

Scalability is usually described and defined (as well as implemented) in two ways: *horizontal* and *vertical*. Stated simply, horizontal scalability applies various techniques to align the infrastructure with system needs, by adding more machines (that is, servers) to the pool of resources, also called *scale out*. Vertical scalability applies various techniques to align the infrastructure with system needs, by adding more compute power (that is, processors, memory, storage) to the existing pool of resources, also called *scale up*. In scale-out architectures, you can partition the data and also apportion the workload into multiple servers in the resource pool and enforce true parallelism and pipelining if architected correctly. Such architectures allow the system to address fault tolerance; that is, the system is able to function even in the event that one resource is down (that is, the second set of resources, supporting the same functions, will take up the workload). In scale-up architectures, you can apportion the workload only to different cores (that is, processor and memory), all within the same server resource.

The one downside of a scale-up technique is that you are putting all your eggs in one resource (server) basket. If it fails, your system is down. Additionally, in the event that, once you hit the upper limit of scaling up and still the system is not able to meet the performance expectations, you have to start thinking of changing the infrastructure architecture from scale up to scale out; in other words, you need to start adding new resources (servers) to the pool. The scale-out architecture, although much more robust and extensible by its very nature, comes with its own set of challenges: the cost of additional server resources along with additional maintenance and monitoring needs.

You should, by now, have a good understanding of how to enforce and manage the QoS of a system by tinkering around with the scalability measures and techniques. You can *split* the system's workload into multiple servers or can *merge* multiple workload variability onto a single node. Of course, the architecture chosen will influence other QoS characteristics such as manageability, maintainability, availability, reliability, and systems management.

Rationalize and Validate the POM

It is essential to ensure that the POM not only is a true instantiation of the COM and SOM but also factors in the variability aspects of federated operations. By "federated operations," I mean a system whose functionality is distributed across multiple physical units. The retail example is a case in point in which there are multiple regional stores and one single back-office operation. It is imperative to identify the possible variations of the POM components between locations and use that as a lever to rationalize.

Iterative rationalization often leads us to standardize on a few variants and use them as a catalog of models to choose from. Consider the retail scenario used in this chapter for illustrative purposes. The operational landscape for the retail scenario has multiple regional store locations and one central back-office location. Consider the fact that there are three store locations in New York, two in London, and one each in Charlotte and Nottingham. One option would be to define a single-sized POM and implement the same for each of the regional stores. If we do so, the POM has to support the maximum workload, which evidently would be geared toward the stores in New York and London. Wouldn't that be a vastly overengineered solution for the stores in Charlotte and Nottingham? Sure, it would be! Alternatively, it may be worthwhile to define two (or multiple) different-capacity-sized POM models for the regional stores by engineering different workload metrics that each of the variants would support. That is your catalog!

Cloud-based virtualization techniques also call for careful consideration. Consider a distributed cloud model in which one data center is in Washington D.C., and the other is in India. The system users are primarily in North America, India, and eastern Russia. It is common sense to route the North American users to the Washington D.C. data center and the users in India to the India data center. However, routing of the users in eastern Russia poses a challenge. If you go just by the geographical distance, you would choose to route the Russians to the India data center. In this scenario, one common oversight is that the very nature of the network pipes laid down both underground and below the sea bed is foundationally different; the network pipes in the Western world are much more robust and bandwidth resilient than their Eastern world counterparts. Just ping a data center in India from a computer in Russia, and you will see a surprising increase in latency from what you would experience when pinging a machine in a data center in the United States. This difference still exists as much as we try to unify our world! Network bandwidth is an important consideration to rationalize your POM.

Trust but verify, as the adage goes. It is important to validate your POM before you make a commitment! Working with the infrastructure and the network architect is essential. You need to walk them through the different use cases, usage scenarios, and NFRs so that they build it to specifications. However, you also need to have a verification checklist of items to validate and test.

With the objective to verify whether the proposed POM would support both the functional needs as well as the service-level requirements, you need to ascertain how

- Performance, availability, fault tolerance, and disaster recovery aspects are addressed.
- Security is enforced for different types of users accessing from different networks (private, public, restricted).
- The system is monitored (through the use of proper tools) and maintained (through the use of proper procedures for support and enhancements).
- Issues would be detected, raised, and resolved (through the proper defect-tracking tools and procedures).

Much akin to the walkthrough I suggested during the SOM activities, you should ideally perform a similar activity for the POM by leveraging the walkthrough diagram technique. The POM should use the physical servers and their interconnections to represent the walkthrough diagrams. Whereas the SOM focuses on the functional validity of the system, the POM walkthroughs should focus on the NFRs around performance (that is, system latency for different workloads, and so on) and fault tolerance (that is, system failures, recovery from failures, and so on). And before I summarize, I would like to point you back to the tabular format shown in Figure 5.4, in Chapter 5, "The Architecture Overview." Some of the details of the OM developed in this chapter may be used to iteratively refine that data and, along with it, your understanding.

This completes our discussion of the three primary activities of operational modeling—COM, SOM, and POM. Before I discuss the Elixir case study, let me add this advice: As a solution architect, you should primarily focus on defining the COM but ensure that the infrastructure and network architects are performing due diligence on developing the SOM and POM. Trust your fellow architects but verify and validate their design rationale and artifacts by leveraging your big picture knowledge. The practical solution architect not only is born but also is mature enough to walk tall among his peers!

Case Study: Operational Model for Elixir

Refer to the high-level components of Elixir that were identified in Table 5.1. Before you continue, I'd suggest you go back to Chapter 5 and refresh your memory regarding the architecture overview of Elixir in the "Case Study: Architecture Overview of Elixir" section.

For the sake of brevity, I focus only on capturing the artifacts of the operational model and do not go into the rationale behind each one of them. The technique followed here is similar to what I described earlier in the chapter relative to the general formulation of the operational model and its various artifacts. In Elixir's OM, the COM components and artifacts are illustrated in greater detail than their SOM and POM counterparts.

COM

The Elixir system, as shown Figure 8.14, has the following zones and locations:

- **Untrusted Zone**—The zone in which the field operations centers (represented as Machine Ops Centers and the place where the actual equipment is operational) and the Service Centers (from where the system will be monitored) are located. No specific security can be enforced in these two locations.

- **Intranet Zone**—The corporate intranet zone that provides a secure corporate network for corporate offices. There could be up to a thousand (1K) corporate offices across the globe. Employees from locations residing in this zone access the system.

- **Demilitarized Zone**—The zone that hosts the Internet-facing machines and servers. There are three such locations: one each for the two regional sites and one for the central site. This zone is also popularly called the DMZ.

- **Secured Zone**—The zone in which most of the servers reside. This zone is not publicly accessible from the Internet and hence restricts access to the servers in which confidential company information resides. There are two such zones, one each in the regional sites and one for the central site.

- **Back Office Zone**—The zone where corporate systems are hosted. This zone is very secure and can be accessed only from the secured zone through specific policy enforcements.

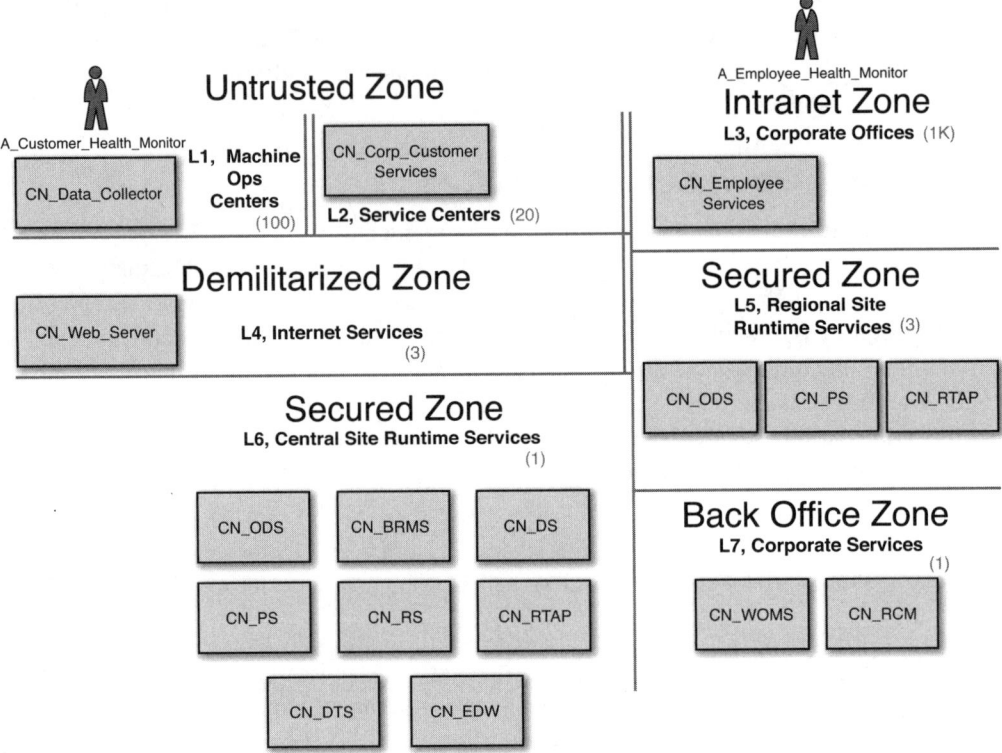

Figure 8.14   The COM for the Elixir system.

The two primary actors that interact with the Elixir system are as follows:

- **A_Customer_Health_Monitor**—Corporate customers who access the services of the system.

- **A_Employee_Health_Monitor**—Corporate employees who access the services of the system.

The following CNs were identified for the Elixir system:

- **CN_Data_Collector**—A conceptual node that collects data from the field operations and gets it ready to be dispatched to the regional or central sites.

- **CN_Corp_Customer_Services**—A conceptual node that allows corporate customers to interact and browse through the system's user interface.

- **CN_Employee_Services**—A conceptual node that allows corporate employees to interact and browse through the system's user interface.

- **CN_Web_Server**—A conceptual node that intercepts all of the user's requests and routes them to the appropriate presentation layer components of the system. Sitting in the DMZ, this node is the only one that has a public-facing IP address.

- **CN_ODS**—A conceptual node that represents the operational data store. There is one instance of this node in each of the regional sites and in the central site.

- **CN_PS**—A conceptual node that hosts the presentation layer components of the system. There is one instance of this node in each of the regional sites and in the central site.

- **CN_RTAP**—A conceptual node that performs the real-time processing of the incoming data and generates the KPIs. There is one instance of this node in each of the regional sites and in the central site.

- **CN_EDW**—A conceptual node that hosts the data warehouse and data marts required to support the various reporting needs of the system. There is only one instance of this node, and it resides in the central site.

- **CN_DTS**—A conceptual node that performs the data exchange between the CN_ODS nodes and the CN_EDW node.

- **CN_RS**—A conceptual node that hosts and supports the various reporting needs of the system. There is only one instance of this node residing in the central site and that caters to all the reporting needs across both the central site as well as all the regional sites.

- **CN_BRMS**—A conceptual node that hosts the various components of the business rules engine. There is only one instance of this node, and it resides in the central site and caters to all the business rules needs across both the central site as well as all the regional sites.

- **CN_DS**—A conceptual node that stores all the user details and its associated authentication and authorization credentials.

- **CN_WOMS**—A conceptual node that hosts the corporate's work order management system.

- **CN_RCM**—A conceptual node that hosts the corporate's reliability-centered maintenance system.

If you referred back to Chapter 5, specifically to Figure 5.5, which depicted the enterprise view of Elixir, you likely noticed the three enterprise applications—PES System, CAD System, and the Enterprise HRMS System—in addition to other ABBs. The COM model, however, does not have any CNs representing these three systems. CAD and Enterprise HRMS are out of scope of the first release of Elixir and hence are not represented. For the PES System, the data would be transferred to the Engineering Data Warehouse; that is, CN_EDW. It was also decided that the IT department of BWM, Inc., would handle the transfer of the required data by leveraging some data integration techniques (see the "Case Study: Integration View of Elixir" section in Chapter 9, "Integration: Approaches and Patterns"). This data transfer is transparent to the rest of the system, and to keep the architecture as simple as possible, these two systems were not depicted. However, it is entirely appropriate to depict them, if so desired. I chose to keep things simple.

Figure 8.15 represents the various PDUs, DDUs, and EDUs of the Elixir system. The deployable units are represented in italics. A brief description of the deployable units is as follows, arranged by the DU categories.

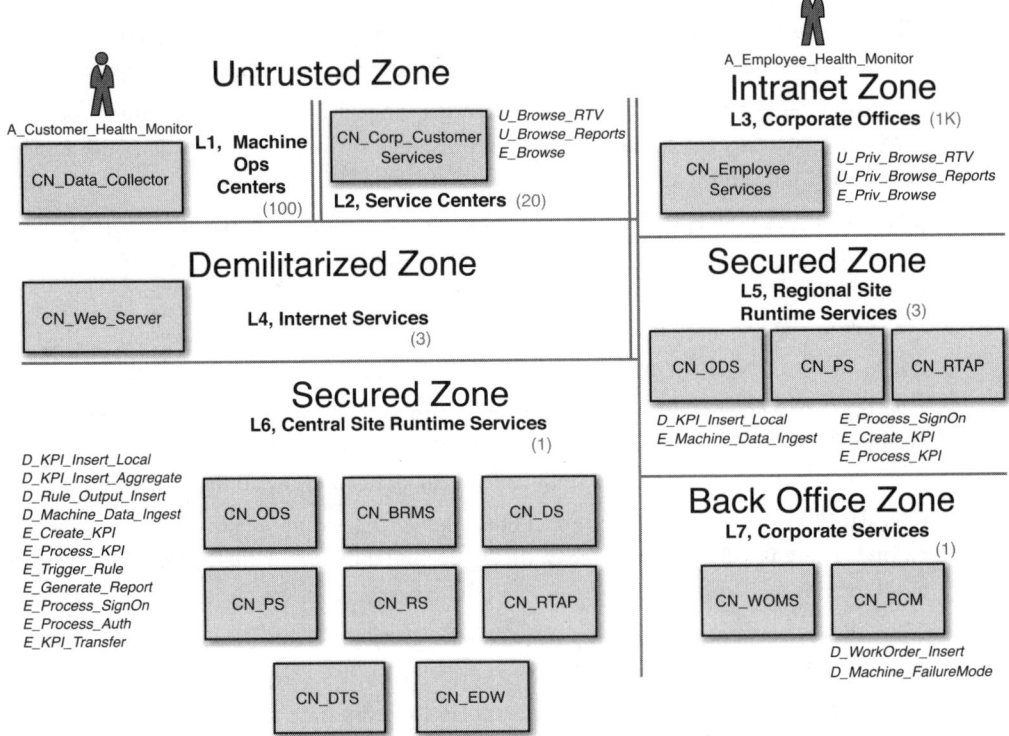

Figure 8.15   COM for the Elixir system with identified DUs.

The PDUs are as follows:

- **U_Browse_RTV**—A PDU that allows corporate customers access to the real-time visualization interfaces.

- **U_Browse_Reports**—A PDU that allows corporate customers access to the suite of business intelligence reports and their visual user interfaces.

- **U_Priv_Browse_RTV**—A PDU that allows corporate employees access to the real-time visualization interfaces.

- **U_Priv_Browse_Report**—A PDU that allows corporate employees access to the suite of business intelligence reports and their visual user interfaces.

The DDUs are as follows:

- **D_KPI_Insert_Local**—A DDU that represents the KPI data entity generated by the CN_RTAP node.
- **D_KPI_Insert_Aggregate**—A DDU that represents rolled-up KPI values aggregated to each cycle of machine operations. This entity is persisted in the CN_EDW node.
- **D_Rule_Output_Insert**—A DDU that represents the data entity encapsulating the outcome of triggered business rules executed on the CN_BRMS node.
- **D_Machine_Data_Ingest**—A DDU that encapsulates a message packet that enters the CN_RTAP node.
- **D_WorkOrder_Insert**—A DDU that represents a work order item that gets created in the CN_WOMS node.
- **D_Machine_FailureMode**—A DDU that represents an entity that gets retrieved from the CN_RCM node.

The EDUs are as follows:

- **E_Browse** —An EDU that is capacity sized to host the PDUs in the service centers.
- **E_Priv_Browse**—An EDU that is capacity sized to host the PDUs in the corporate offices.
- **E_Create_KPI** —An EDU that is capacity sized to meet the service-level requirements of the CN_ODS node.
- **E_Process_KPI**—An EDU that is capacity sized to meet the service-level requirements of the CN_RTAP node.
- **E_Trigger_Rule**—An EDU that is capacity sized to meet the service-level requirements of the CN_BRMS node.
- **E_Generate_Report**—An EDU that is capacity sized to meet the service-level requirements of the CN_RS node.
- **E_Process_SignOn**—An EDU that is capacity sized to meet the service-level requirements of the CN_PS node.
- **E_Process_Auth**—An EDU that is capacity sized to meet the service-level requirements of the CN_DS node.
- **E_KPI_Transfer**—An EDU that is capacity sized to meet the service-level requirements of the CN_DTS node.

Note that no EDUs are identified for the nodes in the Back Office Zone. The reason is that the nodes in this zone already exist as a part of the corporate IT landscape, and hence, no further definition and design for its placement and capacity sizing are required. Again, I tried to keep things as simple as possible—a mantra that I can chant as long as it may take for it to become imprinted into your architect DNA!

SOM

The SOM for the Elixir system is a set of specification-level nodes that are distributed across the various zones of the OM. Figure 8.16 presents the SOM.

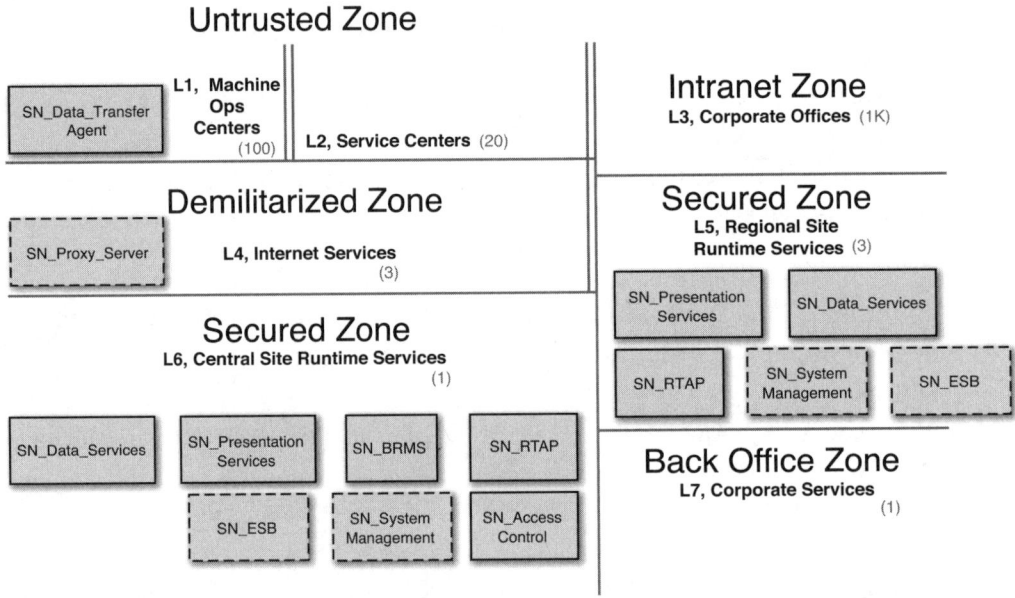

Figure 8.16   The SOM for the Elixir system.

The rest of the section provides a brief description of each of the SOM nodes.

- **SN_Data_Transfer Agent**—A specification-level node that hosts the CN_Data_Collector conceptual node.

- **SN_Proxy_Server**—A specification node, implemented as a technical component, that intercepts user requests and applies load balancing and security checks among other things such as caching and compression, before granting access to the requested application functionality.

- **SN_Data_Services**—A specification node that hosts the data storage and data transfer–related components. It is expected to have two different capacity models. The first capacity model is to support hosting the CN_DTS, CN_EDW, and the CN_ODS conceptual nodes in the Central Site Runtime Services zone. The second capacity model is to support hosting only the CN_ODS conceptual node for each of the Regional Site Runtime Services zones.

- **SN_Presentation_Services**—A specification node that hosts the CN_PS conceptual node.
- **SN_BRMS**—A specification node that hosts the CN_BRMS conceptual node.
- **SN_RTAP**—A specification node that hosts the CN_RTAP conceptual node.
- **SN_Systems_Management**—A specification node, implemented as a technical component, supporting the systems monitoring and management needs for all the components in a given location. This component supports two different capacity models, one each for the Central Site Runtime Services and the Regional Site Runtime Services, respectively.
- **SN_Access_Control**—A specification node, implemented as a technical component, that enables user authentication and authorization along with the application of any required security management runtime policies.
- **SN_ESB**—A specification node, implemented as a technical component, that supports high-speed, low-latency, asynchronous data transfer between the Regional Site Runtime Services and the Central Site Runtime Services locations. The technical component is also capable of supporting mediation, transformation, and routing needs for heterogeneous data sets, message, and transfer protocols.

It is important to note that some of the technical components—for example, SN_BRMS, SN_RTAP, and SN_ESB—are enterprise-level components and hence may be leveraged in multiple enterprise systems (that is, not just for Elixir). Note also, that I have skipped the walkthrough diagrams here; suffice it to say that such due diligence is mandatory as a part of the SOM definition activity.

POM

The POM for the Elixir system is also developed and is represented in Figure 8.17.

It is important to realize that the POM is developed by simulating a real-world customer scenario; the customer had a set of existing technologies that were leveraged—primarily Teradata (for CN_EDW) and Microsoft SharePoint (for CN_PS). Also, the bias toward IBM's analytic capabilities influenced the choice of the IBM technologies. Your solution architecture's POM may well be quite different; in fact, it may not even resemble anything quite like that of Elixir. I presented the POM in this case study as a guideline to drive the design and formulation of the POMs you will forever innovate!

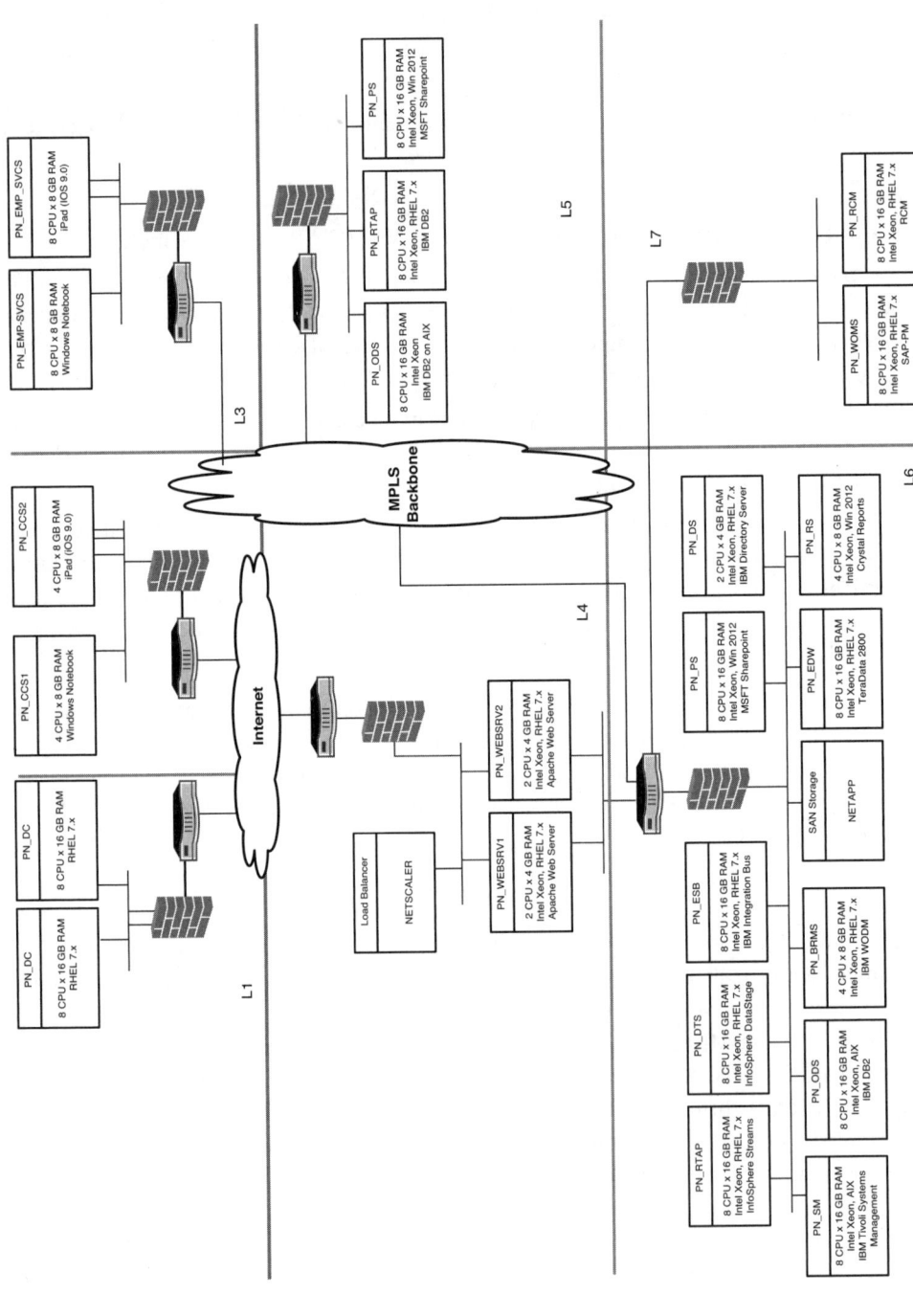

Figure 8.17   The POM for the Elixir system.

Summary

Operational modeling is one of the foundational domains of software architecture focusing on addressing the nonfunctional aspects of the system. It is by no means a trivial subdiscipline of solution architecture. The operational model is iteratively developed through three major phases: the conceptual operational model (COM), the specification operational model (SOM), and the physical operational model (POM). The COM provides a technology-neutral view of the operational model focusing primarily on the application-level components. The SOM turns its attention to the service-level requirements. It not only introduces the executable compute nodes on which the application-level components would run but also identifies a set of technical components that support the system's interconnects, integration needs, systems management, and monitoring needs, along with their required network support. The technical components are identified and their specifications are defined to support the business functions along with their appropriate service-level agreements. The POM provides a blueprint for the procurement, installation, and subsequent monitoring and maintenance of the system. It consolidates the hardware infrastructure along with the physical servers required for the fully operational system.

It is quite natural and realistic to develop the OM through partial parallelism of the phases. The SOM can be split into two iterations. The first iteration may focus on the application-level components, while the second iteration may focus on the technical-level components that are required to support the application components, thereby ensuring that they support the required characteristics. The POM too can be split into two iterative developments. The first iteration may focus on the component selection; that is, identifying the technologies and products that will be used to build the various parts of the OM. The second iteration can, later on, focus on how the technologies will be put together and configured to deliver to the final specifications. It is quite common to perform the first iteration of the POM in parallel with the SOM iterations.

Much like the discussion in the previous chapter about the time-critical nature of almost all IT projects, it is very important to identify every opportunity to parallelize the activities in the various phases of the OM development. Prior knowledge of the system, the IT landscape, the architectural blueprint, the vendor selection policies, and personal or organizational bias must be understood, acknowledged, and appropriately leveraged. Cost and time constraints may push you to start with the SOM and then work your way to a final POM. In such a scenario, here is some advice: you can leverage the first of the two SOM iterations as your virtual COM. In such time-constrained scenarios, my only suggestion would be to add a little bit more time to the SOM phase and tell your project manager that you got rid of the entire COM phase!

As a parting note from this chapter, I strongly recommend that the solution architect in you should mandate that a well-experienced infrastructure architect must be working with you to formalize the OM. Do not shy away from using the help of a network architect either; I call the infrastructure and network architect roles the specialist architects. And although we have not touched upon other areas (for example, security and testing), security architects and test architects also fall under the category of specialist architects. And if you have come this far, you should know enough to be able to engage with your specialist architects—that is, to be able to guide them to build the OM.

The Elixir case study now has an operational model.

Take a step back, relax, take a deep breath, and appreciate the various frontiers of solution architecture that you have mastered so far!

References

"Deployment Operational Models." (n.d.). Retrieved from http://dodcio.defense.gov/Portals/0/Documents/DODAF/Vol_1_Sect_7-2-2_Deployment-Operational_Models.pdf

CHAPTER 9

Integration: Approaches and Patterns

Come together, my building blocks—lego my creation!

Gone are the days when an IT System with only a web front end and a back-end database was good enough for an enterprise to drive competitive advantage through IT automation. Current IT ecosystems are expected to support systems of systems: systems require complex interconnects; data (of wide variety, generated in varied volumes and velocities) needs to be converted into information, information into knowledge, and knowledge into insights. The need for systems integration has never be more demanding than it is now.

This chapter explores some of the essential techniques around systems integration. The focus is on understanding the various patterns of integration and identifying illustrative scenarios in which the patterns may be applicable. The patterns essentially revolve around codifying repeatable techniques to enable the linkage between customer-facing solutions, back-end systems, databases, and external systems. While patterns (in the context of IT Systems) are awesome, their real value is harnessed when one or more such patterns can be instantiated in real-world scenarios to solve architectural problems. This chapter demonstrates how some of the integration patterns, which I present, may also be used in the Elixir system.

And for you, the architect, a strong knowledge of some of the key integration techniques and patterns is destined to be a killer arrow in your architecture quiver!

Why We Need It

Many, if not most, organizations have made huge investments in their IT and legacy systems that, more often than not, they plan to leverage. Treating systems as corporate assets necessitates a conscious and coordinated effort to maximize their shelf life and life span. Increasing customer demands for timely and actionable insights warrants an integration pipeline that generates information from data, knowledge from information, insights from knowledge, and prescriptive actions from insights.

Appropriately integrated systems provide the ability to support business agility—adaptation to rapidly changing business needs and IT's ability to react to such changes. Horses for courses—different integration techniques for different scenarios—are required; some focusing on efficient routing of data, some on adapters to different technologies, some on asynchronous low volume data exchange, and some others on mediation between different systems, among others. A catalog of such integration patterns along with prescriptive guidance on their usage ensures consistency in the ways they are leveraged to address some foundational architectural problems.

Approaches to Integration

As an architect, a practical one at that, you may be frequently confronted with nagging questions regarding how the capabilities of two or more systems can be harnessed in an effective and flexible manner. You may be faced with problem statements like these:

- I have system X and system Y, which have traditionally not talked to each other. How would you go about integrating them?
- What is the best way to interconnect system A with system B and system C such that it does not affect the transactional throughput of system A?

Sound familiar? I bet they do!

There are several approaches to integration. The ones that you may tend to leverage the most to address a majority of your practical integration challenges might be categorized as follows:

- Integration at the glass, a.k.a. user interface (UI)–level integration
- Data-level integration
- Message-oriented integration
- Application programming interface (API)–based integration
- Service-based integration

The integration approaches vary in two respects (see Figure 9.1):

- **The level of integration**—The layer, in the architecture stack, at which the integration takes place. As an example, you can integrate two systems through the services they expose in the services layer, or you can just mash up the components at the consumers (that is, Presentation) layer. (Refer to Chapter 5, "The Architecture Overview," for a recap on the Layered view of the architecture.)
- **The complexity of integration**—The technology challenges and the level of effort involved in implementing the integration. As an example, data-level or API-based integration may be more involved (functionally and also to support the nonfunctional requirements, or NFRs) than integrating presentation logic.

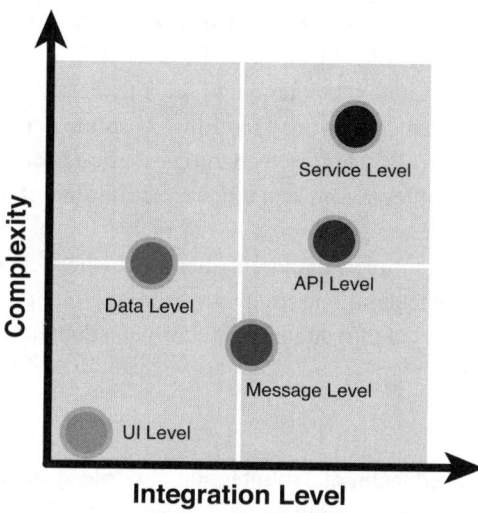

Figure 9.1 Types of integration vary in their level of implementation complexity.

The following sections elaborate on each of the integration approaches.

User Interface Integration

Integration of systems at the Presentation layer (a.k.a. user interface integration) is often used when the systems that are front ended with the presentation layer are too archaic to be integrated at the systems layer. The main reasons for the lack of systems integration are typically attributed to lack of technology skills in legacy back-end systems and hard-to-use exposed APIs. However, often, such legacy back-end systems may require a face lift; that is, a better and more modern user interface, to modernize the look and feel while preserving the rock-solid back-end legacy systems.

Some of the techniques employed in implementing this approach are the following:

- Develop a modern front end for existing legacy systems. Green screens are typical examples of user interfaces (for mainframes and legacy systems) that may require a modern way of user interaction.

- Develop or leverage an intermediary program that can convert the user interactions on the modern front end to a data format and transfer protocol that is used to communicate with the legacy system.

User interface integration has its own benefits and perils. On the upside, the implementation is relatively easier than integrating at one of the systems layers (that is, data, API, or services), requiring no change to the back-end systems and with the potential of reusing the security of the host system. On the flip side, though, the screen limitations (scrolling, absolute screen positions for fields, and so on), along with the lack of skills in legacy technologies, often become problems that are hard to address. The fact that such integrations can extend the lifetime of an otherwise *ready-to-be-retired* system can be either a blessing or a curse—your pick!

Note that, although this is often understood as the simplest integration approach, the archaic nature of legacy systems and the specific user interface technologies that may be used often make such an integration quite a nightmare. So do not be fooled into submission that you adopted the easiest approach!

Data-Level Integration

Data-level integration is often the most commonly used technique to integrate multiple systems. In this approach, two or more data systems are integrated by implementing a set of replication and synchronization processes that link the underlying data models of multiple potentially disparate systems. This technique is commonly implemented when building new systems that need to access data from multiple and disparate existing systems. Rather than re-create the data from scratch, the objective is to reuse the existing data after giving it a shape and form that is more commensurate with the needs of the system to be built.

Data integration techniques can be put into two broad categories: namely, federation and replication. Let's take a closer look at the two categories.

In the federated integration technique, the source data is kept in place. The data needs of the system being built are carefully analyzed, and a semantic data model (see the "Semantic Model" sidebar) is developed. The model provides the level of abstraction that decouples the model user from the underlying physical data sources or systems. The federated integration technique provides a data interface to the consumers of the data while implementing the interface by retrieving the data from one or more source systems, or systems of record (SOR). In this technique, there is no need to physically replicate the relevant data from multiple source systems into a single repository. Keep the data where it is, and provide a data interface that supports the way you need to use it. Figure 9.2 depicts this implementation schematic.

The advantage of this technique is that the source data need not be moved and duplicated. The obvious disadvantage is that the data federation logic is coupled to any change in the underlying systems of records. There are other pros and cons; however, these two primary ones should suffice to give you some guidance on evaluating its adoption.

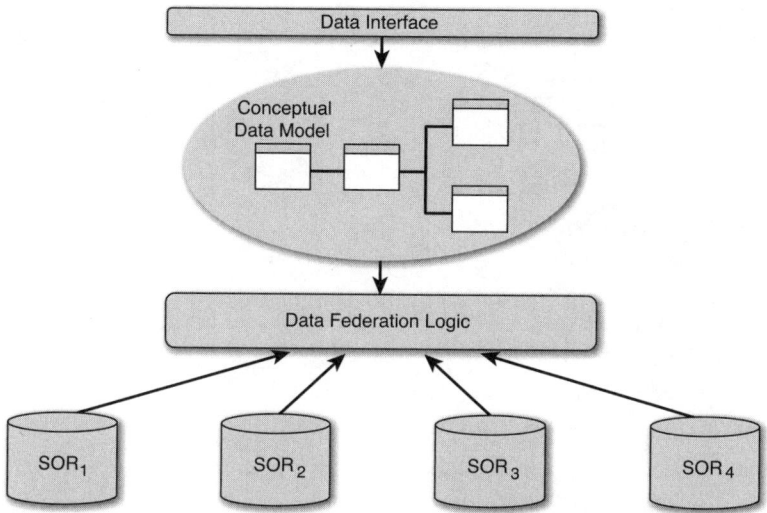

Figure 9.2 The federated data integration technique.

SEMANTIC MODEL

A **semantic model** is an abstract model (at the logical or conceptual level) that defines a set of entities along with the meaning of the entities and how they relate to one another.

The relationships typically follow a subject-predicate-object tuple. As an example, in the sentence "John teaches algebra," John is the subject, "teaches" is the predicate describing, in this case, what the subject does, the action of which is on the object, "algebra." Such a relationship follows human cognition, or the way humans would treat subjects in the real world.

The semantic model, in the context of our discussion, typically manifests itself as a logical or conceptual data model that defines the entities and their relationships. The entities and their relationships follow the subject-predicate-object tuple structure; tuples can be chained to form hierarchical or mesh structures in which subjects may perform multiple actions (predicates) on different objects. Semantic query languages (for example, SPARQL) may be used to query, retrieve, and analyze the entity relationships. Semantic model representations also provide a technology-neutral view of the entities and their relationships as it pertains to their usage patterns.

In the replication technique, data from multiple, possibly disparate, source systems is first copied over, or replicated into, a single data repository. The conceptual data model would thus have a single physical instantiation in the replicated data repository. Figure 9.3 depicts how the technique is implemented.

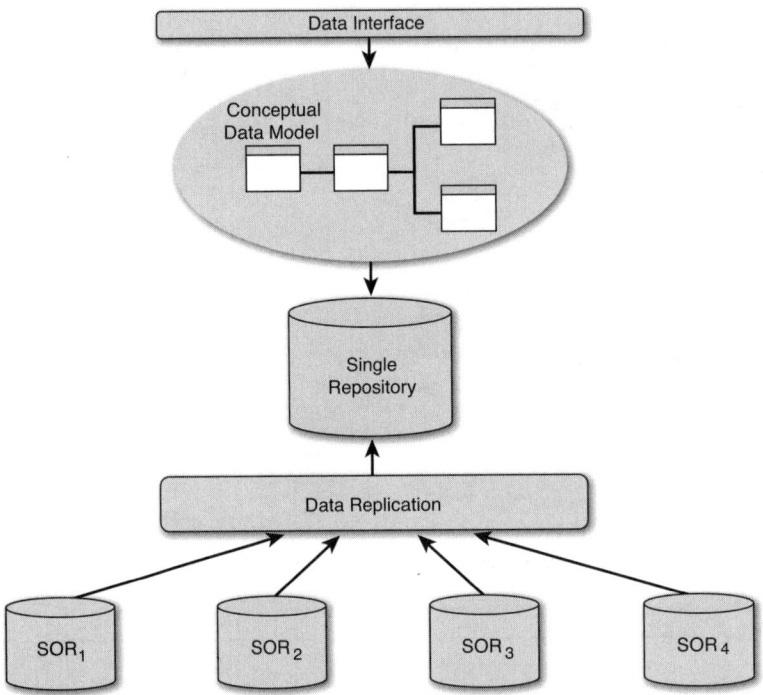

Figure 9.3   The replication data integration technique.

Message-Level Integration

Message-level integration is a technique that facilitates integration with back-end systems and databases based on asynchronous or pseudo synchronous communication. This integration technique is an example of loose coupling between one or more source systems (which are considered to be producers of data) and one or more destination systems (which are considered to be consumers of data).

The unit of communication is a message, which is a textual (most commonly) representation of data exchange between two or more systems. The capabilities are provided by a software system called the *message-oriented middleware* (MOM). The MOM is configured such that paths of communications, called channels, may be established to link the message producers with the message consumers.

In the true asynchronous communication mode, the message producer publishes a message on a message queue. One or more consuming applications can subscribe to the particular message of interest. Each consuming application may have its custom integration methods of consuming the message. In the pseudo synchronous mode, the messaging middleware periodically polls the source system for new data. Once it retrieves the new data, it makes the data available on a message queue. The consumption techniques, for the systems that are message consumers, remain the same. (See the "Message Queue and Topics" sidebar.)

It is important to note that a data producer can also become a data consumer and vice versa. The ability to publish data onto the messaging middleware makes the publishing system a message producer; the ability to consume predefined messages from the messaging middleware makes the consuming system a message consumer; popularly known as the publisher-subscriber (pub-sub) technique of data exchange. In pub-sub, the form of data exchange not only allows multiple consuming applications to subscribe to a single message of interest but also allows the message producer to be a message consumer and vice versa. Figure 9.4 depicts the high-level components for this type of integration.

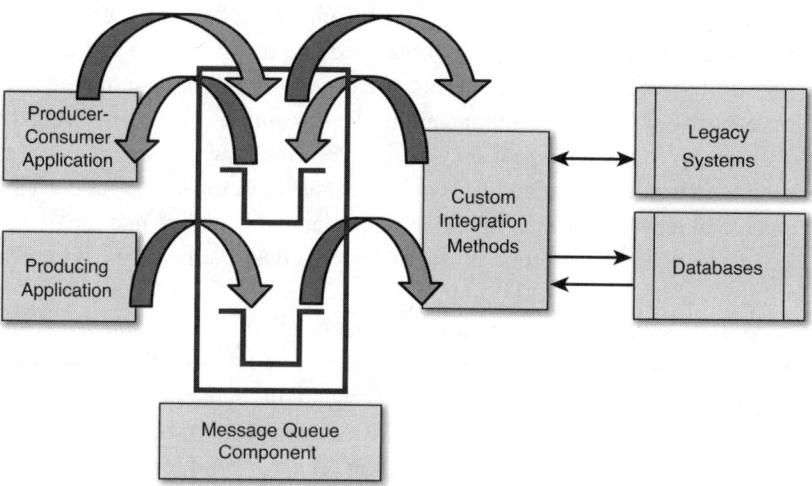

Figure 9.4 A message-level integration schematic.

MESSAGE QUEUE AND TOPICS

A **queue** is a component of any message-oriented middleware (MOM) technology that is used for applications to reliably communicate between one another. A queue supports a point-to-point messaging model that guarantees only one consumer to receive the message. A queue ensures that messages are delivered in the order in which they are received. Recipients can browse the messages in the queue and choose the messages that they want to consume.

A **topic** is a component of any MOM technology that supports the publish-subscribe model. Multiple consumers can subscribe to a single message of interest, and all of them can receive a copy of the message. There is neither any guarantee that messages are delivered in the order in which they are sent, nor any guarantee that each message is processed only once. A topic retains the message as long as it takes to distribute it to the entire list of active subscribers.

Coming back to the concept of loose coupling, the messaging middleware is the trick to decoupling the message producers from the message consumers. Referring to Figure 9.4, the Custom Integration Methods are implemented as adapters. An adapter is a piece of code that provides a technology-specific implementation to interface with specific technology systems. An adapter masks the details of technologies (for example, exchange protocols and data formats) and provides an interface through which data is being translated and transferred to and from an underlying system. You may have come across the terms *JDBC adapter* (implementing the Java for DataBase Connectivity protocol for data communication), *legacy adapters* (implementing the legacy APIs and data formats for data exchange), and so on. The adapters, which are essential to message-level integration between disparate and heterogeneous systems, enable the underlying back-end systems to change independent of the invoking clients and also ensure that the invoking clients may not need to have any knowledge of the underlying data model of the back-end systems.

Message-level integration supports many processing models, of which *send and forget* and *store and forward* are very common. In the send and forget technique, the sending application *sends* the message to the message channel of the MOM, after which the sender can safely *forget* everything about its message-sending responsibility. The MOM takes care of actually transferring the message in the background to the receiving application. The store and forward technique is based on the principle of guaranteed delivery of messages. It is used in scenarios in which the message consumer may be intermittently available. In this technique, the messaging middleware *stores* the message on the physical server of the sending application, *forwards* the message to the receiving application, and *stores* it again in the physical server of the receiving application. Once the receiving application acknowledges the receipt of the message, the stored copy is purged.

This technique, along with its variations, remains one of the most commonly used patterns for loosely coupled integration between systems.

API-Level Integration

Application programming interface (API)–level integration is a technique in which multiple systems are integrated together through a set of invokable functions that are exposed for consumption by the individual systems. Systems—custom applications (for example, developed in J2EE or .NET), packaged applications (for example, SAP, JDEdwards), and legacy applications (for example, IBM mainframe 3270 application)—encapsulate their application-specific functions and expose interfaces through which such functions are made available. The APIs provide a tight integration with the underlying systems. The APIs are primarily synchronous in nature.

API-level integration has been in practice for many decades and has a fairly mature market with system vendors continuously expanding on their offerings. It is quite common to use API-level integration to build higher-end applications as *composite business services*. A composite business service can be built in a couple of different ways:

- **Same function, multiple implementation**—In such a scenario, a common application function (that is, a function that provides the same business functionality; for example, pay by credit card) is exposed by more than one application or system. A standard API is built with a consistent interface (for example, *makePayment*) and exposed for consumption. The same interface is implemented by more than one system. The routing of the interface implementation to one of the multiple systems (that support it) is typically done during the runtime, or invocation, of the interface. The runtime routing is typically controlled by a set of policies based on which a specific API provider, or system, is invoked. An example could be a credit card gateway system that takes MasterCard, Visa, and American Express. While the payment function is the same, the application of transaction fees varies between the card types. The application of the transaction fees is driven by policy and rules that are applied only during runtime; that is, at the time of invocation.

- **Multiple functions combined into a business process**—In such a scenario, an end-to-end business process is implemented by orchestrating functionality that is exposed by different application functions. A business process management (BPM) engine provides the glue to integrate the invocations of multiple APIs, from multiple systems, to realize an end-to-end business process. The BPM engine wires the participating system APIs, maintains the sequence of API invocation, manages the processes' state between subsequent interactions, and also provides transactional integrity for the end-to-end process. Consider an example of an e-commerce application: *browseItems* could be exposed by a legacy mainframe inventory system, *createOrder* exposed by a .NET application, and *makePayment* by a third-party credit card gateway application. Since each of the participating systems is implemented using different technologies, corresponding technology adapters may be used to invoke the exposed APIs.

The main advantage of API-level integration is that the calling programs need not know the underlying data model or application logic of systems that expose the APIs; the underlying business logic and data model can be changed with minimal effect on the integrated application. The challenge lies in the choice of the functionality to be exposed. APIs often may be costly to implement (for example, some technology may be legacy, and skilled resources may be difficult to find). Also, not only does the proper functioning of the API depend on the availability of the back-end system, but also the implementation of an API to work in a distributed environment (for example, CORBA, DCOM) may be expensive. (Refer to the Object Management Group and Microsoft Technet articles in the "References" section.)

Note: The term *API* and its use have evolved to also include Web APIs. *Web APIs* are the defined interfaces through which interactions happen between an enterprise and applications that use its assets, often including mobile applications. Web APIs are what more and more people tend to imply when they are discussing APIs. However, the traditional definition of API, as this section illustrates, still holds true.

Service-Level Integration

Service-level integration is often considered the holy grail of systems integration. One of my colleagues in IBM stated this integration type in a very simple and succinct manner; according to Dr. Ali Arsanjani (2004):

> Service-oriented integration is an evolution of Enterprise Application Integration (EAI) in which proprietary connections are replaced with standards-based connections over an ESB notion that is location transparent and provides a flexible set of routing, mediation, and transformation capabilities.

As stated here, the essential difference between API-level integration and service-level integration is the standardization of a single technology framework to implement, expose, and invoke a piece of business function. Service-level integration, specifically the use of Web Services, its most prevalent implementation technology, is ideal for situations in which out-of-process and distributed (that is, across multiple different physical machines and networks) functions, from different application domains, are required to support the orchestration of a business process.

While this chapter does not go into the details of Web Services, it touches on some of its most commonly used solution topologies:

- **Direct Connection**—In this topology, an application provides either a simple service to access its business data and business functions or a direct access to its underlying database. In such a simple setup, multiple service consumers can invoke the Web Service (which is the technology used to expose the service). The service consumers are expected to have prior knowledge of where the service is located (that is, its endpoint URL) such that it can initiate an early binding to the service interface. See Figure 9.5.

- **Dynamic Binding**—In this topology, the service consumer has prior knowledge only of a service registry (Abeysinghe 2014). The consumer locates the actual service from the service registry during runtime, binds to the service endpoint URL dynamically, and then invokes the service. See Figure 9.6.

- **Composition Service**—In this topology, the service consumer locates the service in the same mechanism as in dynamic binding. However, the located service is a facade over multiple back-end Web Services; the facade Web Service invokes and composes multiple Web Services to deliver the end functionality. See Figure 9.7.

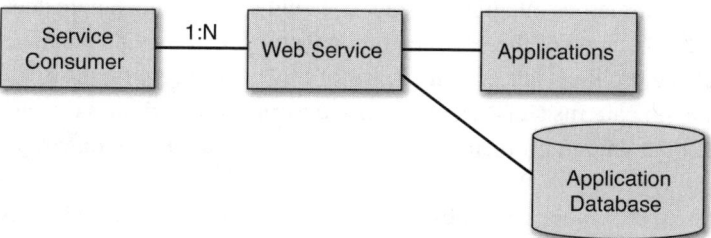

Figure 9.5 Direction Connection Web Service pattern.

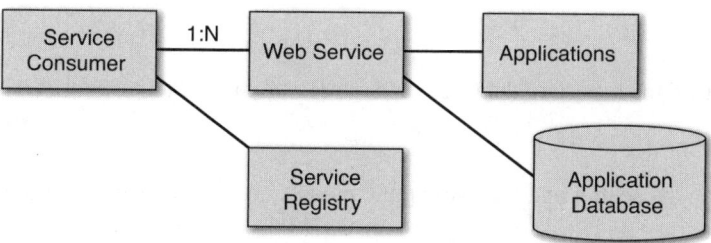

Figure 9.6 Dynamic Binding Web Service pattern.

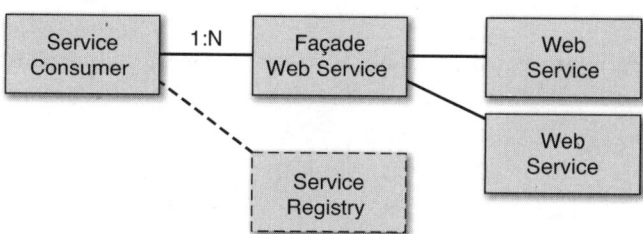

Figure 9.7 Composition Service Web Service pattern.

This discussion completes our brief illustration of the most commonly employed techniques for integration.

Integration Patterns

The various approaches to integration are now in your repertoire. If only you could formulate a set of repeatable and reusable solutions that supplement the various integration approaches. Enter the integration patterns!

A detailed discussion of the numerous integration patterns would require a book unto itself; however, it is necessary to highlight some of the key integration patterns that may be employed to solve a significant chunk of the problem space. In the spirit of this book, I rely on the 80–20 rule: be aware of the most common patterns and then research and learn additional ones that may be required when faced with some unique problems. Or better still: develop a new integration pattern yourself!

The following sections help raise your awareness of the ones that you will practically use more often than not. Fasten your seatbelts for a rapid-fire round of pattern introductions.

Further information can be found in Gregor and Woolf (2003), an entire book dedicated to integration patterns.

Synchronous Request-Response

Problem Statement

How can we send messages from the source to the target and expect an immediate response?

Solution

Establish connectivity between the sender and receiver applications, and use an interface to send the message from the sender to the receiver.

Assumptions

- The source and target applications are simultaneously available, and the message request is processed in real time with the requester application waiting for the response in a synchronous manner.
- Typically, only one message is processed at a time between a request and response turnaround.

Batch

Problem Statement

How can we send messages from the source to the target application in the scenario that the source and target may not be simultaneously available?

Solution

Send data from the source to the target application in periodic intervals.

Assumptions

- No real-time processing is expected.
- The focus is not on real-time processing, and hence, larger (than supported by any optimal request-response) volumes of data may be processed.
- Optionally, a single response may be sent back to the source application upon completion of the processing of the group of messages.

Synchronous Batch Request-Response

Problem Statement

How can we send more than one message and expect them to be processed together?

Solution

Send a group of messages from the sender to the receiver application at the same time and have the receiver application send an acknowledgment back to the sender application on receipt of the message. The results can be made available at a later point in time.

Assumptions

- More than one message typically constitutes the input request.
- The group of messages is expected to be processed together.

Asynchronous Batch Request-Response

Problem Statement

How can we send a large volume of messages and expect them to be processed together?

Solution

Send the large volume of messages in a batch mode; that is, non real time. Expect neither an acknowledgment (of message receipt) nor the results immediately.

Assumptions

- More than one message typically may constitute the input request.
- Large message volumes are expected.

Store and Forward

Problem Statement

How can the sender be assured that the message is delivered to the receiver even under the circumstances of a failure of the messaging system; that is, the MOM?

Solution

The message is persisted to a local persistent store at every point in the message's journey through the MOM. The sender stores a copy of the message in a local persistence store before sending the message to the next recipient in the chain. Only after an acknowledgment is received from the receiver does the send operation actually complete, and the message copy is removed from the local store. This action of locally storing the message before acknowledgment receipt from the next receiver daisy-chains until the message is received at the final destination.

Assumptions

- The MOM technology supports message persistence.

Publish-Subscribe

Problem Statement

How do we send messages simultaneously to multiple recipients?

Solution

Leverage the MOM feature of a message topic that allows recipient applications to subscribe to the message topic. The message, once published in the message topic, is available for all subscribed recipients to consume the message.

Assumptions

- The recipient applications are not known by the source (that is, the sender) application.
- The source application generally does not expect to receive a response.
- Transactional integrity may not be implemented across all the target applications.

Aggregation

Problem Statement

A request from a source application requires functions from multiple target applications to fulfill the request.

Solution

The incoming request from the source application is used to create requests that are specific to the target applications. The target application-specific requests are executed in parallel. The results from all the target applications are collected and grouped (hence, the name Aggregation) together. The response is sent back to the source application.

Assumption

- Intermediate message mediation and routing logic are required to create target application-specific requests and route the requests to the target applications and also to aggregate the responses.

Pipes and Filters

Problem Statement

How can we deconstruct and simplify the processing of complex messages and localize the processing into reusable building blocks?

Solution

Deconstruct the problem into reusable functions and then chain the reusable functions in sequence to obtain the expected outcome. The reusable functions are called *filters*, and the components that connect the output of one filter with the input of the next one are called *pipes*. Each filter has one input and output port, respectively, which the pipes use to establish connectivity between two adjacent filters in the workflow.

Assumption

- The incoming message is complex and requires multiple types of processing in sequence to get to the expected action or result.

Message Router

Problem Statement

How can a message be successfully routed to the receiver if the sender is unaware of the message's final destination?

Solution

Introduce a special type of filter called a router. The router will send the message either to a different output channel or to the next filter in the workflow. The routing logic is based on business rules applied on the message content itself. The content and the rules will direct the message to its final destination.

A variation of this scenario is one in which multiple output destinations (or message channels) can announce their ability to handle a message, based on some conditions and rules. The router evaluates the various conditions (published by different destination channels) upon the arrival of a message and dynamically chooses the destination where the message is sent.

Assumptions

- Business rules, which determine the routing logic, are configured into the MOM and available at system startup.

Message Transformer

Problem Statement

How can the sender and receiver applications communicate if they do not agree on the message format?

Solution

Convert or translate the original request message into a message format (that is understood by the receiver application) before sending the message to the receiver application. The translation is typically done by an intermediate messaging component that is a part of the MOM.

Assumptions

- Sender and receiver applications are heterogeneous and use different technology.

To summarize this section, I elaborated on 10 commonly used integration patterns. There are many variations, some of which can be termed *patterns* in their own rights. It is not uncommon to combine multiple patterns to solve a specific integration challenge.

Keep in mind that this list of integration patterns is not exhaustive; they are intended to give you enough practical knowledge of leveraging integration techniques and patterns for your solution architecture.

Case Study: Integration View of Elixir

The architecture of the Elixir system uses two levels of integration: namely, data-level integration and message-level integration. It also employs two of the integration patterns: the Asynchronous Batch Request-Response and the Message Router patterns.

Let's review the architecture components of Elixir, which were illustrated in Chapter 5. Referring to the components in the Data & Information layer and the Technology Enablers layer, I picked the set of components that are the primary participants of an integration view of Elixir (see Table 9.1). Because I use their abbreviated names, yes, you may have to go back to Chapter 5 and refresh your memory!

Table 9.1   List of Components for Integration

Data & Information	Technology Enablers
PES	DCA
WOMS	BRE
ODS	RTAP
EDW	ESB
CAD	WOMS Adapter

Figure 9.8 depicts a subset of the system's data flow, which takes advantage of either an integration approach or an integration pattern or both.

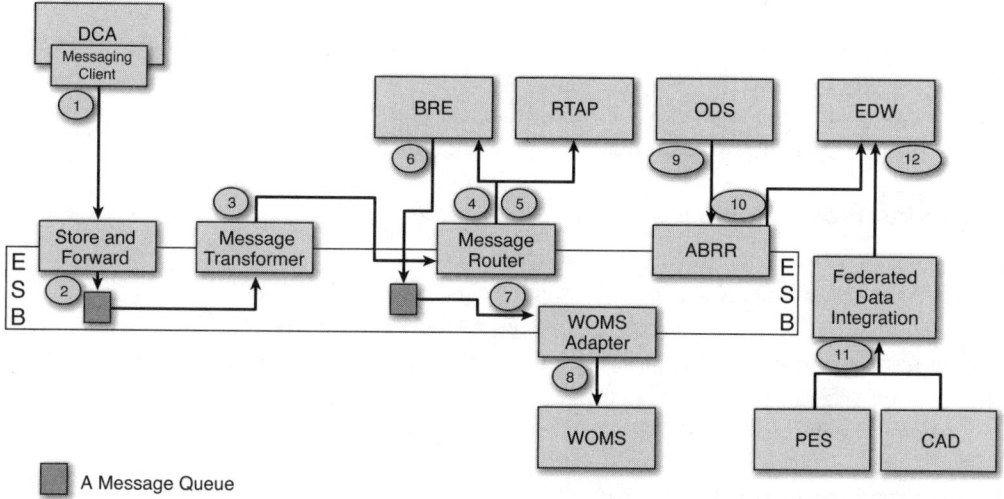

Figure 9.8   An integration view of data and message flow in Elixir.

The following sections walk through the four data flows, highlighting the integration patterns along the way. The walkthrough is broken down into four groups: labels 1 through 5, labels 6 through 8, labels 9 and 10, and labels 11 and 12. The rest of the section illustrates the data flow for each of the four groups.

Following Flow Labels 1 Through 5

The DCA uses a messaging client to connect to the ESB and dispatch the machine data (that is, the messages) to a predefined queue (or set of queues). It uses the Store and Forward pattern to ensure guaranteed delivery of messages. An ESB component, which implements the Message Transformer pattern, picks up the messages and transforms the message format from its native incoming form to a predefined, agreed-upon data format (for example, from sensor time series data format to JSON format). The transformed message is sent to an input node of a Message Router. The router dispatches the messages to two systems: the BRE and RTAP.

Note: I purposefully omitted additional details here for the sake of brevity. As an example, the Message Router executes business rules to determine, in this case, that both BRE and RTAP are eligible recipients, each receiving different subsets of the incoming message. The Message Router component puts the different messages in different queues to which the BRE and RTAP, respectively, listen and subsequently pick up the relevant messages.

Following Flow Labels 6 Through 8

The output of the BRE is a set of recommendations generated by Elixir. These recommendations are asynchronously generated and dropped into a message queue. The WOMS adapter is configured to listen for incoming messages on the queue. Upon arrival of a new message, the WOMS adapter picks up the message, transforms it into a message packet that is understood by the WOMS system, and invokes a WOMS API to transmit the information.

Note: WOMS, in this case, creates a new work order.

Following Flow Labels 9 and 10

Before starting, I must admit I used an abbreviated name in Figure 9.8 that I have not defined before: ABRR stands for Asynchronous Batch Request-Response.

The data in the ODS needs to be moved to the EDW in periodic intervals; the amount of data moved in each invocation is very high in volume. The Asynchronous Batch Request-Response message pattern is used to trigger the asynchronous, periodic, bulk movement of data.

Note: The data in the EDW is used for business reporting and analysis.

Following Flow Labels 11 and 12

The EDW aggregates data from more than one system of record. Elixir uses one of the data-level integration patterns called the Federated Data Integration pattern (see Figure 9.2) to consolidate data from the CAD and PES systems and move a replicated copy of the necessary data (from each of the two source systems) into EDW.

Note: Mapping this flow from Figure 9.8 to the elements in Figure 9.2, the CAD and the PES are the two SORs, the federated data integration is the data replication, and the EDW is the single repository. Note also that the CAD system is out of scope of the initial release. However, the integration pattern used would be very similar to the one used to integrate with the PES system. Hence, the CAD system is depicted in the flow. In the first release, the CAD integration will not be implemented.

And now, the Elixir system architecture has leveraged a set of integration patterns!

Summary

This chapter focused on two main areas: integration approaches and a set of integration patterns. It discussed five major approaches to integration—UI level, message level, data level, API level, and service level—and also ranked them in their varying order of complexities (from an implementation standpoint), discussing the pros and cons of each of them along the way. While all the approaches are in use, the message-level integration approach is the most pervasive, has been tested the most over the years, and has the most number of variants. The UI-level integration approach finds a very niche usage when trying to modernize legacy systems by giving them a facelift. The data-level integration is also quite commonly used and has also been around for many years, tried and tested. The API-level integration sprung into existence when vendors tried to expose their software capabilities through a set of interfaces in an effort to participate in larger systems integration efforts. The service-level integration took the API-level integration approach up a few notches and standardized the ways in which distributed systems could interact and participate to foster an ecosystem of capabilities that could be choreographed and orchestrated to build complex systems.

This chapter also described 10 fundamental integration patterns that not only are used in their own rights but also are capable of being coupled together to solve specific integration problems. Although the 10 integration patterns discussed in this chapter can provide a very solid foundation, they are not exhaustive by any means. If these patterns, or their combinations, fall short of solving an integration problem, you should research other patterns. That said, this list should give you a firm base from which there is only one way to go—higher!

The solution architecture of Elixir now has an integration view that can be further elaborated and refined. A data flow view of the system was chosen to depict how the various integration approaches and patterns can be bundled together to realize a subset of the solution—the integration aspects of the solution, that is.

Integration approaches and patterns—the techniques and know-how to leverage them in the architecture and design of enterprise solutions—are among the fundamental abilities that any established solution architect must possess. In fact, one of my key criteria to verify the credentials of a solution architect is the viability of her capabilities in the integration space; if she does not have knowledge of too many software products and technologies, that is still okay, as she can pick them up. However, lacking integration skills does not serve a solution architect too well, at least when looking at her through my eyes in search of any suitable solution architect.

If you have successfully come this far in the book, you are fast gaining a distinct advantage over your budding solution architect peers who are not following this script the way you are; the distinctness of the advantage is much more palpable against those who have not picked up this book yet!

Where next from here?

References

Abeysinghe, A. (2014, July 24). API registry and service registry. *Solution Architecture Blog.* Retrieved from http://wso2.com/blogs/architecture/2014/07/api-registry-and-service-registry/

Arsanjani, A. (2004, November 9). Service-oriented modeling and architecture: How to identify, specify, and realize services for your SOA. *IBM developerWorks.* Retrieved from http://www.ibm.com/developerworks/library/ws-soa-design1.

Gregor, H., & Woolf, B. (2003). *Enterprise integration patterns: Designing, building, and deploying messaging solutions.* New York: Addison-Wesley Professional.

Microsoft Technet. (n.d.). Distributed component object model. Retrieved from https://technet.microsoft.com/en-us/library/cc958799.aspx

Object Management Group (OMG). (n.d.). The CORBA specification. Retrieved from http://www.omg.org/spec/CORBA/

CHAPTER 10

Infrastructure Matters

The road is built; the tires ready to screech—game on!

In everyday life, you may hear the question "How good is the infrastructure?" This question is applicable to a wide array of disciplines—from politics to transportation to health care and many more. Software development is not too different in this regard. The hardware infrastructure—the network, hosting, and servers—is among the most critical components that are instrumental in making a system operational; that is, for it to be deployed, accessible, and usable. Your system's ability to support its nonfunctional requirements relies heavily on the shape, size, and placement of the infrastructure components.

This chapter briefly explores some of the essential considerations regarding hosting, which promotes better efficiency and utilization of the compute (processor speeds and families, processor types, memory) and storage resources; how availability and reliability measures can be met through infrastructure; network characteristics that provide optimal bandwidth; and also metrics to consider while deriving the capacities of some of the key architecture building blocks of IT Systems. We also demonstrate how some of the infrastructure considerations influence the deployment model for the Elixir system.

Note: The term "compute" is used often in this chapter to denote different types of processors for dedicated functions, processors with different rates for processing instructions, and the capacity of the processor family along with the memory specifications.

And practically speaking, you, as a solution architect, need to know enough to be able to oversee the design of the right-sized infrastructure for any of your solutions. To be able to wear the infrastructure hat and facilitate design discussions around capacity sizing and hosting will make you even more formidable. You'll have a quiver full of *architecture* arrows!

Before jumping in, look at these two formal disclaimers for this chapter:

- This chapter, by no means, makes any claim to provide an exhaustive treatment of infrastructure architecture as a discipline. The aim is to provide the solution architect with some of the essential considerations that must be addressed for most systems.

- The intent of this chapter is not to make you an infrastructure architect. However, it is intended to provide you with some key concepts around some of the infrastructure areas that commonly recur in most medium to complex IT Systems.

Why We Need It

The need for a well-defined and appropriately architected infrastructure for any IT System is paramount. In the yin and yang analogy, while a system's functionality ascertains its expected behavior (the yin), the infrastructure platform on which the system operates (the yang) ensures that the expected behavior is made available in a timely, responsive, and resilient (to failure) manner. The salient point here is that an IT System has both a functional and a nonfunctional component, and only when they complement each other will the use of the system be effective.

The options around infrastructure have significantly increased with the introduction of cloud computing and the many opportunities around federation and virtualization of computing. Network technologies have also seen tremendous advancements; technologies such as IBM Aspera® (IBM "Aspera high-speed transfer") use breakthrough transfer protocols, which use the existing infrastructure, to handle the largest data requirements at maximum speed, regardless of data type, size, distances, or network conditions. The infrastructure buzz is real, and companies are already harnessing significant returns on investment (ROIs) by adopting the right infrastructure technologies. The fulfillment of the physical operational model (see Chapter 8, "The Operational Model") requires commensurate diligence in designing the system's IT infrastructure.

From a business perspective, a study conducted by IBM Institute of Business Value (n.d.) revealed that "while 71% of all modern organizations say that IT infrastructure plays an important role in enabling competitive advantage or optimizing revenue and profit, only less than 10% report that their IT infrastructure is fully prepared to meet the demands of modern day computing demands around mobile technology, social media, big data and cloud computing." The role of infrastructure assumes even greater significance with the advancement in computing paradigms.

Seat belts fastened? Off we go!

Some Considerations

As a practical solution architect, you have to always keep one hand on the infrastructure steering wheel. The direction you're heading should be correct!

The following sections focus on five essential aspects of infrastructure:

- Networks
- Hosting
- High availability and fault tolerance
- Disaster recovery
- Capacity planning

Networks

A network infrastructure model is influenced by the size of the site or the data center, the volume and frequency of data transfer, and a subset of the service-level agreements (SLA) around performance, throughput, and system uptime. Although data centers abstract the underlying network models, topology, and physical interconnects, this section briefly touches upon some of the high-level fundamentals that help influence and determine the network topology.

The network model has been standardized to follow a three-tier hierarchical model consisting of the Access, Distribution, and Core layers (see Figure 10.1):

- **Access layer**—This layer provides network access to the users and devices. The number of system users typically determines whether a switch (which is faster and more expensive) or a hub (which is slower and cheaper) is used. Both wired and wireless access to the devices and users may be provided.

- **Distribution layer**—This layer mediates between and provides the Access layer entities with the connectivity to the Core layer. It also facilitates communication between multiple Access layers. Routers and multilayer switches are typically used as the network devices at this layer. The network devices are typically deployed in pairs to ensure redundancy and, hence, reliability of the network.

- **Core layer**—This layer provisions the application services and storage services. The network devices at this layer are responsible for aggregating multiple Distribution layer networks, facilitate their interconnections, and also provide very high speed network access for and between the services offered at this layer.

Cisco (2008, April 15) provides more details on the three-tier hierarchical network model.

The size and complexity of a set or data center determines the level of sophistication (around, for example, redundancy, reliability, bandwidth, processing capacity, and distribution topology) of the network components and devices (that is, hubs, switches, multilayer switches, switch blocks, routers, and network cabling) to support the desired network workload to meet the required SLAs.

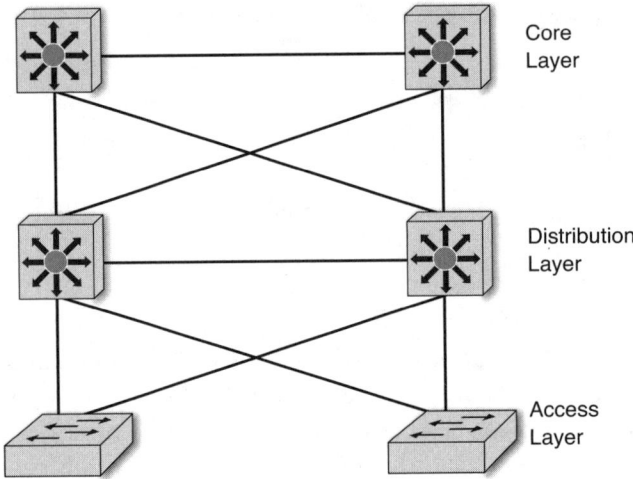

Core
Layer

Distribution
Layer

Access
Layer

Figure 10.1   A standard three-layer network hierarchical model.

Any standard data center is expected to provide capabilities at all three layers. In a standard setup, the functions of all three layers are placed in a single switch, and popular wisdom advocates that, except in the most trivial of network topologies, there is at least a pair of such switches to support basic network redundancy (see Figure 10.2). However, in scenarios in which the infrastructure components (that is, servers, server interconnections, and so on) outgrow the capacity of a switch, the network topology is typically broken down into multiple tiers (as opposed to all functions being in a single switch). With cost, economies of scale, and SLAs in mind, the Core layer gets a dedicated switch, while the Access and Distribution layers continue to be supported by a single switch (see Figure 10.3). In such a multitier network topology, there are more connections and, hence, commensurate opportunities exist to foster redundancy and reliability at the network level for the IT System.

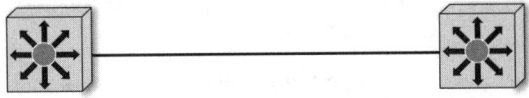

Single Tier with Access, Distribution, and Core Functions

Figure 10.2   A single-tier network topology with functions of all three layers.

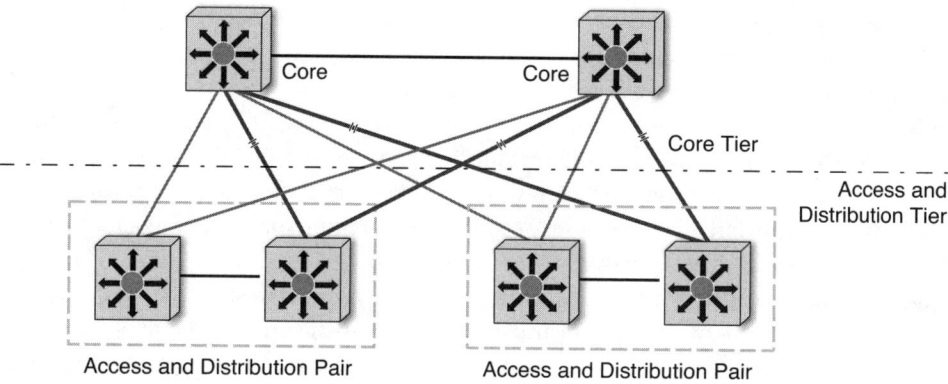

Figure 10.3   A multitier distributed network topology.

The network layer can also be used to implement segmentation, ensuring that the infrastructure resources are shared in a manner that is secure and appropriately apportioned according to utilization requirements. Access layer segmentation is typically implemented using a virtual local area network (VLAN), which enables multiple groups of Access layer devices and servers to share a single switch. For the Distribution and Core layers, although quite a few options exist, the most commonly used technique is based on MPLS/VPN technology. Virtual firewalls can also be attached (that is, plugged into the switches at the Distribution layer) if an additional level of user and application security is required.

MPLS/VPN

MPLS stands for Multiple Protocol Label Switching, and *VPN* stands for Virtual Private Network.

MPLS is a standards-based technology that supports very fast transmission of network packets across multiple network protocols. For example, such protocols include Internet Protocol (IP), Asynchronous Transport Mode (ATM), frame relay, and so on.

VPN uses a shared telecom infrastructure such as the Internet to provide secure access in ways that are usually cheaper than using dedicated or leased trunk lines.

You actually read the term *MPLS/VPN* as "MPLS over VPN," which is to say that this technology supports very fast data packet transmission over a secure VPN network channel. Said in a different way, the MPLS/VPN technology ensures end-to-end virtual communication that is highly scalable, reliable, fast, and secure.

Pepelnjak and Guichard (2000), Pepelnjak et al. (2003), and SearchEnterpriseWAN (n.d.) provide a more detailed treatment of MPLS and VPN.

You typically create a virtual data center by using VLANs in the Access layer, virtual firewalls in the Distribution layer, and MPLS/VPN at the Core switches.

Quality of Service (QoS) is a key metric used to measure the efficacy of the network backbone. QoS is a set of techniques to manage bandwidth, delay, jitter, and packet loss within the network. It is often used to influence a prioritization scheme for serving a class of applications over others. The trick is to differentiate the network traffic by the class of users accessing a class of applications that are differentiated by a set of service-level requirements, among other criteria.

If you have not had deep network architecture and design experience, relax! Having an understanding of the concepts shared in this section will help you set the stage, facilitate, and ask pertinent questions of the network or infrastructure architect to ensure that the appropriate due diligence and rigor are applied to design the network layer. In this era of cloud computing when networks are offered through an *As-a-Service* model, networking has become more about *picking your choice* rather than having to build everything on your own.

Hosting

The main objective of hosting is to ensure that fragmented, inefficient islands of computing are not fostered; instead, a virtualized, efficient, resilient, and secure infrastructure platform is leveraged to support dynamic provisioning of infrastructure services and its associated services management.

Although traditional enterprise IT, on-premise, and in-house data centers are not going to fade into obsolescence, cloud computing is abundant in its hype, focus, and buzz; it is positioned to be the hosting strategy for most enterprises. According to Gartner (2009), "Cloud is emerging at the convergence of three major trends: service orientation, virtualization and standardization of computing through the Internet." In its current state in 2015, this prediction is not only spot on, but cloud computing is also poised to take off more aggressively in the upcoming years. Cloud hosting started with two broad categories of cloud-based hosting: namely, *private* clouds and *public* clouds. However, hybrid cloud topology and deployment models have become so commonplace that it is now safe to consider three cloud hosting models: *public*, *private,* and *hybrid* (of public and private).

Cloud Hosting Models

Public cloud deployment models provide cloud-based services (either or all of IaaS, PaaS, SaaS) to multiple large enterprises. The resources are typically shared among the enterprises while their management and maintenance are supported by the cloud service provider. The resource sharing model makes it multitenant. This model is typically suited for organizations that do not want to lock in upfront investments in computational backbone while being able to develop, test, deploy, and scale applications that typically required large computational workloads.

Private cloud deployment models are operated for and dedicated to a single enterprise. The hosting could either be on premise or off premise and may be supported and maintained either by in-house IT or by an external cloud service provider. This model is typically used in situations in which security requirements are stringent and adherence to regulatory laws is paramount.

Hybrid cloud deployment models, as the name suggests, are a mixed bag of private and public cloud deployment components. The hybrid model is the best of both worlds, so to speak: It provides dedicated compute infrastructure and security on a private cloud along with cost savings by using the public cloud for systems and applications that do not have strict security and privacy requirements and can coexist in a shared workload environment. This model is applicable to a multitude of organizations that need the flexibility of the mixed bag for a variety of reasons.

Choosing the hosting strategy often may turn out to be a time-consuming and detailed undertaking. The "Cloud Hosting Models" sidebar may provide some hints to help guide you.

From a hosting architecture perspective, the physical components (that is, the servers, network, hardware, compute, storage, and facilities where they all get hosted) are foundational; the traditional IT enterprise has been using them for decades. Where hosting has taken off, in an exponential manner, is with its adoption of the *As-a-Service* model. The cloud model abstracts the foundational components and exposes and offers their capabilities *As a Service* for consumption; the consumers can remain ignorant of their physical location and placement—the boon of virtualization! Speaking of which, there are three layers of virtualization in the cloud hosting architecture, each with increasing levels of abstraction; that is, the higher you go up the three layers, the less you know or care about the physical components. Although cloud service providers such as IBM, Google, and Amazon are continuously innovating and adding higher levels of *As-a-Service* offerings, there still are three foundation virtualization layers.

Let's look further at the three layers of virtualization: Infrastructure as a Service (IaaS), Platform as a Service (PaaS), and Software as a Service (SaaS).

- **IaaS**—Physical resources: Servers, compute, network, hardware, storage, and data centers are virtualized and available for quick provisioning and use. In effect, the compute, storage, and interconnects (network, data center backbone) are virtualized. The virtualized environment is typically offered as virtual machines (VMs) that are owned, hosted, managed, and maintained by the cloud hosting provider. IBM SoftLayer® (Softlayer n.d.), Amazon EC2 (Amazon n.d.), Google Compute Engine (Google n.d.), and Azure Virtual Machines (Microsoft n.d.) are examples of IaaS service providers.

- **PaaS**—Middleware components: Databases, development tooling for application development and orchestration, runtime environment (for example, .NET, J2EE runtime), and application deployment tooling, all of which support a complete end-to-end application development, test, and deployment platform. The platform, exposed *As a Service*, builds on top of and abstracts the underlying hardware, network, and server components; that is, the IaaS layer. The platform facilitates an almost instantaneous subscription to a complete environment tailored to the user's preferences and choices. The user is not tied to these choices and has the freedom to subscribe to more (or less) compute and environment capabilities on demand. IBM Bluemix™ (IBM n.d.) and Google App Engine (Google n.d.) are great examples of PaaS offerings as of this writing.

- **SaaS**—Application: This layer provides complete end-to-end applications exposed and accessible through a multitude of delivery channels, such as desktop browsers and native mobile applications. The user interfaces, data, and middleware components along with the storage, network, servers, and compute are all hidden from the user and managed by the hosting service provider. Custom-built applications; CRM, ERP, and HR applications; industry-specific applications; and business processes are examples of SaaS offerings.

Innovative companies and solution providers are pushing the SaaS envelope and chartering specialized offerings such as *Solution as a Service* and *Analytics as a Service*. Other similar or more innovative offerings are also viable and are highly probable to come up.

From a hosting standpoint, both traditional enterprise IT Systems and modern cloud-based hosting solutions have one thing in common: the need for physical resources such as server, storage, hardware, compute, middleware, networks, and related peripherals. They also must exercise the same rigor to size and procure, install, and configure these resources. However, that is where the commonality ends. The cloud-based hosting philosophy takes off from there—riding on the paradigm of virtualization, fostering ease of use, minimal to zero upfront cost and setup time (for end users), and no management overhead (now, which enterprise IT department wouldn't love that?!). With the ease of usability and ramp-up, dished out to the IT community, someone has to do all the heavy lifting ("free and easy" is relative!) and charge a premium in order to make a living. There is an entire discipline around cloud services management that is pivotal for the cloud-based computing business to flourish.

Cloud Management Services (CMS) is an entire discipline unto itself; I do not provide an exhaustive treatment of it here. Rather, I touch on the aspects that are, in my experience, not only the most practical and common but also are the most frequently touched-on discussion topics related to solutioning. A solution architect needs to be able to participate in such discussions, if not contribute to the same. Some of the topics are shown in Table 10.1.

Table 10.1 An Illustrative (Not Exhaustive) List of Offerings and Features of a Typical Cloud Management Service

CMS Subject Areas	Subject Area Subdomains
Infrastructure Management	**Provisioning**—Process to install and configure all hardware, compute, servers, storage, middleware, network, and related peripherals.
	Capacity Management—Process to monitor and manage the data center capacity relative to hardware, compute, storage, and so on—essentially for all components that have been provisioned.
	Monitoring—Tools and processes to monitor the use and health of the infrastructure components for proactive detection of failures and outages.
	Backup & Restore—Tools and processes for backing up and restoring servers, application and operating system images, virtual machines, storage, disks, and other necessary peripherals.
	High Availability—Network, hardware, and server configurations designed for resiliency and redundancy such that there is a definitive uptime of systems running on the overall infrastructure.
	Disaster Recovery—Tools, technology, and processes to ensure graceful failure and efficient recovery of all infrastructure components along with the data center itself; for example, power, cooling devices, and security, among other related components.
	Security—Technology, protocols, and cryptography techniques supporting secure access to resources.
Services Lifecycle	**Service Creation**—Processes and tools to package the capabilities at each layer into a set of exposable and discoverable services targeted at monitoring the services' health and usage.
	Service Request Processing—Processes, tools, and technology to monitor, accept, and provide access to user requests for services from one or more of the IaaS, PaaS, or SaaS layers.
	Service Provisioning—Installation and configuration of offered services for easy discovery and access by users.
	License Management—Process of managing the validity, expiry, and renewal of users' rights to use the services, for which there is a premium fee for usage.
Subscription Management	**Service Catalog**—Published list of usable cloud hosting services that can be managed by the vendor and used by the user community.
	Service Ordering—Process (automated or manual) for users to subscribe to (typically for a fee) one or more offered services.
	Service Pricing—Price catalog of services categorized by service type and their expected usage.
	Service Metering—Tools to monitor and report on the usage of a service by a user or user community. Policies around pricing of service usage are based on SLAs and user contracts.

It should be quite evident by now that the real work is managed behind the scenes by the cloud service providers. Although the list of CMS features is not exhaustive, you, as a solution architect, should be able to ask a pertinent set of questions when working with, directing, and overseeing the infrastructure architect to ensure the appropriate hosting solution is designed and implemented for your solution. You might ask questions like these: *Which PaaS features are offered by Vendor X? What are the different levels of SLAs supported for premium service? Are the subscription fees of Vendor X competitive in the marketplace?* Asking these questions, and many more tough ones, should not be scary!

High Availability and Fault Tolerance

High availability (HA) defines the ability of an application to provide and adhere to a consistent uptime, either for the entire application or for its most critical parts, in a manner that is predictable and deterministic. It is the ability of the application to be tolerant to system faults and is a measure of its resiliency to system failures—an effort to move toward continuous operations. The terms *high availability* and *fault tolerance* are often used synonymously.

From an architecture standpoint, HA falls under the nonfunctional requirements, ensuring that the architecture supports the requirements around system uptime and resiliency criteria. A thorough assessment covering the operating systems, middleware, databases, storage, network, and applications is ideally required to identify, determine, and address the various points of system failures in the end-to-end system topology. The assessment may optionally include a component failure analysis, transaction flow monitoring through the infrastructure, and analysis of a real or potential outage, and it ultimately may influence the disaster recovery architecture and plan (which is the topic of the next section).

In a nutshell, the general technique to address a system's HA architecture follows a few simple steps (but, of course, you need to pay attention to the details):

1. Identify the single points of failure (SPoF) in the system.
2. Assess the probability of the SPoF and its cost to fix or recover.
3. Introduce redundancy in the component that is deemed to be a critical SPoF.
4. Develop a detailed diagrammatic (often geeky and esoteric looking) representation depicting the HA system topology.

Note: I have not included cost impact analysis as a part of the preceding steps. While I could argue that it is not an aspect of architecture, there is no discounting the effects of cost and budget on a solution's practicality of implementation in an organization.

Table 10.2 identifies the most commonly addressed SPoFs along with, generally speaking, their relative cost to fix.

Table 10.2 The Most Common SPoFs of a System

SPoF	Cost to Fix
Network	High
Hardware	High
Operating System (OS)	Medium
Disk Subsystem	Medium
Database	Low
Application	Low

In the previous section, you learned about some potential network architectures that can aid in minimizing or avoiding its failure. In the following sections, I highlight some techniques to support fault tolerance and introduce HA for the SPoFs identified in Table 10.2.

Let me make a few simplifying assumptions to illustrate some of these techniques:

- A unit of physical address space is defined by a single virtual machine that runs a copy of an operating system.
- All of the application components run on a single operating system.
- The cardinality of redundancy is two and not too many!
- The operating system is Linux.
- The web application serves static content and runs on an HTTP server.

Hardware HA

System failure may occur at the physical hardware. If the hardware (on which the operating system and the application components runs) fails, you have a problem.

Redundancy at the hardware level can be implemented in two ways. In the first approach, you can have two (or more) physical machines built with the exact same hardware architecture and configuration as well as the software and applications that run on it. In such a scenario, there should be an external means to switch from one physical machine (the primary) to another in the event the primary physical machine fails. The second approach is a bit more innovative and much more cost effective; it employs the general principles of virtualization. The approach uses a technique called *logical partitioning* (LPAR) that packages a subset of the computer's hardware resources and virtualizes the same as though it is a separate compute environment. Each separate LPAR hosts its own copy of the operating system and can be used independently. Of course, a management component at the physical machine level manages the LPARs and also manages the traffic between the LPARs. Resources are either statically allocated and remain fixed for each of the LPARs or may be dynamically allocated based on computational needs; the dynamic variations are often called dynamic LPARs, or DLPARs.

The LPARs are massively cost effective because they run multiple environments—for example, development, test, and production environments—in a single physical machine. They also can be used to support resiliency to hardware failures through dynamic resource allocation based either on internal intelligence or on external triggers.

IBM has been the pioneer of LPAR technology. IBM mainframes run exclusively in LPAR mode running on the z/OS® operating system. With the introduction of the POWER5® architecture and higher-end processors, even the midrange IBM pSeries supports hardware virtualization features. Fujitsu, with its PRIMEQUEST line of servers, and Hitachi Data Systems, with its CB2000 and CB320 blade systems, also provide support for LPAR.

Note: In some cases LPAR configuration changes may require a reboot of the LPAR. So there is always a catch!

Operating System HA

When multiple instances of the operating system run simultaneously, each hosting a replicated instance of the application, the OS SPoF can be addressed. A failure of the Linux server still allows the application to run on the other server and hence eliminates system downtime. There could be at least two topologies if the hardware configuration supports LPARs. In the first topology, which is an example of vertical scaling, a single LPAR can run multiple instances of the operating system. Meanwhile, in the second topology, which is an example of horizontal scaling, two or more different LPARs run the two or more instances of the OS, one on each LPAR.

While the second topology can take advantage of the hardware HA, the first topology requires that the server workload needs to be carefully designed. In one of the scenarios in the first topology, the two application instances can be configured to run concurrently and share the workload between them. In another scenario in the first topology, the two application instances may be configured to run in hot standby mode: one instance is active and serving the users, whereas the other is on standby mode and ready to run in the event the first instance goes down. If the underlying hardware architecture supports the sharing of all compute resources among all the virtual machines running the operating systems, the failure of one virtual server frees up all its compute and makes it available for the others to consume. In this case, no additional workload care is required. However, when the hardware architecture does not support resource sharing, each of the server instances must be appropriately sized and configured accordingly to pick up the entire workload with dedicated compute resources.

A tad complicated, isn't it? Take a look at the two topologies shown in Figures 10.4 and 10.5, which can at least be worth the nearly 300 words I used in the preceding paragraphs!

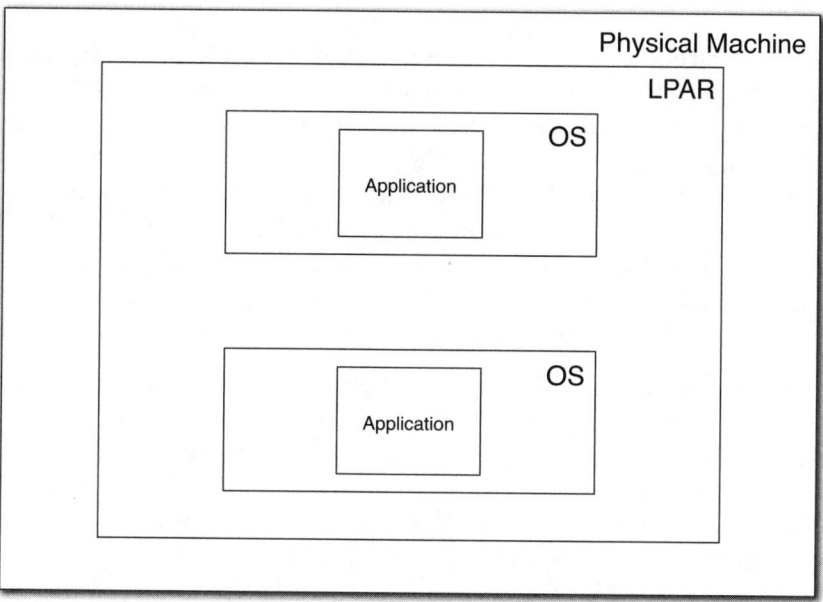

Figure 10.4 In the first topology, a single LPAR runs multiple OS instances.

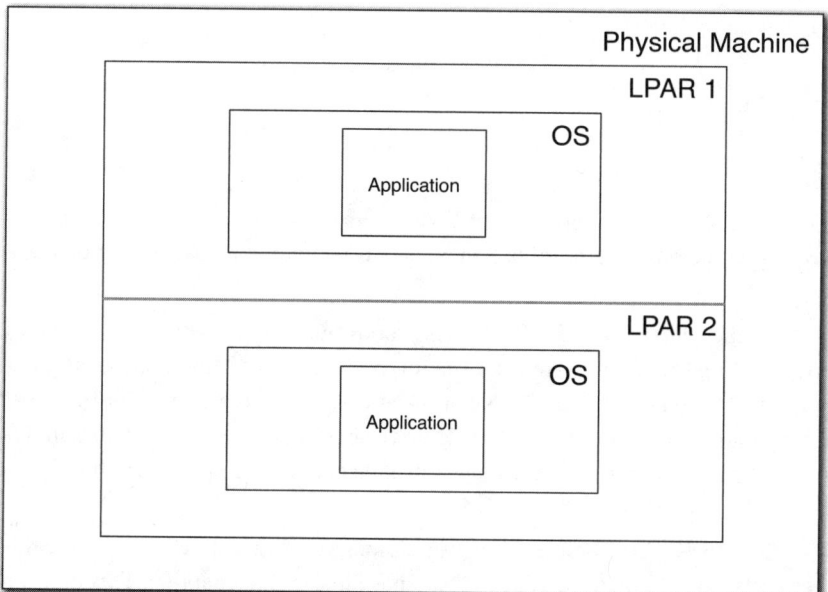

Figure 10.5 In the second topology, individual LPARs run dedicated instances of the OS.

Disk Subsystem HA

The disk subsystem is a critical element of the overall high availability of the solution. If the disk subsystem fails, any of the application's persistence (that is, storage) requirements will not be met. Disk fault tolerance is implemented using the most commonly used disk redundancy technique called Redundant Array of Inexpensive Disks, or RAID. There are a multitude of configurations of the disk subsystem: RAID 0, RAID 1, RAID 5, RAID 6, and RAID 10. However, the two most commonly used ones, in practice, are the RAID 5 and RAID 10 configurations. For the sake of simplicity, assume no more than two, three, or four disk drives, depending on the RAID configurations. The actual number of disk drives can be more, however.

The most commonly used RAID configurations are as follows:

- **RAID 0**—Also called *striping*, RAID 0 uses a configuration in which the data is spread across (that is, *striped*) more than one disk. The data *blocks* (a unit of data that is read or written to and from a disk subsystem) are distributed in the disk drives, for example; only alternate data blocks are stored in each disk drive. This configuration offers no fault tolerance; the failure of a disk drive implies loss of data and should typically be used in systems where storage loss is noncritical. Figure 10.6 provides a depiction.

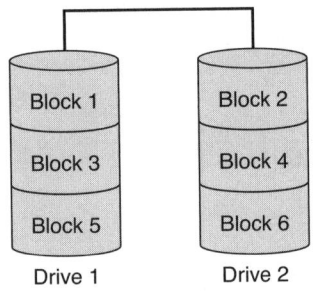

Figure 10.6   A typical RAID 0 configuration with two disk drives.
(*Note*: In Figure 10.6, the data blocks are striped; that is, distributed across multiple disk drives.)

- **RAID 1**—Also called *mirroring*, RAID 1 uses a configuration in which all the data is replicated (that is, *mirrored*) in more than one drive. The exact same copy of the data is stored in multiple drives; all data blocks are written to all drives. This configuration supports the redundancy required at the disk drive level and is suited for use in systems where storage loss is critical and may not be acceptable. Figure 10.7 provides a depiction.

- **RAID 5**—RAID 5 uses a configuration that combines striping with a technique called *parity checksum* (see the "Parity Checksum" sidebar later in this chapter). This configuration requires three or more disk drives. A data block is striped (that is, broken down into constituent blocks), and each block is written to different disk drives. The parity checksum of all the data is computed and written randomly to any one of the existing disk drives. The parity checksum is used, if required, to calculate the data in one of the data blocks in the event that the data block is no longer available. This configuration not only allows data to be available in the event that one disk drive fails but also allows the data on the failed drive to be recovered (through the parity checksum calculations). Keep in mind that access to data becomes slower in the event of a disk failure owing to parity checksum computation needs. Figure 10.8 provides a depiction.

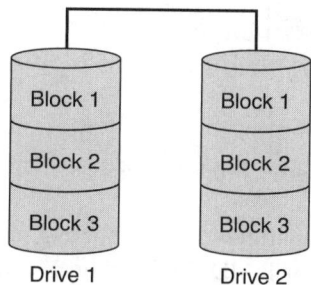

Figure 10.7 A typical RAID 1 configuration with two disk drives.
(*Note*: In Figure 10.7, the data blocks are mirrored; that is, replicated across multiple disk drives.)

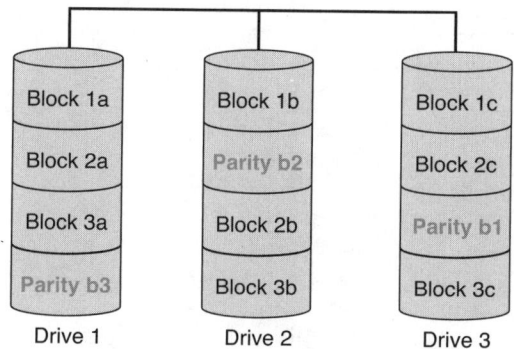

Figure 10.8 A typical RAID 5 configuration with three disk drives.
(*Note*: In Figure 10.8, the data blocks are striped across the disk drives along with parity bits for each block.)

- **RAID 6**—RAID 6 is similar to the RAID 5 configuration with the added sophistication of maintaining two (or more) copies of the parity bit in separate drives. With the parity data also being redundantly available, this configuration has the potential of surviving two failures happening at overlapping times. Figure 10.9 provides a depiction.

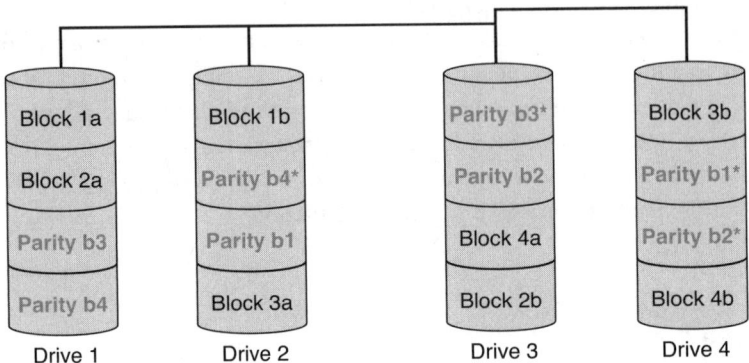

Figure 10.9 A typical RAID 6 configuration with four disk drives.
(*Note*: In Figure 10.9, the data blocks are striped, and the parity bits are mirrored across disk drives.)

- **RAID 10**—RAID 10 is a hybrid of RAID 0 and RAID 1 configurations combining the speed of access of RAID 0 striping with the redundancy of RAID 1 mirroring. It can also be thought of as mirrors that are striped. This configuration not only provides complete data redundancy (through mirroring) but also is efficient in data access and transfer (through striping). Figure 10.10 provides a depiction.

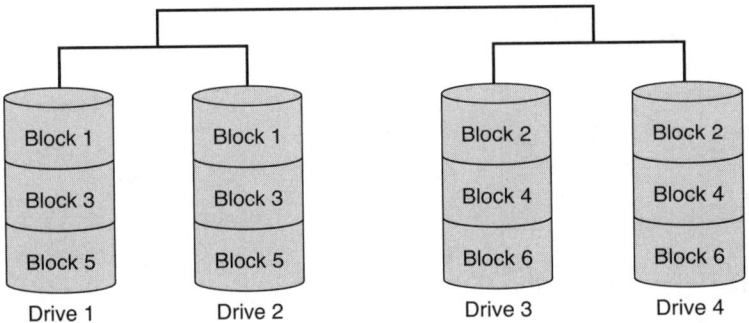

Figure 10.10 A typical RAID 10 configuration with four disk drives.
(*Note*: In Figure 10.10, the data blocks are striped as well as mirrored across multiple disk drives.)

It is very important to note that each RAID configuration not only has different levels of fault tolerance, or lack thereof, but also varies, often significantly, in its overall read-write performance and cost of implementation. While I don't get into a detailed analysis and discourse of the "whys" of performance and cost here, let me just state the following:

- Striping, in general, increases the overall throughput and performance of the disk subsystem, whereas mirroring, in general, facilitates fault tolerance in the event of one or more disk drive failures.

- RAID 1 is the simplest of configurations with the greatest cost of drive capacity usage (for example, in the case of two disk subsystems, it can use only 50 percent of the total disk capacity owing to full mirroring across drives).

- RAID 5 and its use of the parity checksum not only make disk writes slower (parity checksums need to be calculated) but also pay a penalty in disk rebuilds (owing to the parity computations). The cost of disk capacity usage is better than that of RAID 1 and gets better with a higher number of disks (the percentage of disk space usage increases).

- RAID 6 configurations are quite popular, owing to its ability to tolerate multiple simultaneous disk failures.

- RAID 10 is the most costly solution and, if affordable, is often the best solution.

While you, as the solution architect, may not be expected to be the jack-of-all-infrastructure-matters (certainly not an expert on the disk subsystem, at least), having a good understanding and appreciation for the different RAID configurations, coupled with the nonfunctional requirements around system performance, would put you in a powerful position to facilitate important disk-related design decisions. Your value as a solution architect knows no bounds!

PARITY CHECKSUM

Parity checksum is an algorithmic technique to detect any error that may have been introduced during either the transmission or storage of digital data. The technique uses a checksum function on the input data to calculate an output that is either the same as the input (in cases in which there is no error) or different (in cases in which an error is introduced).

The technique, in its simplest form, uses an extra bit, called a *parity bit*, for the sequence of input bits. The parity bit is calculated using the Boolean XOR logic, which states that the output is 1 if and only if one of the bits is different.

This technique is used in recovering data loss from one disk drive; that is, a disk drive failure. A certain parity function is calculated for the predefined sizes of data blocks that form the unit of data storage. If one disk drive fails, the missing data block is recalculated using the checksum function.

Database HA

High availability of database systems is often the most commonly seen scenario. At the end of the day, the data and computational results have to be persisted somewhere, with minimal to zero loss of information. Not having a database available during system operations is not a good story to tell.

Database technology has been around for many decades; it has been perfected and hardened over the years. Although the fundamental theories of database management systems still apply, vendors have developed innovative, specialized, and differentiated capabilities to win the competitive race toward a monopoly. HA solutions vary from one vendor to another and often quite dramatically as proprietary techniques and technologies are being applied. As an example, IBM DB2® uses its proprietary High Availability & Disaster Recovery (HADR) (IBM Redbook 2012) and Tivoli® System Automation (TSA) technologies to implement automatic failover between multiple instances of the database server. Oracle, on the other hand, practices what it calls the Maximum Availability Architecture (MAA) (Oracle 2011), which is based on Oracle's proprietary HA technology—Oracle Flash technology, Automatic Storage Management (ASM), among a slew of other related technologies. Other vendors use their own versions of HA implementation. The bottom line is that most vendors have a pretty robust HA solution; the choice of vendor product will dictate your database's HA approach.

Application HA

The application can be configured to work in a clustered environment. The two most common cluster configurations are the ones in which the first variation has both of the application instances (primary and secondary) simultaneously active. The second variation has one instance (the primary) active at any time and the second instance (the secondary) in passive mode, ready to be brought up and activated.

In the first variation, the primary processes the requests while the secondary has a heartbeat exchange with the primary. As long as the heartbeat is healthy, only the primary keeps processing the requests. When the heartbeat fails, the secondary considers the primary to be down and immediately picks up the processing tasks in a way that is completely transparent to the user request. In the second variation, an external intermediary component is typically required; it first identifies the failure of the primary, activates the secondary, and starts routing the user requests to the secondary.

To summarize, it is important to note that HA and fault tolerance implementations often vary significantly between multiple vendor products. The product-specific HA implementation best practices and configurations are necessities that should influence the final HA topology of your system. While you should be well versed with the general techniques and approaches for each of the SPoFs, I highly recommend that you call on and rely on an infrastructure architect to come up with the final HA topology. Now, doesn't that bring a big sense of relief?

Disaster Recovery

Disaster recovery (DR) establishes a process to develop, maintain, and implement plans that assist organizations in handling disasters or interruptions that make critical client and systems support unavailable for any period of time. The main constituents of a DR process are as follows:

- **DR Plan**—A plan that consists of the disaster recovery organization structure, the escalation process, an inventory of the critical applications along with their contact information, and alternate site details, among other processes that are collected, documented, stored, and shared.

- **Communication Management Plan**—A plan that manages the communication either within your organization or between your organization and your clients. It supports the execution of the organization's business goals and strategies around disaster recovery.

- **Application Recovery Plan**—Process steps that need to be followed to support a rapid restoration of a critical application following a disaster or interruption. Each application has a unique plan identifying its points of failure, data backup and restoration processes, and the latest point in time until when the application may be restored.

- **Maintenance Strategy**—Periodic or simulated event-triggered reviews of disaster recovery plans put in place so that, when a disaster actually occurs, accurate plans and execution strategies are available to deal with this interruption.

DR does not typically fall under the purview of the solution architect and may or may not be considered as success criteria for the system architecture. Your interface with the DR team primarily occurs in the form of assistance in developing the Application Recovery Plan. The DR team may expect the solution architect to help identify the most critical applications, their points of failure, and their data backup and restoration needs.

Capacity Planning

Capacity planning is one of the last "points of attraction" (that is, activity of importance) in this tour through the infrastructure kingdom! By this time, the technology architecture, which is defined by the set of middleware product as well as the infrastructure, should be well defined; that is, the network and servers on which the middleware products and application components will not only be hosted but also communicating with each other. Each server, hosting a set of middleware components, needs to be capacity sized; that is, the amount of compute power and storage needs required to run the application components. Each application component has unique characteristics that ultimately drive the capacity and throughput needs of the server on which it is hosted. As an example, a web server that front-ends user requests needs to support a given number of concurrent user requests without compromising on expected latency for user request fulfillment. A database server that back-ends an application needs to support a given number of transactions (reads, writes, and so on), among other requirements, in a given unit of time without compromising on the transactional latency. The bottom line is that the nonfunctional requirements of the application primarily dictate the capacity of the servers on which certain middleware is hosted, supporting different application components.

Capacity planning—or I should say the outcome of a capacity-planning analysis—varies from one middleware product to another. As an example, for databases, the recommended compute and storage capacity for IBM DB2 could be different from the Oracle RDBMS (relational database management system). The reason may be attributed to the internal architectures of the middleware products.

This section describes three main components and discusses some of the most generic attributions that aid in the capacity-sizing analysis. I describe the web server, application server, and database server. Although I highlight the consideration factors that I believe to be imperatives, product vendors get the final say in the factors that they consider to be the most important to size their middleware appropriately. Yes, vendor product specialists and subject matter experts get to have the final say!

For the web server, the most commonly recurring factors to consider may be the following:

- Is the web server external (Internet) or internal (intranet) facing?
- What is the total number of users who will be accessing the web server?
- How many concurrent users will be accessing the web server?
- How many web pages will the web server serve?
- What is the average transaction size?
- Is the web traffic continuous, or does it come in bursts?
- Are there expected spikes in web traffic; for example, seasonal traffic?
- What is the distribution between static and dynamic web pages that are being served?
- For dynamic content, what is the nature (for example, multimedia, text, images, streaming data) and complexity of the generated content?
- What is the availability requirement for the web server serving the presentation components of the IT System?
- What is the expected growth (for example, number of users, number of served pages, type of content served) of the presentation components of the IT System?
- Do the user sessions require being stateful in nature?

The sizing should typically recommend the memory requirements for the underlying operating system, the application itself, and the cache size. It also provides the maximum number of child processes that may be spawned as well as the total disk space requirements. The vendor may choose to recommend additional criteria for optimal usage of its middleware products.

For the application server, the most commonly recurring factors to consider may be the following:

- How many concurrent users will require service?

- How many concurrent database connections must be supported across all database instances to which access may be required?

- How many applications or application components will be installed; that is, the total workload on the application server?

- How many applications will be active and concurrently accessed?

- What additional workloads will be installed on the same box or machine?

- What is the total size of the applications that are installed; that is, the application's disk requirements?

- What is the total size of the applications that are simultaneously active?

- How active and busy will the active applications be; for example, their hit rate?

- Will session persistence be required? If so, what is the size requirement (that is, memory and disk space) of each session?

- What is the expected average and peak CPU utilization?

- Is the application server workload expected to be executed on a single machine, or is it expected to be shared among multiple machines or servers?

- Is vertical scaling (running multiple clones of the application server on the same box) a part of the deployment plan?

As the solution architect, you must decide or influence how the application workload may be distributed. As an example, consider whether all applications or application components will be hosted on a single server and a single instance or whether vertical or horizontal scaling will be required as a part of the operational model. The plans for application scaling, for expected server busy times, for hit rate variations, and for session requirements, among other parameters, are critical considerations to right size the servers.

For the database server, the most commonly recurring factors to consider may be the following:

- What is the complexity of the transactions; in other words, what are the query workload characteristics?

- How many concurrent transactions need to be supported?

- How many concurrent connections need to be available?

- What is the database size on which transactions will be executed?

- What is the size (smallest, largest, and average) of the tables?
- What is the ratio of read versus write (and delete) queries?
- What are the I/O (input, output) workload characteristics?
- What is the size of the raw data to be stored in the database?
- What are the availability requirements?

The sizing outcome typically recommends the processor and memory needs (or specifications) for the operating system and the database server, the disk space needed to store the data, the processing power of the hardware (using memory requirements as one of the inputs), and the database cache size and file system cache size (used in conjunction with the database cache).

For capacity sizing in general, there are some standard, well-accepted rules of thumb to calculate the metrics for specific genres of applications and middleware components. However, churning out the numbers is better left to the product vendors. The considerations are typically submitted to the specific product vendors either in the form of a questionnaire or through some tooling utility. Vendors are expected to provide the suggested compute and disk space requirements. They may also provide recommendations on the hardware and chip specifications for optimum performance, which is also an aspect of the compute. The hardware recommendations are more pervasive in the context of cloud computing; the cloud service providers typically have multiple different hardware machine specifications to choose from.

Capacity planning combines both art and engineering. Getting the exact or the most optimum capacity-sized infrastructure is often not realistic. When the system undergoes performance testing, quite a few surprises may surface. As a solution architect, you have to be amenable to accept these surprises, leave your ego outside the door, and keep an open mind. Both the project team and the project plan should factor in contingency to mitigate the risks that arise from the possibility of making mistakes.

Case Study: Infrastructure Considerations for Elixir

The technology architecture of the Elixir system leveraged three of BWM, Inc.'s existing technologies: Teradata, Microsoft SharePoint, and Crystal Reports. The rest of the products came from an integrated IBM software stack. There is no real value in explaining the inner guts of the capacity-planning techniques. Suffice it to say that, in this case, the IBM workload and capacity estimator tools were leveraged for each individual IBM middleware product. Similar techniques were used for Teradata, Microsoft SharePoint, and Crystal Reports to arrive at the computational capacities and server specifications for each node. You may want to refresh your memory with the architecture components of Elixir illustrated in Chapter 5, "The Architecture Overview," as well as the operational model in Chapter 8.

Figure 10.11 depicts a technology architecture view of Elixir annotated with the hardware and server specifications for each of the nodes in the operational topology.

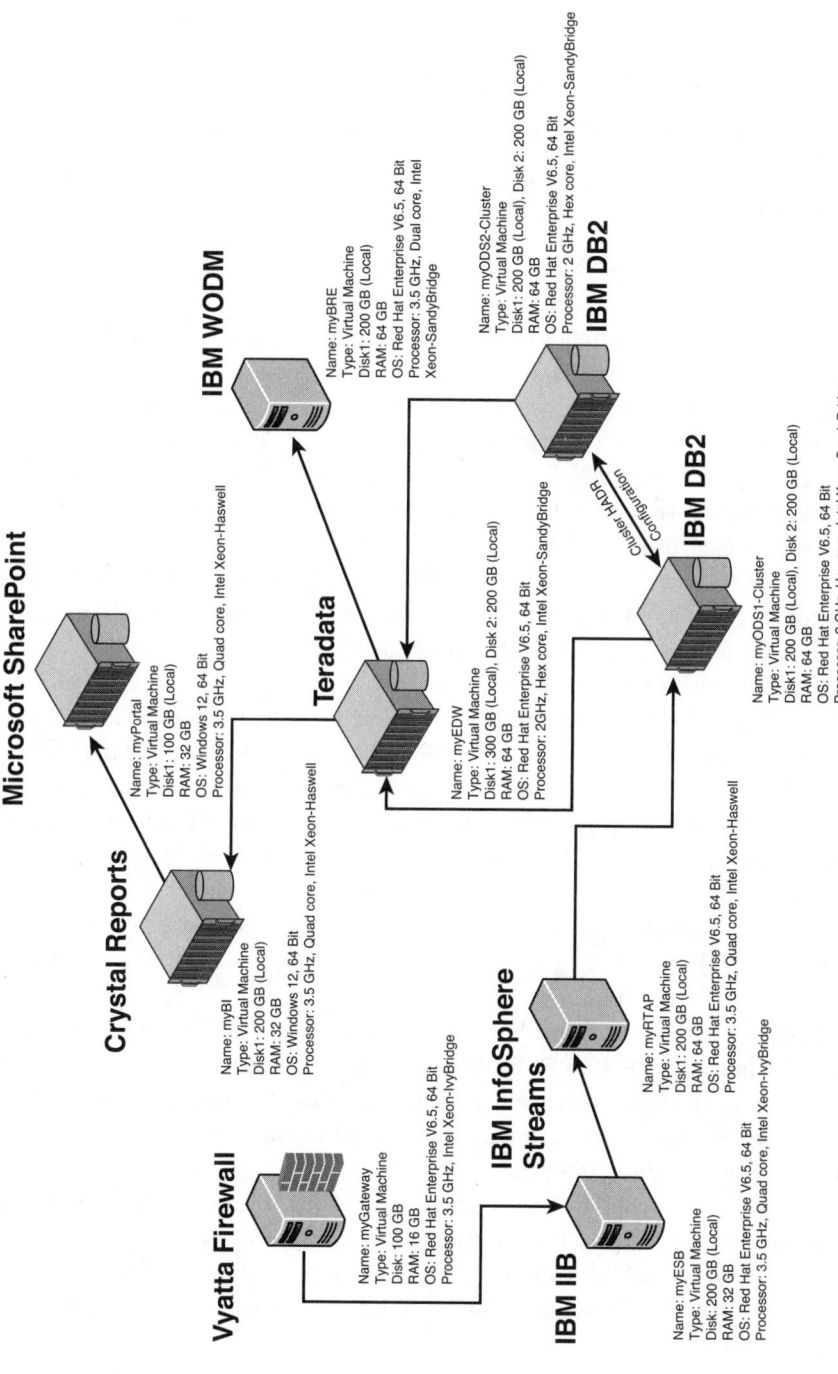

Figure 10.11 The technology architecture view of Elixir.

Note: Figure 10.11 uses a few abbreviations for product names. The actual names for the abbreviations are as follows:

- **IBM IIB**—IBM Integrated Information Bus
- **IBM WODM**—IBM WebSphere® Operational Decision Management

And now, the Elixir system has a technology architecture with capacity-sized hardware and middleware for the most critical components of the system.

Summary

This chapter covered a wide array of topics on infrastructure matters. If you have reached this far, you surely have realized that this chapter did not transform you into an authority on all infrastructure-related aspects that warrant focus and attention in any typical medium to complex IT Systems development initiatives. However, the purpose was to inform and provide you with the major disciplines and topics that are paramount to make your system functional and usable by happy users. The chapter covered five major areas of infrastructure: networks, hosting, high availability and fault tolerance, disaster recovery, and capacity planning.

In the network domain, this chapter discussed how you can design the network architecture to help the IT System support its SLAs. You do so by designing the placement of the Access, Distribution, and Core layer hubs; switches, multilayer switches, and routers; and use of VLANs, virtual firewalls, and MPLS/VPN network technologies.

In the hosting domain, the chapter focused primarily on the cloud hosting model and introduced three foundational layers—IaaS, PaaS, and SaaS—while acknowledging that higher-order services such as *Solution as a Service* and *Analytics as a Service* are becoming mainstream. I highlighted the magic that has to happen behind the scenes in order to provide high-valued hosting services to the end-user community. The back-end activities, which are collectively called the Cloud Managed Services, at a high level, can be divided into three main subject areas: Infrastructure Management, Services Lifecycle, and Subscription Management. I touched on the various subdomains within each subject area that you ought to consider to harden any industry-strength CMS offering.

In the HA and fault-tolerance domain, the focus was to identify the most commonly recurring single points of failure (SPoF) in an IT System: the network, hardware, operating system, disk subsystem, database, and application itself. I discussed various techniques for each identified SPoF to throw light on some of the techniques that may be considered to introduce HA at various layers of the overall system architecture.

In the disaster recovery domain, the discussion assumed that it is neither a direct responsibility of the solution architect nor may it be considered a fundamental constituent of the solution architecture. I briefly discussed the standard set of process steps while drawing a link to the application architecture and how the solution architect may get to influence the technical aspects of the disaster recovery plan.

And finally, the chapter touched on the capacity-planning domain. Capacity planning of the application, which often gets influenced by the final HA topology, is the key to put up an infrastructure on which the application may be hosted such that both its functional and nonfunctional capabilities are finally integrated and brought to life by making the applications available for use. I focused on the three main and most commonly used components of any custom application: the web server, database server, and application server. For each of the three components, the factors to consider are different because they serve a different class of workload; for example, the web server serves user requests, the database server serves read and write transactions, and the application server serves the processing of the business logic. The workload characteristics drive the factors to consider, which were illustrated through the three components considered here.

And finally, you got to see a glimpse of how the detailed technology architecture for Elixir would look—the physical server specifications, compute, and operating systems that run on each box that hosts the operational components. I hope that upon being asked whether infrastructure matters or not, you answer with a resounding "*Sure, it does!*"

Where next from here? Before we consider venturing anywhere else, let's take stock of where we stand. A good idea, isn't it?

So Where Do We Stand?

This book started with a discussion of why we need software architecture—its essence and value, the need to allocate commensurate effort in its formulation, and some of the pitfalls if we choose to ignore it. From then, in a step-by-step manner, we captured the various frontiers of any typical software architecture: the *system context*, which identifies the external systems and actors; the *architecture overview*, which provides a high-level functional and operational view of the evolving system; the *architecture decisions*, which demonstrate how the most significant decisions that underpin the solution's architecture may be documented; the *functional model*, which elaborates a prescriptive technique on how to deconstruct the architecture into a set of functional building blocks focusing on supporting the functional requirements; and the *operational model*, which structures the distribution of the functional components onto distributed nodes and defines the connections and network necessary to support the required interactions between the functional components. The preceding chapter introduced a set of *integration approaches and patterns* that are critical to solve some of the recurring problem patterns. Finally, this chapter discussed *infrastructure matters*—how networks, hardware, disk subsystems, and database systems all need to work in tandem to operationalize an IT System.

From the conceptualization of an IT System, expected to address a set of business challenges or requirements, to how the end product (that is, the IT System) is finally made available for end-user consumption, such that both the functional as well as the service-level agreements are met, we essentially have come full circle on how we can build a software architecture in a way that is lean and practical, capturing just the essentials and no more. The combination of allocating commensurate time to the essential tenets of the architecture along with practical wisdom on what is *just enough* brings us to this confluence where we can stand and declare how software architectures can be built by a seasoned software architect in ways that embody practicality in both the doer (the architect) and the final product (the architecture).

Mastering the preceding task is what I believe is essential to succeed as a practical software architect and to be able to develop the Minimum Viable Architecture (MVA) for any system, successfully and repeatedly. And for what it's worth, if not anywhere else, you are ready to apply for a position as the Lead Solution Architect at Best West Manufacturers (for whom you built the Elixir system); I do not even have to push your case through!

So where do we go from here? You can just stay here and master the aforementioned tasks. That said, while custom application development and packaged application implementations will not go away, it is getting increasingly apparent that analytics and analytically powered applications are being considered among the few options left for enterprises to gain competitive advantage in the marketplace. As a software architect working for any enterprise, you should not be surprised if the next system you are asked to build is based on analytics. Allow me, if you will, to introduce the foundational elements of an analytics architecture model in the next chapter and hope that it will come in handy for you sooner rather than later!

Stay right here, or charter the field of analytics—you are the winner!

References

Amazon. (n.d.). Amazon Elastic Compute Cloud (EC2) platform. Retrieved from http://aws.amazon.com/ec2/.

Cisco. (2008, April 15). Enterprise Campus 3.0 architecture: Overview and framework. Retrieved from http://www.cisco.com/c/en/us/td/docs/solutions/Enterprise/Campus/campover.html.

Gartner, Inc. (2009, July 16). Hype Cycle for Cloud Computing, 2009. Retrieved from http://www.gartner.com/doc/1078112?ref=ddisp.

Google. (n.d.). Google App Engine platform. Retrieved from https://cloud.google.com/appengine/docs.

Google. (n.d.). Google Compute Engine Cloud platform. Retrieved from https://cloud.google.com/compute/.

IBM. (n.d.). Aspera high-speed transfer: Moving the world's data at maximum speed. Retrieved from http://www-01.ibm.com/software/info/aspera/.

IBM. (n.d.). IBM Bluemix DevOps platform. Retrieved from http://www-01.ibm.com/software/bluemix/welcome/solutions3.html.

IBM. (n.d.). IBM Institute of Business Value study on IT infrastructure's vital role. Retrieved from http://www-03.ibm.com/systems/infrastructure/us/en/it-infrastructure-matters/it-infrastructure-report.html.

IBM Redbook. (2012). High availability and disaster recovery options for DB2 for Linux, Unix and Windows. Retrieved from http://www.redbooks.ibm.com/abstracts/sg247363.html?Open.

Microsoft. (n.d.). Microsoft Azure Cloud platform. Retrieved from http://azure.microsoft.com/.

Oracle. (2011). Oracle's Database high availability overview. Retrieved from http://docs.oracle.com/cd/B28359_01/server.111/b28281/toc.htm.

Pepelnjak, I., & Guichard, J. (2000). *MPLS and VPN architectures.* Indianapolis: Cisco Press.

Pepelnjak, I., Guichard, J., & Apcar, J. (2003). *MPLS and VPN architectures, Vol. II.* Indianapolis: Cisco Press.

SearchEnterpriseWAN. (n.d.). MPLS VPN fundamentals. Retrieved from http://searchenterprisewan.techtarget.com/guides/MPLS-VPN-fundamentals.

Softlayer. (n.d.). IBM Softlayer Cloud platform. Retrieved from http://www.softlayer.com.

CHAPTER 11

Analytics: An Architecture Introduction

If the universe can be mathematically explained, can we use math for competitive business advantage, I wonder?

IT business units in enterprises have reached a local optimum (that is to say, they are maxed out or close to it, in automating business processes): Almost every enterprise business unit—for example, HR, Accounting, Payroll, Operations, and so on—has standard IT Systems and automation. The standardization of IT Systems and automation minimizes options that may be used to drive any differentiation between competing organizations. While standardization has advantages, it also brings organizations to a level playing field.

Data has been touted the currency of the twenty-first century and for all good reasons. The advent of modern technology that can emit, capture, ingest, and process data on the order of petabytes and zetabytes is becoming commonplace. By using this data to drive insights and using these insights to drive proactive decision making and actions, enterprises can drive competitive and differentiated advantages (Davenport and Harris 2007; Davenport et al. 2010)—the survival kit! *Analytics* is the discipline that leverages data (of any size, form, and variety) to drive insights and support optimized decision making. It has become the most commonly referenced and sought-after discipline in both business and IT. There is hardly any organization of repute, credibility, or potential that does not have analytics as a part of its business strategy.

In this chapter I briefly touch upon the value of analytics and its various forms and also provide an architectural teaser around some key functional building blocks of an analytics blueprint. Such a blueprint may be used as a baseline to further expand on, customize, and develop analytics reference architectures supporting an enterprise's business strategy around analytics and its adoption road map.

And as has been customary throughout this book, my hope is to drive another feather in your cap, to add more wood behind the tip of your architecture arrow, and armor you with some key know-how around designing analytically powered enterprise solutions. Your quiver gets fuller with more potent arrows!

199

Disclaimer: This chapter is not intended to provide a detailed discourse of analytics, covering all of its architectural aspects such as context diagrams, operational models, and infrastructure considerations. This is a conscious decision because such an exhaustive treatment would require a book unto itself—maybe a hint to myself!

Why We Need It

The need for software architectures for any domain (in this case, analytics) was discussed earlier in this book. Here, let's discuss in more detail why analytics, in itself, is important. In the interest of brevity, I want to keep this discussion to *just enough*: a plethora of additional information is available on the Internet anyway.

Analytics is the new path to value creation—the value that holds the key to unlocking the major traits of effective decision making. The effectiveness of making a decision is characterized by its timeliness, the confidence levels around its accuracy, and a streamlined process to execute and act on it in ways that position the enterprise to seize the opportunity.

Let's start by looking at an excerpt from an informative research work that the IBM Institute of Business Value (IBV) conducted and published as a paper titled "Analytics: The Speed Advantage." Based on IBV's extensive research:

- 63% of organizations realized a positive return on analytic investment within a year.
- 69% of speed-driven analytics organizations created a significant positive impact on business outcomes.
- Use of analytics is primarily focused on customer-centric objectives (53%) with operational efficiency not lagging too far behind (at 40%).
- An organization's ability to convert analytical insights into decision making actions is influenced by the pervasiveness of the usage of analytics across the organizations along with the breadth of technical capabilities leveraged to support analytics. Those who are the leaders in that pack are the ones who can act with the speed required for competitive advantage with 69% of the ones studied reporting a significant impact on business outcomes, 60% reporting a significant impact of revenues, and 53% of them reporting gaining a significant competitive advantage.
- The leaders in the pack (see the bullet above) are the ones who are the most effective in their speed to acquire data, to analyze data and generate insight, and to act on it in a timely and opportune manner to drive positive impact and competitive advantage for the enterprise. (IBM Institute of Business Value n.d.)

The paper goes on to provide supporting evidence regarding why data-driven organizations are winning the race in the marketplace.

While all the points highlighted here are relevant to why analytics and its adoption have become essential for any enterprise to foster competitive advantage, the last point is particularly interesting, especially in the light of an analytics architecture. Acquiring data, analyzing it to extract information, and being able to generate optimized recommendations to act on the data require a foundational technology underpinning.

If analytics is relevant, essential, and imperative for an enterprise, it surely needs a good architecture treatment.

Dimensions of Analytics

Just as DNA holds the secret to all human characteristics, insight lies encoded in the various strands of data: what DNA is to humans, data is to business insights. The various forms of data (that is, its *variety*), the various rates at which data is generated and ingested (that is, its *velocity*), the various sizes in which data is generated (that is, its *volume*), and the trustworthiness of the data (that is, its *veracity*) typically constitute the four key characteristics (that is, variety, velocity, volume, and veracity) of data that influence and provide clues on how the analytical imprints can be unlocked. It suffices to say that the staggering rate at which the expansion of data volumes and velocity continues to be relentless, the veracity index of the data comes more and more under scrutiny.

Analytics is being leveraged in a multitude of ways to foster better decision making. The use of analytics can be broadly classified into five categories or dimensions:

- Operational (real-time) Analytics
- Descriptive Analytics
- Predictive Analytics
- Prescriptive Analytics
- Cognitive Computing

The various forms of analytics form a spectrum and address a continuum for supporting business insights, starting from what is happening right now (that is, at the point of business impact) and extending to acting as an advisor to humans (that is, an extension to human cognition).

Let's explore the continuum!

Operational Analytics

Operational Analytics focuses on highlighting what is happening right now and brings it to the attention of the relevant parties as and when it is happening. The "right now" connotation implies a real-time nature of analytics. Such an analytics capability, owing to its real-time nature, requires the generation of insights while the data is in motion. In such scenarios, in which the decision latency is in seconds or subseconds, data persistence (that is, storing it in a persistence store before retrieving it for analytics) is not conducive to generating insights in real time. Analytical insights need to be generated while the data is in motion—that is, at the point where the data is first seen by the system. The data flows through continuously (that is, it is streaming) while analytics is applied on the data in the spectrum of the data continuum. It is referred to by various names: data-in-motion analytics, Operational Analytics, or real-time analytics. Some examples of operational or real-time analytics are

- Providing stock prices and their temporal variation every second
- Collecting machine instrumentation (for example, temperature, pressure, and amperage) of fixed or moving assets (for example, pipelines, compressors, and pumps) and monitoring their operational patterns, in real time, to detect anomalies in their operating conditions
- Detecting motion detection in real time, through video imaging and acoustic vibrations (for example, analyzing video feeds, in real time, from drones to detect political threat)

Descriptive Analytics

The form known as Descriptive Analytics focuses on highlighting the description and analysis of *what already happened* and providing various techniques to slice and dice (that is, get different views of the same data or a subset thereof) the information in multiple intuitive ways to drive analytical insights of historical events. It is also called after-the-fact analytics, owing to its nature of describing what happened in the past. Traditional business intelligence (or BI, as we know it) was primarily this. The power of BI lies in the various techniques used to present information for analysis such that the root causes of business events (for example, historical trends for car battery recall reasons, efficiency and productivity losses in the manufacturing assembly line) are easier to analyze, comprehend, and understand. Owing to its after-the-fact nature, it is performed on data at rest; that is, on persisted data. Some examples of Descriptive Analytics are

- Performing comparative analysis on production metrics across multiple similar production plants such as oil platforms and semiconductor fabrication assembly lines
- Comparing the productivity of field operators across multiple shifts in a day
- Comparing how the average availability of a machine degrades over the years

Predictive Analytics

Predictive Analytics primarily focuses on predicting *what is going to happen* in the future by either analyzing how something happened in the past or by detecting and learning patterns used to classify future behavior. Predictive Analytics relies on building predictive models that typically transform known data representing an entity into a classification, probability estimation, or some other relevant measure of future behavior. Predictive models are typically built using algorithms that look at large volumes of historical data. Algorithm-based models are primarily data driven; that is, various statistics of the data define the characteristics of the model. Models are developed using various statistical, probabilistic, and machine-learning techniques to predict future outcomes. Supervised learning and unsupervised learning form the basis of the two broad categories of machine-learning techniques. Building reliable and effective models generally requires transformation of the raw data inputs into features that the analytical algorithm can exploit. Some examples of Predictive Analytics are

- Predicting the chances of a given patient having a certain form of skin cancer given a sample of her skin
- Predicting the remaining life of a critical component of any expensive heavy equipment such as coal-mining equipment
- Predicting whether a person applying for a bank loan will default on his payment

Note: I encourage you to research further into supervised and unsupervised machine-learning techniques. You may start by understanding the fundamentals of regression, classification, and clustering schemes.

Prescriptive Analytics

The form known as Prescriptive Analytics focuses on answering the question around *what you should be doing* (that is, prescribe) if something were to happen (that is, predictive) in the future. Stated differently, Prescriptive Analytics addresses how and what to provide as recommendations and actions that may be taken based on some future event that is predicted to happen.

Prescriptive Analytics relies on optimized decision making. It typically considers one or more predictive outcomes and combines them with other factors to arrive at an optimized recommendation that is typically actionable in nature. It may leverage tools and techniques, around business rules, optimization algorithms, or a combination thereof, to come up with recommendations. Whereas Operational, Descriptive, and Predictive Analytics tell us what is happening now, what happened in the past, or what is going to happen in the future, Prescriptive Analytics actually prescribes what to do or what actions to take if such events were to happen. Rules engines correlate multiple input events that take place across both space (that is, in multiple locations) and in time (that is, at different points in time) along with external events such as weather, operating conditions, maintenance schedules, and so on, to come up with actionable recommendations. Because this form of analytics may be a bit esoteric, in the spirit of practicality, let me provide an example as illustration.

An elderly man is driving his relatively new BMW M5 on a bright sunny Sunday morning on May 24, 2015. Imagine that a predictive model predicts this man's car gearbox will stop functioning in the next 30 days and flashed an alert on the car dashboard. Other than getting upset, this man may not know to do anything else other than turning around and making plans to immediately take the car to the dealer. A Prescriptive Analytics module comes in and intervenes! It figures out that the car has free servicing, under warranty, on June 14, 2015 (that is, in the next 21 days and that the confidence level of the predictive outcome does not change too much between 21 days and 30 days; in other words, as an example, the model predicts that the gearbox can break in 21 days from now with a confidence level of 85 percent and that it can break in 30 days from now with a confidence level of 88 percent). Given these three data points (that is, the time window of opportunity, confidence levels, and upcoming warrantied scheduled service maintenance window), the Prescriptive Analytics system performs a business-rules–based optimization and subsequently sends out a notification to the car owner with a precise recommendation: "Bring in the car for service on June 14; your car is going to be just fine, and we will take care of it free of charge!" This is an example of a prescriptive and actionable recommendation.

Some examples of Prescriptive Analytics are

- Recommending creation of a work order (along with job procedures) to fix equipment
- Recommending deferring the maintenance of a high-valued equipment component close to its planned maintenance window
- Recommending an optimum price point to sell a specialty chemical (for example, an oxy-solvent) at which there will be a decent profit margin and also a higher probability of the buyer's acceptance of the price

Cognitive Computing

Cognitive Computing focuses on systems that "think" to generate insights that are human-like; at least, that is the basic idea! This is a relatively new paradigm because there is a fundamental difference in how these systems are built and how they interact with humans. Traditional systems generate insights at various levels—descriptive, predictive, prescriptive, and so on— where humans perform most of the directing. Cognitive-based systems, in contrast, learn and build knowledge, understand natural language, and reason and interact more naturally with human beings than traditional programmable systems. Cognitive systems extend the capabilities of humans by augmenting human decision-making capacity and helping us make sense of the growing amount of data that is germane to a situation—a data corpus (that is, its sheer volume and wide variety) that is typically beyond the capacity of a human brain to process, analyze, and react to in a period of time that fosters competitive decision-making advantage.

Cognitive Computing is very much in its infancy stages (IBM Institute of Business Value n.d.), leaving various opportunities in its potential evolution. Organizations need to set realistic expectations, and they certainly should set long-term plans instead of trying to achieve immediate gains from it. Expecting immediate gains would not only be frustrating to the enterprise but also would not be acknowledging the true potential of Cognitive Computing; *potential* is the operative word here.

Cognitive systems, such as the technology behind the IBM Watson™ computer that participated and won the *Jeopardy* event, are based on an open domain question-answering technique called DeepQA (IBM n.d.). The technique, at a very high level, leverages sophisticated and deep natural language processing capabilities, along with advanced statistical and probabilistic algorithms, to arrive at the best possible answer to any question. The corpus of data on which it applies the techniques is primarily unstructured and semistructured in nature and can be a combination of data available in the public domain and privately held enterprise content. Some examples of cognitive systems are

- IBM Watson participating in the popular *Jeopardy* television show and winning the competition against the top-ranked *Jeopardy* participants

- An advisor system that assists oil and gas engineers detect a potential "stuck pipe" situation in an oil rig

- A cognitive system that can streamline the review processes between a patient's physician and his health plan

The preceding discussion provided a brief introduction to the various dimensions of analytics. Each dimension is a field unto itself, and professionals could easily spend their entire career in any one discipline perfecting expertise and then building into adjacent domains, fields, and dimensions.

It is important to understand that those organizations that will enjoy competitive advantage in the marketplace are the ones that will break away from the traditional approaches of human intuition and expertise-based *sense and response* mode of business automation. They will move to one from which the next-generation efficiencies and differentiation will be achieved by providing precise, contextual analytics at the point of business impact, thereby adopting a real-time, fact-driven *predict and act* modus operandi. This fundamental shift will be made possible only through a serious investment in analytics as a part of the organization's business strategy. Any such strategic business reason, to invest in analytics, needs to be supplemented with an innovative solution approach that is built on a strong foundation of complementary advanced analytics techniques that collectively will provide a 360-degree view of whatever it takes to provide insightful decisions.

Regarding advanced analytical techniques, a strong architectural foundation is paramount to consolidate the required features, techniques, and technologies to support the organization's business strategy—a perfect segue into our next section!

Analytics Architecture: Foundation

Any nontrivial IT System must have an architecture foundation. What I describe in this section is a functional model of an analytics reference blueprint (or architecture or model). This blueprint addresses each layer of the architecture stack and strives to address a wide coverage of use-case scenarios in which analytics applications may be implemented across businesses that consider analytics to be a strategic initiative focused on developing a distinctive business advantage. You can also think of it as an analytics capability model describing a set of capabilities that may be required for any enterprise to consider when it embarks on its analytics journey. This model does not require to support all of the capabilities—at least not all at once. The maturity of an enterprise's adoption of analytics, along with its prioritized business imperatives, typically dictates the iterative rollout of the capabilities.

Quite frequently, I have stumbled upon analytics architecture models (or blueprints) that focus on developing subsets of data architectures along with their access management and integration. An analytics reference architecture or model should assign primary focus on analytics while addressing data architecture to the extent that is commensurate in enabling an analytics framework or platform.

It is important for the technical community to realize that, while making data and information accessible and actionable is imperative (that is, analyzable), the core discipline of analytics focuses on building *systems of insight* and hence requires a different mindset and focus. Systems of insight, the focus of analytics, aim at converting data into information, from information to insight, and from insight to actionable outcomes, and subsequently sharing that information, insight, and actionable outcomes with the appropriate personas. The interaction with users forms the basis of what we call *systems of engagement*—putting a user in the driver's seat while arming her with the information, insight, and actionable outcomes (which forms the core of the systems of insight) required to drive home successfully. The type of information, insight, and actionable outcomes generated, along with the required analytic capabilities, may be categorized by the user type or personas. The following are some illustrative examples of user types and their analytics focus:

- Business executives may be interested only in business metrics and, hence, on reports that highlight one or more performance measures with the ability to view the same data but through different views (for example, revenue by region, revenue by product, and so on).

- System engineers may be interested in root-cause analysis and, hence, expect to be able to drill down from a metrics-based view to a summary view and further down to a detailed and granular root-cause analysis, to determine the actual cause of critical events (for example, operations shutdown or random maintenance episodes).

- Data scientists are responsible for performing ad hoc analysis on a multitude of data sets, across heterogeneous systems, leveraging a wide variety of statistical and machine-learning algorithms to identify patterns, trends, correlations, and outliers that may be used to develop predictive and prescriptive analytic capabilities for the enterprise.

If we study the usage patterns and the expectations to extract intelligence from data, we can categorize analytics into five dimensions, as described earlier. These categories or dimensions define the five pillars of corporate intelligence into which the discipline of analytics can be constructed. It is important to acknowledge that the focus of analytics is fundamentally different from that of data and its management, focusing primarily on generating systems of insight that drive systems of engagement between the human and "things" (machines, processes, and the entire connected ecosystem).

Let's dive a little deeper into the reference model.

The Layered View: Layers and Pillars

Figure 11.1 depicts the layered view of an analytics architecture reference model. The layers and pillars, along with the capabilities discussed, are meant to be used as guidelines and not a strict prescription for adherence. Architectures and architects alike need to have enough flexibility to be both adaptive and resilient; principles, guidelines, and constraints aim to provide such flexibility and resilience.

Before we get further ahead, let me state my intentional use of the terms *analytics reference model* (ARM), *analytics reference blueprint* (ARB) and *analytics reference architecture* (ARA) interchangeably; ARM, ARB, and ARA are one and the same for the sake of this discussion. You never know which phrase will stick with your team and your customers; having three options to choose from is not bad!

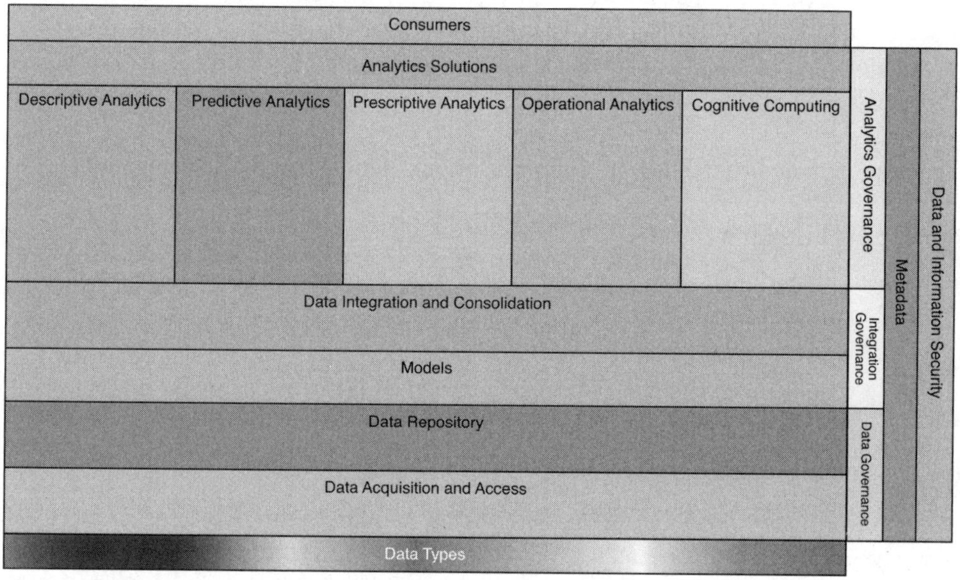

Figure 11.1 A layered view of an analytics reference architecture.

ARA is composed of a set of horizontal and cross-cutting layers. Some of the horizontal layers are focused on data acquisition, data preparation, data storage, and data consolidation, whereas some others cover the solutions and their end-user consumption. The cross-cutting layers, as the name suggests, provide a set of capabilities that are applicable to multiple horizontal layers.

ARA introduces the concept of pillars, representing the five dimensions of analytics (just below the Analytics Solutions layer in Figure 11.1). Pillars represent a set of related capability.

The capabilities supported by each of the pillars can cross-pollinate, comingle, or coexist (because they are at the same level and hence adhere to the fundamental principles of a layered architecture). They not only harness the capabilities from all of the horizontal layers that lie below (the pillars) but also can leverage the capabilities from the vertical cross-cutting layers.

Although some of the key characteristics of each layer may be highlighted, they are by no means fully exhaustive. In the spirit of *just enough*, my goal here is merely to introduce you to the concepts and provide a foundation on which you can build your ARA!

ARA/ARM/ARB is composed of seven horizontal and three vertical cross-cutting layers. The horizontal layers are built from the bottom up, with each layer building on the capabilities and functionalities of the layers below. The layers are Data Types, Data Acquisition and Access, Data Repository, Models, Data Integration and Consolidation, Analytics Solutions, and Consumers. The five layers from the bottom—Data Types, Data Acquisition and Access, Data Repository, Models, and Data Integration and Consolidation—form the data foundation based on which the analytic capabilities are built. The Analytics Solutions layer describes the various analytically powered solutions that can be offered to the consumer. The topmost layer (that is, the Consumers layer) represents a set of techniques that may be leveraged to interface with the end users—the visual interfaces.

The next sections elaborate on the horizontal layers, vertical layers, and the pillars.

The Horizontal Layers

The following sections define each of the horizontal layers and the collective functionality each one of them is expected to provide in the overall ARB.

Data Types

The lowest layer in the ARB, Data Types, acknowledges the fact that the various data types and data sources are spread across a broad spectrum ranging from traditional structured data to data types that are categorized as unstructured in nature.

This layer enforces the expectation of the ARB to address the broad spectrum of data sources and types that may be ingested into the system for further processing. Examples of structured data types include transactional data from routine maintenance, point-of-sales transactions, and so on. Semistructured data types represent common web content, click streams, and so on, whereas unstructured data is represented by textual content (for example, Twitter feeds), video (for example, surveillance camera feeds), audio (for example, acoustic vibration from operating machines), and so on.

Data Acquisition and Access

The Data Acquisition and Access layer focuses on supporting various techniques to acquire and ingest the data from the gamut of Data Types (the layer below) and make the data ready and available for provisioning and storage. The architecture components in this layer must support the abilities to acquire transactional (structured) data, content (semistructured) data, and highly unstructured data, while being able to accommodate various data ingest rates—from well-defined periodic data feeds to intermittent or frequent data feed updates to real-time streaming data.

Data Repository

The Data Repository layer, as its name suggests, focuses on provisioning the data. The purpose of this architecture layer is to focus on supporting the capabilities required to capture the ingested data from the Data Acquisition and Access layer and to store it based on the appropriate types of data. The layer should also provide storage optimization techniques to reduce the total cost of ownership of IT investments on technologies required to support the expected capabilities.

Models

The Models layer focuses on abstracting physical data and its storage into a technology-agnostic representation of information. The capabilities of this layer can also be viewed as consolidating and standardizing on the metadata definitions for an industry or an enterprise; the business and technical metadata collectively satisfies the metadata definition.

Some organizations may adopt a well-known industry standards model (for example, ACORD in insurance (ACORD n.d.), HITSP in health care (Healthcare Information Technology Standards Panel [HITSP] n.d.) and try to organize their own enterprise data around such standards. Some other organizations may develop their own versions, whereas some others prefer meeting in the middle: starting with a relevant industry standard and extending it to fit their own enterprise data and information needs and guidelines. Regardless of the approach an enterprise adopts, a metadata definition of both the business and technical terms is essential; it shields the interfaces used to access the data from the underlying implementation of how data is persisted in the Data Repository layer.

The architectural building blocks in this layer aim to formulate a metadata schema definition that may be used to define the data and their relationships (semantics or otherwise) on entities provisioned in the Data Repository layer.

Data Integration and Consolidation

The Data Integration and Consolidation layer focuses on providing an integrated and consolidated view of data to the consuming applications. Components in this layer may serve as a gatekeeper and a single point of access to the data that is provisioned in the various components within the Data Repository layer. The components in this layer may leverage the metadata definitions enforced in the Models layer in an effort to standardize on a prescribed mechanism to access and interpret the enterprise data, allowing applications and users to formulate business-aligned information retrieval queries.

Consolidated data requires various integration techniques to either physically collate data from multiple, often disparate, data sources or to provide a set of virtual queryable view interfaces to the physically federated (in multiple systems) data. Physical data consolidation activities and techniques often manifest themselves as data warehouses or domain-specific data marts.

Data virtualization techniques aim at providing virtual queryable view interfaces to data sets that are physically distributed in multiple data sources and repositories.

Analytical Solutions

The Analytical Solutions layer focuses on classes of solutions that are powered by analytics at its core. Solution classes are typically industry specific (for example, retail, health care, oil and gas, mining, and so on); even within an industry, there are differences between the solution's manifestations in different organizations. As an example, if a Question Answering Advisor is a type of solution, it could be implemented as a Drilling Advisor supporting deep sea oil drilling as well as a Maintenance Advisor supporting optimized maintenance of costly equipment.

The solutions at this layer leverage one or more capabilities from the various dimensions of analytics and integrate them to support a specific genre of analytics solutions.

Consumers

The Consumers layer focuses on providing a set of user interface facades that may be leveraged to interact with and consume the features and functions of the analytical solutions.

The components in this layer ensure that existing enterprise applications can leverage the analytical solutions; there also exist user interface widgets (either standalone or integrated) that expose the analytics outcomes and allow users to interact with the solutions.

In the spirit of fostering collaboration and knowledge sharing, components in this layer have a collective responsibility to extend the value reach of analytics into the broader enterprise IT landscape.

The Vertical Layers

The three cross-cutting (that is, vertical) layers are as follows:

- **Governance**—This is a discipline in its own right. Rather than illustrating governance as a foundational discipline, I focus on the three subdisciplines of governance—namely, data governance, information governance, and analytic governance.
- **Metadata**—This defines and describes the data used to describe data.
- **Data and Information Security**—This layer addresses the security underpinnings of how data needs to be stored, used, archived, and so on.

Note: Figure 11.1 does not depict Governance as a cross-cutting layer; rather it shows the three subdisciplines.

Data Governance

Data Governance focuses on managing data as an enterprise asset. It defines and enforces processes, procedures, roles, and responsibilities to keep enterprise data free from errors and corruption by leveraging practical disciplines. The purpose is to address business, technical, and organizational obstacles to ensuring and maintaining data quality.

Some of the areas that may be addressed under data governance include

- **Data Quality**—Measuring the quality, classification, and value of the enterprise data.

- **Data Architecture**—Modeling, provisioning, managing, and leveraging data consistently through the enterprise, ideally as a service.

- **Risk Management**—Building trusted relationships between various stakeholders involved in the creation, management, and accountability of sensitive information.

- **Information Lifecycle Management (ILM)**—Actively and systematically managing enterprise data assets throughout their lifetime to optimize availability of an organization's data assets; support access to information in a timely manner; and ensure that the information is appropriately retained, archived, or shredded.

- **Audit and Reporting**—Ensuring proper routing and timely audit checks are exercised and appropriate reports communicated to those who either need to take action or be informed about any data stewardship issues.

- **Organizational Awareness**—Fostering a collaborative approach to data stewardship and governance across the enterprise, paying particular attention to the most critical areas of the business.

- **Stewardship**—Implementing accountability for an organization's information assets.

- **Security and Privacy Compliance**—Ensuring the organization has implemented commensurate controls (for example, policies, processes, and technology) to provide adequate assurance to various stakeholders that the organization's data is properly protected against misuse (accidental or malicious).

- **Value Creation**—Using formulated metrics to quantify how an organization realizes returns on investment in its use and potential monetization of enterprise data.

Integration Governance

Integration Governance focuses on defining the process, methods, tools, and best practices around consolidating data from federated data sources to form an integrated and intuitive view of the enterprise business entities. The discipline also drives the adoption and usage of metadata that provides a technology-agnostic definition and vocabulary of business entities and their relationships, which may be leveraged to exchange information across applications and systems in a consistent (and ideally standardized) manner.

The areas covered by Integration Governance may include

- Developing best practices around integration architecture and patterns to consolidate data from multiple data sources

- Developing a standards-based canonical metadata and message model

- Exposing integration services for consumption and governing their use by other layers of the architecture

Analytic Governance

Analytic Governance focuses on managing, monitoring, developing, and deploying the right set of analytic artifacts across the five disciplines of Descriptive Analytics, Predictive Analytics, Prescriptive Analytics, Operational Analytics, and Cognitive Computing. The discipline defines the process and policies that should be formulated and executed to manage the life cycle of artifacts created from the various analytics pillars.

This relatively new construct exists in acknowledgment of the fact that analytics is a separate discipline requiring its own life-cycle management. This layer is evolving and therefore will only mature over time.

The focus of Analytic Governance may include

- Developing the best practices, guidelines, and recommendations that may be leveraged to maximize the value generated through analytics
- Developing processes, tools, and metrics to measure the use of and the value harnessed from analytics in an enterprise
- Developing processes around managing, maintaining, and monitoring the analytics artifacts across their life cycle
- Developing analytics patterns that may drive the use of a multitude of capabilities from and across the different analytics pillars to build analytic solutions
- Developing processes, methods, and tools on how analytic functions and capabilities may be exposed *As-a-Service* for use and consumption

Metadata

The Metadata layer focuses on establishing and formalizing a standardized definition of both business terms and technical entities for an enterprise. The architectural building blocks and their associated components in this layer encourage building a metadata schema definition that may be used to organize the data and their relationships (semantics or otherwise) on entities provisioned in the Data Repository layer. Such metadata definitions form the basis of the information models in the Models layer.

Data and Information Security

The Data and Information Security layer focuses on any additional data security and privacy requirements that assume importance in the context of analytics. Data, as it gets prepared and curated for analytics, needs to be cleansed of any personal information and anonymized, masked, and deduplicated such that identity is masked and privacy not compromised. During the data preparation tasks, the components in this layer enforce just that.

The Pillars

ARA/ARM/ARB is composed of five pillars, each of which focuses on each of the dimensions of analytics. The five pillars are Descriptive Analytics, Predictive Analytics, Prescriptive Analytics, Operational Analytics, and Cognitive Computing. The combined capability supported by the five pillars aims at providing a reasonably well-addressed platform for providing holistic coverage of analytics capabilities for any enterprise.

The following sections provide high-level definitions of each pillar and the collective functionality each one of them is expected to provide in the overall ARB.

Descriptive Analytics

Descriptive Analytics, also known as after-the-fact analytics, focuses on providing intuitive ways to analyze business events that have already taken place—that is, a metric-driven analytical view of facts that have occurred in the past. It uses historical data to produce reports, charts, dashboards, and other forms of views that render insights into business performance against the strategic goals and objectives. For example, a mining company's business goal may be to maintain or increase the amount of coal produced per unit time. *Tonnage Per Hour* is a key performance metric or measure for such an enterprise. A business goal for an electronics manufacturing company may be to reduce the rate of scraps generated during the manufacturing and assembly of electronics circuit boards. *Cost of Product Quality* could be a key performance metric for such an enterprise.

Some of the key characteristics or capabilities expected from the components in this pillar may include

- Leveraging predefined performance measures and metrics around strategic goals and objectives and using them to leverage the design of the reports and dashboards.

- Supporting different views of the analytical data for different personas (that is, user roles) and user communities. Examples include executive dashboards displaying only a few top-level metrics and a field supervisor's view of performance data for each equipment product line (such as for a truck, loader, or bulldozer). Also, they may provide drill-down (into reports) capabilities to perform root-cause analysis across one or more dimensions of the analytical data.

- Providing metadata definitions to support both precanned and ad hoc reports on data, which is consistent and quality controlled.

- Supporting the optimized retrieval of data from multiple database and data warehouse systems in ways such that the heterogeneity (of the data systems) is abstracted from the reporting widgets.

Predictive Analytics

Predictive Analytics focuses primarily on developing statistical and probabilistic models to predict the occurrence of business critical events; it also qualifies the models with a confidence level quantifying the probability of its occurrence.

As mentioned earlier in the chapter, the modeling techniques are categorized broadly into two categories: supervised and unsupervised learning. Supervised learning uses historical data, which contains instances of the past occurrences of a particular business critical event, to build predictive models that can predict the future occurrences of the same (or similar) business-critical event. Unsupervised learning does not have the luxury of any known business-critical events in the past; it finds patterns in a given data set that it uses to group (or cluster) the data without having prior knowledge of the groups. Components and techniques in this layer support the two broad classifications of modeling techniques.

Continuously analyzing and looking for new trends and patterns necessitates access to data for intensive computations on a variety of data sources. As such, a dedicated analytical development sandbox with dedicated computational workload influences some of the capabilities and components required to be supported in this layer.

The primary user of the capabilities in this layer is the data scientist community (the ones who are in the highest demand in this millennia!). These users leverage sophisticated statistical, stochastic, and probabilistic techniques and algorithms to build and train models that can predict the future with a high enough level of confidence scoring.

Once some trend or pattern can be detected and proven to be able to predict a business event that drives value, its underlying analytical models may influence the metric-driven objectives and goals that are used in the Descriptive Analytics pillar. Hence, new reports (in the Descriptive Analytics pillar) often become relevant and important based on the outcome from the continuous analysis performed in this pillar.

Some of the key characteristics or capabilities expected from the components in this pillar may include

- Empowering and enabling data scientists with commensurate tools and infrastructure to perform exploratory and intensive data crunching and computing tasks
- Using a broad range of statistical techniques
- Supporting an integrated development environment (IDE) to automate model-building and deployment tasks

Prescriptive Analytics

Prescriptive Analytics focuses on optimizing the results of multiple, possibly disparate, analytical outcomes coupled with external conditions and factors. The main components in this pillar are the ones that provide various tools and techniques for developing mathematical optimization models and for correlating (typically business rules based) multiple events to generate prescribed outcomes that are both optimized and actionable.

An example of a mathematical optimization technique may be a linear programming model that provides an optimized price point for a spot price of any raw goods such as copper or gold. An example of a rules-based optimization may be to identify the most opportunistic time to decommission any costly production equipment for maintenance (based on a combination of a prediction of the equipment's failure and its upcoming nearest window of time for planned maintenance).

Some of the key characteristics or capabilities expected from the components in this pillar may include

- Optimization engines with complex mathematical models and techniques for constraint-based optimization of a target outcome
- A business rules engine that is capable of correlating multiple discrete events that may occur at different locations (that is, in different coordinates in space) and at different times, and navigating decision trees to arrive at one of many possible recommendations

Operational Analytics

Operational Analytics, or real-time analytics, focuses on generating analytical insights from data in motion. It employs techniques to bring the analytical functions to the data. In traditional techniques, the data is at rest, and processing functions such as SQL or SQL-like queries are applied to the data that is already persisted. In Operational Analytics, the analytical functions and algorithms are applied at various times, knowing fully well that the data set on which the processing operates may be radically different between two points in time. As an example, if a sentiment analysis algorithm is being put to test (during the cricket world cup finals) across a streaming data set from Facebook and Twitter, it is quite possible that, in a particular time window, the analytical algorithm works on a data set that has no Facebook data and contains only Twitter data, while in another time window, the same analytical algorithm has to work on a data set that has an equal volume from Twitter and Facebook feeds.

Some of the key characteristics or capabilities expected from the components in this pillar may include

- Support for ingesting data at very high frequencies and generating insight from the streaming data (that is, on data in motion) before it is stored
- Ability to operate on newly generated data in operational data warehouses; this can apply complex event-processing techniques to correlate events from multiple systems and trigger alerts
- Ability to invoke the predictive analytical models in real time; that is, on streaming data
- Support for both structured as well as unstructured data with an emphasis on generating insight from continuous streaming semistructured and unstructured data

Cognitive Computing

Cognitive Computing represents a relatively new field in the computing era, one in which computing systems are not just a slave of humans (that is, they process based on how humans program them) anymore but can build their own knowledge and "learn"; they can understand natural language and can engage and interact with humans more naturally and intuitively. Such systems are expected to provide insights and responses that are backed by confidence-weighted supporting evidence (supporting the responses). As an example, a healthcare advisor may be a cognitive system that can advise doctors on the possible diagnosis of patients and suggest appropriate medical care. Of course, the doctor would have the discretion to accept or reject the advice.

Some of the key characteristics or capabilities expected from the components in this pillar may include

- Ability to provide expert assistance to humans in a timely and effective manner
- Ability to make decisions (and augment the human cognition) based on supporting evidence that keeps growing as the body of relevant information in the world continues to grow
- Ability to exploit the vast body of available information by deriving contextual relationships between entities and continuously generate new insights

I hope this description of the layers and pillars provides a base foundation for you to develop an analytics architecture blueprint. The architecture building blocks that further elaborate the capabilities of each layer may provide the next level of detail.

Architecture Building Blocks

This part of the chapter briefly touches on some of the main architecture building blocks that enable the realization of the capabilities in each of the layers and pillars of the ARA.

I do not claim to be exhaustive and complete in identifying every single hitherto conceived building block, for two main reasons. First, the discipline of analytics has still not fully matured; therefore, the list of such architecture components will only change, mature, or be enhanced over time. Second, in the spirit of flexibility, it is important not to pigeonhole architects into a set of basic architecture building blocks; we need room to innovate—combine the pieces, nix some, and introduce some more—all in the context of addressing the problem at hand and the solutions we seek!

So, the intent of the following sections is to get you thinking and may just get you started. I first address the ABBs in the horizontal and vertical (that is, cross-cutting) layers before addressing the same for the five analytics pillars.

Figure 11.2 provides an illustrative depiction of how an ARB might look. Yes, it may morph—changing its shape, size, content, form, and other dimensions. But we always look for a good starting point, don't we?

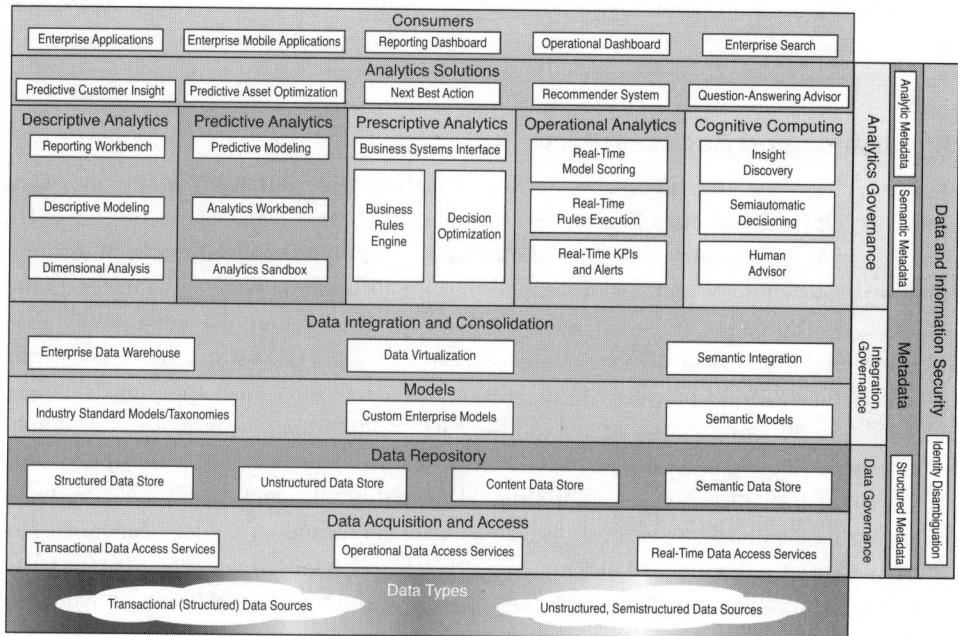

Figure 11.2 Illustrative architecture building blocks of an analytics architecture blueprint.

The following sections focus on highlighting the architecture building blocks (ABBs) in each layer. The descriptions, by intent, are kept short, some shorter than others. Therefore, you must research deeper into the capabilities on your own.

Data Types ABBs

I do not illustrate any specific architecture building blocks in the Data Types layer. However, it is important to recognize that this layer must be able to inform the other layers about the different variety of data types that may be required to be ingested into and supported by the system.

Structured data is typically well formed, which means it is amenable to following a well-defined and designed data schema. Data that is grouped into semantic chunks has the same attributes, follows the same order, and can be consistently defined. Examples are transactional data from trade executions, point-of-sales transactions of consumer retail products, and so on; they can be provisioned in relational databases, data warehouses, or data marts.

Semi-structured data can typically be organized into semantic entities such that similar entities (which may or may not have the same attributes) can be grouped together and can be formulated through semantic relationships between entities. Examples are data captured from web clickstreams and data collected from web forms and so on.

Unstructured data does not have any predefined format; can be of any type, shape, and form; and is not amenable to any structure, rules, or sequence. Examples include free-formed text and some types of audio.

Data Acquisition and Access ABBs

The Data Acquisition and Access layer is shown to support three ABBs: *Transactional Data Access Services*, *Operational Data Access Services*, and *Real-Time Data Access Services*. The services in this layer facilitate the ingestion of data of different types and generated at different rates. Appropriate technology components supporting the different services also reside in this layer.

Transactional Data Access Services focuses on Extract, Transform, Load (ETL) techniques used to acquire the data primarily from transactional data sources and applying data transformations and formatting necessary to convert the data into the standard format as dictated by the schema designs of the database systems where the data is expected to be provisioned. As a part of the data transformation process, appropriate data quality rules and checks are expected to be applied to ensure that the data conforms to the metadata definitions of the data standards. This ABB primarily transfers data in a batch mode, from the transactional source systems to the target data repository. The frequency of the batches may range from hourly to once or multiple times in a day.

Operational Data Access Services focuses on acquiring data from sources where the frequency of data generation is in real time (more or less) and hence is much higher in frequency than the data sources from where data is acquired by the Transactional Data Access Services ABB. It is important to note that the data source could still be transactional systems; however, the rate of data generation is far more than what may be supported by traditional batch-oriented systems. Various services are leveraged to acquire the data. A technique known as Change Data Capture (CDC) may be leveraged to move the data from the source to the data storage in a way that minimizes the additional workload on the transactional data source. In situations in which the traditional execution time intervals for batch data transfers may not be adequate, techniques like CDC may assist in mitigating risks of failure in long-running ETL jobs. Micro Batch is another technique that may be leveraged; it facilitates supporting a much shorter batch window of data acquisition. The difference between CDC and Micro Batch is in the specific techniques used to ingest the data. A third technique may be Data Queuing and Push, which uses a different process to acquire operational data, relying on asynchronous modes of sending the data from the data sources to the appropriate data storage. Asynchronous data push, similar to CDC, adds minimal workload on the transactional source systems.

Real-Time Data Access Services focuses on acquiring data from source systems that generate data at rates that are not possible to commensurately support the ingestion by even the Operational Data Access Service ABB; this resides in the realm of near real-time to real-time data feeds, and the types of data typically range between semistructured to unstructured. There is a limit to which the window for batch data acquisition (supported by the other two services in this layer) can be reduced. Beyond this, different capabilities are needed to support the high to ultra-high data volumes and frequencies. This service may employ techniques such as Data Feed Querying or socket- or queue-based continuous data feeds to ingest data in near real time to real time. When the data is acquired, it may be normalized into a set of <key, value> pairs among other formats (for example, JSON), which flattens the data into its basic constituents that encapsulate the information.

Data Repository ABBs

The Data Repository layer is shown to support four ABBs: *Structured Data Store, Unstructured Data Store, Content Data Store,* and *Semantic Data Store.* Each of the ABBs addresses specific capabilities.

Structured Data Store focuses on storage for data sets that are inherently structured in nature; that is, it follows a well-defined data schema that is often called *schema on write,* which implies that the data schema is defined and designed before data is written to the persistent store. As such, the storage components are primarily relational in nature, supporting various data normalization techniques.

Unstructured Data Store focuses on storing primarily unstructured data sets. Examples of such data sets may include machine-generated data, from trading floor transactions (for example, from telephone conversations between customer and trader for trade transactions), and from social networking sites and the Internet in general (for example, customer sentiments on product, stock prices, world affairs affecting oil prices, weather patterns). The data stores are typically schema-less, which implies that data of any structure and form may be provisioned (also referred to as "dumped" in colloquial IT lingo). It is often called *schema on read*, which implies that the structure and semantics may be defined during retrieval of data from such data stores.

Content Data Store focuses mainly on storing enterprise content. Enterprise documents (for example, technical specifications, policies, and regulation laws) typically fall under this category. A separate class of technology called Content Management Systems (CMS) is purpose built to store, retrieve, archive, and search massive amounts of heterogeneous enterprise content.

Semantic Data Store focuses primarily on storing semistructured data sets that may have undergone semantic preprocessing. Triple Store is a technology that may be used to store semantic-aware data sets; it stores data in the form of a triplet (that is, a triplet tuple). Each tuple consists of a <subject, object, predicate> construct. A Search Index Repository technique, as its name suggests, may be used to store the indexes that are created after applying semantic processing to all searchable content.

Models ABBs

The Models layer may have three ABBs: the *Industry Standard Models*, *Custom Enterprise Models*, and *Semantic Models*.

Industry Standard Models represent an industry standard data, information, or process model that is agreed upon, at the industry level, to be a standard and is typically maintained by some standards body or consortium. ACORD in insurance and HITSP in patient care are examples of such standards. Organizations that either want to or are required to (by regulation laws) adopt an industry standard for information exchange adopt the standard models (either in whole or in part) to implement data exchange between their IT Systems.

Custom Enterprise Models represent information or data models that are typically developed indigenously within an organization. Such models may either be a derivative, extension, or customization of an industry model or a completely home-grown model. The intent of the model is the same as that of an industry standard model—that is, to work as a facade between the physical representation of the data and the means by which it is exchanged and consumed by systems and applications.

Semantic Models focus on developing ontology models representing specific business domains or subsets thereof. The word *ontology* is typically used to denote at least three distinctly different kinds of resources that have distinctly different kinds of uses, not all of which lie within the realm of natural language processing (NLP) and text processing. Such models are used to develop an interface to navigate and retrieve data from semantic stores, for consumption and use by components in other layers in the ARB. (Refer to the "Semantic Model" sidebar in Chapter 9, "Integration: Approaches and Patterns.")

ONTOLOGY

Ontology is a capture of knowledge (terms and concepts) within a particular domain. Typically, it takes the form of taxonomies or taxonomy, dictionaries, entity relationships around elements, and concepts within a domain. An ontology is typically defined as a taxonomy with rules.

A large percentage of ontologies are really controlled vocabularies, organized as taxonomies or a thesaurus. These are not really "ontologies" in any sense of the word, because they contain none or very little relational information between concepts (also called entries or entities). They are useful for establishing standard use of vocabularies and other pieces of information, and organizing, sorting, and modifying databases. These ontologies can grow into millions of pieces of data, because they have no mechanism for cross-categorizing and specifying within each datum. This is in contrast to true ontologies that contain conceptual information, meaning that each individual entry is no longer a single datum, rather a compilation of data about an entity. Ontologies of this sort are not only able to relate entities to each other in a variety of ways but also to make cross-comparisons of the properties of the entities. Because entries for entities are more complex or, in current measures, are not just one triple, but several triples of information, they are likely to contain far fewer entries, probably in the order of tens of thousands.

The collective capabilities of the representative ABBs in this layer are intended to facilitate a technology-agnostic and highly resilient integration approach as it pertains to efficient data and information exchange.

Data Integration and Consolidation ABBs

The Data Integration and Consolidation layer may be supported by three ABBs: *Enterprise Data Warehouse*, *Data Virtualization*, and *Semantic Integration*. These ABBs foster consolidated and virtualized access to heterogeneous data and are ideally expected to leverage the components and artifacts in the Models layer (refer to Figure 11.2) to standardize on a contextual representation (of the consolidated data) and access (through virtualization) to the data.

Enterprise Data Warehouse focuses on developing and providing a consolidated representation of the most critical enterprise information and knowledge—for example, performance metrics, business financials, operational metrics, and so on; this information is critical for enterprise reporting and insights into business operations and performance and is often considered to be a trusted source of enterprise information. Data marts, data warehouses, and their operational data warehouse variation typically fall under this category. Operational data warehouses support data feeds at a frequency that is much higher than the data currency maintained in a traditional data warehouse without compromising on the data read performances. Data marts represent a subset of the data that is stored in a data warehouse. Each subset typically focuses on a specific business domain—for example, customer, product, sales, inventory, and so on. Data marts can also represent subdomains within each business domain in scenarios where the business domain is complex and requires further classification. Examples of such subdomains may be product pricing and product inventory.

Data Virtualization focuses on providing virtualized access to multiple federated data repositories in ways such that the technology complexities of federated and distributed queries are encapsulated in this building block (thereby shielding the complexities from the consuming applications and systems). One of the key functionalities that may be expected would be to package and prefabricate frequently occurring correlated queries and expose the collection as a single-query (that is, retrievable) interface to the consuming and requesting applications. A typical technology implementation could be to take a user-defined or an application-specific query request and abstract the routing of query subsets to potentially different data sources and subsequently combine or consolidate the individual query subset results into a single integrated result set to return to the consuming applications.

Semantic Integration focuses on providing a set of interfaces that facilitate semantic query building and executing. SPARQL (which stands for SPARQL Protocol And RDF Query Language; see W3C 2008) is an example of a semantic query language for databases in which the data is typically stored in the form of a triple store (for example, in a Semantic Data Store).

It is important to highlight that the integration facilitated through the Semantic Integration and Data Virtualization ABBs is runtime in nature, whereas Enterprise Data Warehouse is typically a physical integration or consolidation construct.

While not mandatory for the layers and pillars above (that is, the Descriptive Analytics, Predictive Analytics, and so on) to leverage the functionality exposed by the ABBs in this layer, best practices often advocate exercising due diligence to leverage the capabilities of this layer as a mechanism to virtualize information access.

Analytics Solutions ABBs

The Analytics Solutions layer hosts prefabricated end-to-end solutions that focus on solving a specific class of business problem. It is impractical to point out specific building blocks at this layer because the components at this layer are not really ABBs but more of packaged solutions. I kept the *ABBs* in the heading to maintain consistency and not confuse you by introducing YAT (Yet Another Term)!

In the spirit of consistency, or at least the look and feel of the ABB view of the ARB, I depicted some representative solutions:

Predictive Customer Insight (IBM 2015) focuses on extending the benefits of an organization's marketing and customer service systems. It does so by leveraging a combination of advanced analytics techniques to deliver the most important customer-related KPIs by leveraging data around buyer sentiments and delivering personalized customer experience.

Predictive Asset Optimization (IBM n.d.) focuses on leveraging a combination of various advanced analytic techniques to improve the Overall Equipment Effectiveness (OEE) of critical enterprise assets (for example, heavy equipment, factory assembly-line machines, rotatory and nonrotating equipment in an oil and gas platform, aircraft engines, among many more). It does so by predicting the health of costly and critical assets relative to potential failures, much ahead of time, such that proper actions may be taken to reduce costly unplanned downtimes of the most important and critical assets.

Next Best Action (IBM 2012–2013) focuses on developing and providing optimized decisions and recommending actions that may be taken to minimize the potential adverse impact of a business-critical event that may be forthcoming. Optimized decision making can be applied to various types of enterprise assets: customers with regard to increasing loyalty, products with regard to reduced cost of production, employees with regard to reducing attrition rates, and so on.

Recommender Systems (Jones 2013) focuses on generating contextual recommendations to a user or a group of users on items or products that may be of interest to them, either individually or collectively. It leverages multiple machine-learning techniques such as collaborative filtering (CF), content-based filtering (CBF), hybrid approaches combining variations of CF and CBF, Pearson correlations, clustering algorithms, among other techniques, to arrive at an ordered (by relevance) set of recommendations. Netflix and Amazon employ such recommender systems, or variations thereof, to link customer preferences and buying or renting habits with recommendations and choices.

Question Answering Advisor focuses on leveraging advanced natural language processing (NLP); Information Retrieval, Knowledge Representation & Reasoning; and machine-learning techniques and applying them to the field of open-domain question answering. An application of open-domain question answering is IBM's DeepQA (IBM n.d.), which uses hypothesis-generation techniques to come up with a series of hypotheses to answer a specific question, and uses a massive amount of relevant data to gather evidence in support of or refuting the hypotheses, followed by scoring algorithms to ultimately arrive at the best possible answer. IBM's Watson is a classic example of such a solution.

Consumers ABBs

The Consumers layer is represented by five ABBs: *Enterprise Applications*, *Enterprise Mobile Applications*, *Reporting Dashboard*, *Operational Dashboard*, and *Enterprise Search*. The focus on the ABBs in this layer is to provide different channels to expose analytics capabilities and solutions for enterprise consumption. The ABBs are strictly representative in nature, implying that other components may be supported in this layer.

Enterprise Applications represent the classes of applications in an enterprise that are used either by one or more lines of business or by the entire organization. Such applications may require interfacing with the analytics capabilities or solutions to extend the value of their legacy enterprise applications. As an example, a SAP Plant Maintenance (SAP PM) system may receive a recommendation to create a maintenance work order from a decision optimization analytic solution.

Enterprise Mobile Applications represent a relatively new and upcoming class of enterprise applications that are primarily built for the mobile platform. Such applications benefit from receiving notifications for actions from analytic solutions. In other cases, an analytic application may be fully mobile enabled—that is, built as a native mobile application on the iOS or the Android platform. One such example is an application for airline pilots to help them decide on the optimized refueling for the aircraft, running natively on an iOS platform (think iPads) and powered by analytics.

Reporting Dashboard provides a platform to build, configure, customize, deploy, and consume reports and dashboards that not only are visual manifestations of data in data marts, cubes, or warehouses but also serve as various means to slice and dice the information and represent it in multiple intuitive ways for analysis.

Operational Dashboard provides a visual canvas and platform to render data and information that is being generated and obtained in real time—that is, at a rate which is faster than it is possible to persist and analyze before being rendered. An example may be collecting data from a temperature and pressure sensor on a valve in an oil platform and visualizing the data as a real-time trend immediately upon its availability.

Enterprise Search represents a class of consumer applications that focus on providing different levels of analytical search capabilities to retrieve the most contextual and appropriate results from the body of enterprise content. It can also act as a front end to analytic solutions such as the Question Answering Advisor (refer to Figure 11.2).

Metadata ABBs

The Metadata layer is represented by three ABBs: *Analytic Metadata*, *Semantic Metadata*, and *Structured Metadata*. The ABBs in this layer work in close conjunction with the ABBs in the Models layer in an effort to develop a standardized abstraction to information management and representation.

Analytic Metadata focuses on defining, persisting, and maintaining the gamut of metadata required to support the various facets of analytics in an enterprise. The most common analytic metadata is for capturing the data definitions required for all the precanned reports that are typically executed either periodically or upon user requests. Reporting requires its own metadata definitions, which determine how the data elements on the reports are constructed and are related to each other and to the data sources from where the content needs to be retrieved to populate the reports. Additionally, the navigation design for multiple visual pages and widgets is also considered analytic metadata. Similarly, data model representations required to train and execute predictive models are also part of the analytic metadata. The definition of business rules, along with its input parameter set, is also considered analytic metadata. The scope of analytic metadata is determined by the variety of analytics supported in an enterprise.

Semantic Metadata focuses on the foundational components required to build a semantic information model for the entire information set or its subset thereof. Language models based on a dictionary of terms, a thesaurus, grammar and rules around semantic relationships between entities and terms, may define ontologies that form the underpinning of semantic metadata.

Structured Metadata focuses on defining the metadata definitions for business entities along with their constraints and rules that influence how the Structured Data Store ABB (in the Data Repository layer) may define its schema definitions. It needs to address different types of metadata, for example, Business Metadata, Technical Metadata, and Metadata Rules. The Business Metadata may encapsulate the business entity concepts and their relationships; the Technical Metadata may be used to formulate the constraints on the attributes that define the business entities; the Metadata Rules may define rules and constraints governing the interrelationships between entities and their ultimate realization as physical schema definitions for the Structured Data Store ABB.

Data and Information Security ABBs

The Data and Information Security layer is represented by only one ABB: *Identity Disambiguation*. This is admittedly sparse; the field of information security is starting to get the attention it deserves in the light of data being increasingly considered as an enterprise asset. This will continue to grow and mature over time. As an example, with Internet of Things (IoT) becoming increasingly pervasive, connectivity and interaction with the device instrumentations (which run critical operations, such as oil production, refinery operations, steel productions, and so on) require more secure networks and strict access mechanisms, to interact with the device instrumentations.

Identity Disambiguation focuses on ensuring that the proper masking and filtering algorithms are applied to disambiguate the identity of assets (especially humans) whose data and profile information may be leveraged in analytical decision making.

We've concluded our treatment of the representative ABBs in the various layers of the ARA. With the layers given some attention to identify a set of representative ABBs, now let's apportion equal attention to the analytics pillars. They too deserve some further discussion.

Descriptive Analytics ABBs

The Descriptive Analytics pillar is represented by three ABBs: *Reporting Workbench, Dimensional Analysis,* and *Descriptive Modeling.*

Reporting Workbench provides and supports a comprehensive set of tools to define and design analytical reports that support a set of predefined business metrics, objectives, and goals. It should additionally support the ability and tooling to test and deploy the reports and widgets onto a deployment runtime. Some nonfunctional features worthy of consideration may include (but are not limited to)

- Ease of use to configure and define the reports and widgets by business users
- The richness, fidelity, and advanced visual features to support attractive, intuitive, and information-rich visualizations
- Customizability capabilities to connect to different data sources and graphical layouts

Dimensional Analysis provides the capability to slice and dice the data across various dimensions to develop a domain-specific view of data and its subsequent analysis. This ABB also supports tools and techniques for developing data marts and data cubes to represent data for specific domains and targeted analytical reports on historical data.

Descriptive Modeling develops data models that specifically cater to the generation of business reports that can describe, in multiple ways, how users may like to analyze (and hence display) the information. Such models are built on top of the data models in data warehouses and data marts, focusing on generating flexible reports.

Predictive Analytics ABBs

The Predictive Analytics pillar is represented by three ABBs: *Predictive Modeling, Analytics Workbench,* and *Analytics Sandbox.*

Predictive Modeling focuses on employing data analytics along with statistical and probabilistic techniques to build predictive models, which can predict a future event supported by a degree of confidence of the event's occurrence. It leverages two broad classes of techniques: *supervised* and *unsupervised* learning. As illustrated earlier in the chapter, in supervised learning, the target outcome (or variable), which is to be predicted, is known ahead of time (for example, failure of an aircraft engine). Statistical, algorithmic, and mathematical techniques are used to mine and analyze historical data to identify trends, patterns, anomalies, and outliers and quantify them into one or more analytical models containing a set of predictors that contribute to predicting the outcome. In unsupervised learning, neither the target is known ahead of time, nor are there any historical events available. Clustering techniques are used to segregate the data into a set of clusters, which help determine a natural grouping of features, and more importantly of behavior and pattern, in the data set.

Analytics Workbench provides an integrated set of tools to help the data analysts and data scientists perform the activities around data understanding, data preparation, model development and training, model testing, and model deployment.

Some of the capabilities provided by the workbench may be (but are not limited to)

- Mathematical modeling tools and techniques (for example, linear and nonlinear programming, stochastic techniques, probability axioms and models)
- Ability to connect to the analytics sandbox
- Coverage of the most common techniques (for example, SQL, SPARQL, and MapReduce) for introspecting data from multiple storage types (that is, data warehouses, semantic data stores, and structured data stores)
- Ability to perform text parsing
- Ability to build semantic ontology models

Analytics Sandbox provides the infrastructure platform required to perform all activities necessary to build, maintain, and enhance the Predictive Analytics assets. The sandbox needs to ensure that commensurate capacity (shared or dedicated) is available to compute and run complex, intensive algorithms and their associated number crunching against very large data sets. The sandbox is expected to provide data scientists with access to any and all data sources and data sets that may be interesting or required to perform a commensurate level of data analysis necessary to build predictive models.

Some considerations may be (but are not limited to)

- A dedicated sandbox environment where the necessary data and tools are made available for analysis
- A shared sandbox environment that is configurable, appropriately partitioned, and workload optimized

Prescriptive Analytics ABBs

The Prescriptive Analytics pillar is represented by three ABBs: *Business Systems Interface, Business Rules Engine*, and *Decision Optimization*.

Business Systems Interface addresses having the output of Prescriptive Analytics outcomes available to the various enterprise business systems of the organization. It exploits the capabilities of an Analytical Data Bus (a new term I just introduced!) to push the generated insights (from this layer) to the business systems.

Note that although the Analytical Data Bus is not represented explicitly in the reference architecture, its physical realization may be the standard Enterprise Service Bus (ESB), which is usually present in most IT integration middleware landscapes.

Business Rules Engine focuses on providing the necessary tooling and runtime environment to support building, authoring, and deploying business rules. The intent of this component could be to provide the flexibility for business users to author business rules by combining and correlating the outcomes from, for example, predictive models, external factors (such as environmental conditions and human skill sets), actions, and event trigger outputs. The purpose is to correlate them both in space (from multiple locations) and in time (occurring at different times) to come up with more prescriptive outcomes. It may serve as an enabler to the *Decision Optimization* building block.

Decision Optimization builds on top of capabilities realized from ABBs within the Prescriptive Analytics tower and from other analytics towers; it focuses on applying optimization techniques. Constrained and unconstrained optimization methods, linear programming, and nonlinear programming (such as quadratic programming) are some of the techniques used to formulate maximizations or minimizations of objective functions. Examples may be to maximize the profit margin of an energy and utilities company or to minimize the cost of servicing warrantied items for a retail company.

Operational Analytics ABBs

The Operational Analytics pillar may be represented by three ABBs: *Real-Time Model Scoring, Real-Time Rules Execution,* and *Real-Time KPIs and Alerts.*

Real-Time Model Scoring focuses on executing the predictive models in real time; that is, on the data in motion. It allows the predictive models to be invoked at the point where data is ingested into the system, thereby enabling real-time scores that allow the business to take actions in near real time. As an example, a predictive model can determine whether a semiconductor fabrication will have quality issues and hence result in scrap. Such a model can be invoked at the time the fabrication assembly line produces the data from the robotic equipment. This results in early detection of scrap and thus reduces the Cost of Product Quality (COPQ), which is a key business metric in the semiconductor manufacturing industry.

Real-Time Rules Execution focuses on executing the business rules in real time, that is, on the data in motion. It allows the business rules to be invoked at the point where data is ingested into the system, thereby enabling real-time execution of business rules. As an example, rules that can determine whether a credit card transaction is fraudulent can be invoked at the time when the transaction data is being captured.

Real-Time KPIs and Alerts focuses on computing key operational metrics defined as key performance indicators. The KPIs, which can range anywhere between simple formulations to complex state machine derivations, may be calculated on the data in motion. That is, they are calculated as and when the generated data is available in the system. Such KPIs can be annotated with thresholds and other measures that, when compromised, can result in the generation of alerts that can be notified to the relevant users in near real time. As an example, the deviation of the operating conditions of a mining machine (for example, equipment working underground to produce coal) can be formulated into a set of complex state machines and associated KPIs. These state machines and KPIs can be computed in real time. Alerts can be generated to inform the operators that the machine is not being used to its optimum capacity. Such real-time KPIs and alerts enable the operators to make necessary changes so that they can obtain maximum production in shift operations.

Cognitive Computing ABBs

The Cognitive Computing pillar may be represented by three ABBs: *Insight Discovery, Semi-Autonomic Decisioning*, and *Human Advisor*.

Insight Discovery focuses on continuously mining the combination of new and existing information corpora to discover new relationships between entities in preparation of supporting more enriched evidence when faced with complex real-world questions.

Semi-Autonomic Decisioning focuses on parsing real-world questions, breaking down the questions into smaller constituent questions, generating multiple hypotheses for each subquestion, gathering evidence in support or refutation of each hypothesis, and then leveraging confidence weightages (that is, statistical and mathematical techniques to derive the best outcome) to finally combine and generate the best possible response. The component, in its current state of maturity, still serves as an aid to the human decision-making system (hence, semi-autonomic) with the ultimate future goal to be the decision maker!

Human Advisor focuses on combining the capabilities of the insight discovery and the semi-autonomic decisioning components to function as an interactive guide (with a rich and intuitive graphical user interface) to humans, helping them through question-answering sessions to arrive at a well-informed and evidence-supported answer.

This completes our illustration of the ABBs of an ARB!

It may be worthwhile to note that the market, geared toward providing the components in the layers and pillars, is competitive by its very nature. The product vendors will continue to keep coming up with enhanced capabilities in support of a combination of features and functions. Do not be surprised if you come across vendor products supporting multiple features within or across layers or pillars in the ARB.

Summary

The analytics clock should keep ticking, generating moments of insight.

Analytics is at work. Most organizations that are serious about identifying innovative ways of lowering costs, increasing revenue, and differentiating themselves for competitive advantages are making analytics a mainstream business strategy.

This chapter identified five foundational subdisciplines within analytics that form the analytics continuum: Descriptive Analytics, Predictive Analytics, Prescriptive Analytics, Operational Analytics, and Cognitive Computing.

Descriptive Analytics answers the question *what already happened?* Predictive Analytics attempts to *foretell what may happen* in the future. Prescriptive Analytics attempts to prescribe *what we should do if something happens.* Operational Analytics brings the *application of analytics to where data is generated.* Finally, Cognitive Computing attempts to *aid the human as an advisor.*

One theory postulates that an organization's analytics maturity should follow this order—that is, start with Descriptive Analytics and then move into Predictive, Prescriptive, and then Cognitive. Another theory postulates that an organization can simultaneously mature itself in most if not all of the analytic disciplines. There is no one correct answer, and the choice depends on the business imperatives and strategy. Operational Analytics does not need to follow the sequence because it caters to real-time analytics on data in motion; not all organizations may require it, nor would it strictly depend on the other analytic disciplines as a prerequisite.

I framed an analytics reference architecture consisting of seven horizontal and three vertical, cross-cutting, layers along with five pillars (representing the analytics continuum). The architecture layers address how different *data types* require different *data ingestion techniques*; different *data storage capabilities* provision the data; leveraging a *model-based approach,* driven *by metadata definitions,* to *consolidate and virtualize* the data for consistent and standardized access; ensuring proper *governance around data, integration, and analytic* assets with appropriate *data and information security* measures. The pillars focus on the five analytic disciplines: *Descriptive -> Predictive -> Prescriptive -> Operational -> Cognitive.* Often a reference architecture is met with an unnecessary waste of energy in analyzing whether it is a reference architecture or not; in such situations, it is okay for us, as practical architects, to give it different, less-conflicting, titles such as analytics reference model, analytics architecture blueprint, and so on.

It is important to acknowledge that the reference architecture serves as a guideline to define a baseline from which you can innovate, improvise, and develop an analytics architecture that supports not only the business strategy and objectives but also acknowledge the IT capabilities of an organization. Furthermore, I illustrated all concepts in exhaustive detail; I meant to make you aware of their relevance and hence the imperative nature to exercise self-driven research in such topics (for example, ontologies, cognitive computing, industry standard information models).

For a practical software architect, having a firm understanding of analytics and its capabilities could be an important differentiation!

Like all good things, this book too needs to come to an end. I reflect back on the topics that I tried to cover and feel that I was able to address the areas in software architecture that I had in mind when I conceptualized this book. However, just as with anything close to our hearts that we do not want to leave or finish, I keep thinking about what else I could have shared with you. I made up my mind to dedicate one last chapter to sharing some of the experiences that I have picked up over my professional years. The next chapter, thus, is a collection of a few such experiences. Although they were gathered the hard way, they were rich in the lessons I learned from them.

References

ACORD. (n.d.) Retrieved from http://www.acord.org/. This insurance industry standards specification also consists of a data and information standard.

Davenport, T., & Harris, J. (2007). *Competing on analytics: The new science of winning.* (Boston: Harvard Business Review Press).

Davenport, T., Harris, J., & Morison, R. (2010) *Analytics at work: Smarter decisions, better results.* (Boston: Harvard Business Review Press).

Healthcare Information Technology Standards Panel (HITSP). (n.d.) Retrieved from http://www.hitsp.org. This site shares information across organizations and systems.

IBM. (2012–2013). Smarter analytics: Driving customer interactions with the IBM Next Action Solution. Retrieved from http://www.redbooks.ibm.com/redpapers/pdfs/redp4888.pdf.

IBM. (2015). The new frontier for personalized customer experience: IBM Predictive Customer Intelligence. Retrieved from http://www-01.ibm.com/common/ssi/cgi-bin/ssialias?subtype=WH&infotype=SA&appname=SWGE_YT_HY_USEN&htmlfid=YTW03379USEN&attachment=YTW03379USEN.PDF#loaded.

IBM. (n.d.) FAQs on DeepQA. Retrieved from https://www.research.ibm.com/deepqa/faq.shtml.

IBM. (n.d.) Predictive asset optimization. Retrieved from http://www-01.ibm.com/common/ssi/cgi-bin/ssialias?infotype=SA&subtype=WH&htmlfid=GBW03217USEN.

IBM Institute of Business Value. (n.d.) Analytics: The speed advantage. Retrieved from http://www-935.ibm.com/services/us/gbs/thoughtleadership/2014analytics/.

IBM Institute of Business Value. (n.d.) Your cognitive future. Retrieved from http://www-01.ibm.com/common/ssi/cgi-bin/ssialias?subtype=XB&infotype=PM&appname=CB_BU_B_CBUE_GB_TI_USEN&htmlfid=GBE03641USEN&attachment=GBE03641USEN.PDF#loaded.

Jones, T. (2013). Recommender systems. Retrieved from http://www.ibm.com/developerworks/library/os-recommender1/.

W3C. (2008, January 15). SPARQL specifications. Retrieved from http://www.w3.org/TR/rdf-sparql-query/.

CHAPTER 12

Sage Musings

In deep meditation ... can I reach me in a parallel universe?

In the din and bustle of life's frantic pace, we cannot seem to slow down, take a step back, and reflect over the experiences we learn and gather. Nor can we always make an effort to look for avenues to share our invaluable experiences with the broader community and foster a collaborative ecosystem of knowledge sharing. I share my part in these vices of not doing the same—at least not as much as I would have liked to. I wonder how much of a prisoner of events I have become and whether I can own and drive my own action plans.

This chapter, albeit a short one, is my effort to practice what I would like to preach. That is, my goal is to share some real-world experiences that I find helpful in grounding myself in times when I fail to see the bigger picture during the madness of project execution.

I humbly share some of my revelations with you and my architect colleagues, to whom I remain forever grateful. My learnings and experiences are not elaborate and extensive; rather, they highlight some bits and pieces of over-a-drink musings!

Agility Gotta Be an Amalgamate

We are now at a point where the industry is convinced that there is enough value in applying agile principles to software development for companies to consider the adoption of agility as an enterprise manifesto.

We tend to develop our own views of agility and how it may be incorporated and adopted into IT. No two individuals I have talked to have the same point of view! I have started to wonder whether it is about time for us to get to a simple and crisp viewpoint that a team can agree on and hence simplify putting agile disciplines into action.

Being agile is as much a cultural statement of intent and mindset as it is to have an underlying and supporting IT framework to support its instantiation.

The culture of agility, in my experience, can be boiled down to four fundamental statements of intent:

- Clarity over uncertainty
- Course correction over perfection
- Self-direction over command-and-control teams
- Talent density over process density

Clearly defined, well-documented, properly understood, and appropriately communicated project objectives are worthy of being pinned to the walls of IT project team members. Reading them out loud before the start of the day often helps in clearing noise from the head and focusing on working toward the stated objectives. I believe that every single team member has an equal right to stand up and question any deviation from the stated project intent. Setting clear, precise, and objective goals goes a long way. Look at what the Fitbit did for me: I get out of my seat and walk around every now and then just to reach my daily goal of 10,000 steps!

You cannot strive for perfection; expecting that every single project artifact will be on target in its first incarnation is unrealistic by the very nature of this thinking. Instead, an environment that fosters quick learning and prototyping and that does not penalize failure but rather encourages failing fast and correcting course promotes a dynamic, fast-paced, and self-driven project setting, one in which team members thrive and perform better.

A project environment in which team members believe and practice course correction over perfection automatically builds self-driven teams. As a result, team members are not only crystal clear in their understanding of the project objectives but also know how to prototype, learn, course correct if required, and bring innovation and dynamism in attaining their project goals. Such teams do not require much hand holding or commanding and controlling of their work activities; micromanaging them usually proves to be a deterrent.

Organizations these days are more geographically distributed than ever. We see projects, whose requirements are understood and documented in one country, and then their development is shipped to another country; some organizations even go to the extent of shipping testing phases to yet another country. Projects in which there is such a clear delineation between project team activities often end up building isolated teams and hence skillsets that become highly specialized. The project's resource and skill profiles become waterfall driven (that is, much like sequential and often specialized tasks in a project plan, skillsets too become specialized with team members entering and exiting project phases)! One aspect of infusing agility in IT projects is to cross-train individuals to pick up adjacent skills. Consider a scenario in which the same team members who gather the requirements also perform system testing. Such cross-training of skills not only helps the team members become multifaceted but also builds a knowledge continuum. I have seen teams that focus on talent density through team colocation and cross-training to be more successful in their project execution than their counterparts.

In my experience, while the culture, mindset, and execution modus operandi is necessary, appropriate measures should also be put in place to convert agile thinking into agile deliverables. One of my colleagues once pointed out that there is often a tendency to treat agility as being different from DevOps. Agility is used to deliver business value, not just IT projects. Commensurate tooling and infrastructure support, which fosters iterative and incremental software system development, is critical if you want to harness tangible outcomes from practicing agile adoption in IT projects. Management ought to invest in setting up a framework and not only let individual project teams leverage the framework's capabilities but also be empowered to customize it to further fit their development methodology. Some of the tooling infrastructure aspects may include

- **Environment Setup (Development, System Test, Production)**—These elements may be leveraged by similar projects on a shared platform; for example, Docker containers or virtual machines in the cloud.
- **Test Automation Engine**—This tool supports continuous testing of regularly developed code.
- **Automated Build Engine**—This tool supports and fosters continuous integration between new codebases with existing system features.
- **Automated Deployment Engine**—This tool supports continuous deployment and testing.

I submit that the infrastructure framework for agile development is an amalgamation of the mind (culture and mindset) as well as the means (rapid development, testing, and deployment tools) to realize its true benefits.

Traditional Requirements-Gathering Techniques Are Passé

For business analysts, the process of gathering requirements and formalizing them into painfully long documents has been trite for the past few decades. We generate reams of textual documents and package them up into use cases and functional specifications.

What has struck me in the past few years is that this traditional approach to gathering requirements is not as effective in the present-day setting wherein mobility and mobile applications have become the de facto standard for humans to interact with machines and systems. In a few experiments that I have personally undertaken, in a few software development initiatives, team members were encouraged to assume that technology has no bounds and it can do anything and everything. Team members were then asked to engage with the user community; that is, the people who would be the real users of the system. The engagement approach had simple objective outcomes:

- How do the users like to interact with the system?
- What information would they like to have available to them?
- In which ways should the information be rendered and viewed?

The focus changes from textual documentation to information visualization and user interactions through intuitive infographics. A premium is placed on the intuitiveness and innovativeness in visual rendering and on elements of human psychology as it pertains to how visual processing of information triggers synaptic transmission. Easing neurotransmission in the human brain is a natural way to increase human acceptance—in this case, the intuitive adaptation with the IT System and having user acceptance as a given before even constructing the system! (Yes, I know what you're thinking about nonfunctional requirements, or NFRs; let's keep that issue aside for a moment.)

Design thinking advocates such a philosophy. Apple, as an enterprise, practices such a philosophy; the world's acceptance and usage of its products is a standing testimonial!

Next time you come across an IT System that you have to architect, try considering the design-thinking approach.

The MVP Paradigm Is Worth Considering

If you are adopting agile development practices, shouldn't the product being built ship sooner? After all, you are being lean in your execution, using prioritized epics and user stories, and managing your backlogs efficiently. (Epic, user stories, and backlog are foundational concepts in agile methodology.)

In my experience, it is critical to think of a product or a project as having continuous releases. Traditional product release cycles have been six months to a year. Although the cycles need to be shortened (no one waits that long these days!), the principle is very much applicable. I have seen that a six-week release cycle is a nearly ideal target. However, there are some questions and challenges:

- What would we be releasing?
- What would the first release look like?
- Who would it cater to?

This is the point where the concept of an MVP, or what I call, in this context, the *Minimal Valuable Product*, comes in. The definition of MVP should take center stage. An MVP addresses the leanest product features that should be packaged and made available. The *leanest* aspect can be dictated or influenced by different factors, most of which are more business than IT imperatives and are usually value driven. Here are some of the dictating factors I have come across:

- Establish a presence in the marketplace as the first mover.
- Establish a presence in the marketplace as one who is not lagging behind in the industry.
- Develop a set of features that have an immediate effect on either decreasing operational costs or increasing revenue.

- Enable a particular workforce (certain set of user personas) that has a compelling need for some features—for example, those users who have been taking significant risks in their decision making and traditionally have had to face tough consequences.

Features and capabilities are only as good as the means through which users interact with a system to exploit and leverage them; this is where the design-thinking paradigm assumes utmost significance, along with the standard analysis around data and integration, of course. Be sure to drive it through design thinking!

An objective focus on deciding on the MVP feature list and its corresponding user interface drives such a behavior and increases chances of getting something (which is business value driven) out the door and in the hands of the practitioners and users as early as possible.

Subsequent iterations will obviously follow the MVP!

Try it out if you like, and if the opportunity presents itself, lead by using an MVP paradigm. Or better still, *create the opportunity*!

Do Not Be a Prisoner of Events

As a software architect, as you make projects successful, you will increasingly attract the attention of your organization, the cynosure of their eyes. It is human instinct to gravitate toward success. You will be in demand and hence pulled in multiple project engagements and strategy discussions.

As I reflect on my personal experiences, I have had to stumble upon repeated realizations regarding my valiant attempts to simultaneously execute on multiple fronts, making every effort to satisfy multiple parties and juggle (possibly disparate) activities all at the same time.

Popular wisdom advocates focusing on one task at hand and executing it with your best effort. If you are bored working on one major activity, it is okay to work on two (at most) activities simultaneously. Some people find it refreshing to have a change. However, in general, the cost of context switching is very high and often proves to be detrimental.

Time will evidently prove to be the most precious resource: something that you will increasingly be chasing. However, you will be doing so in vain if you try to address too many tasks and satisfy multiple groups. You will end up just being a prisoner of events. If you cannot manage yours effectively, people will dexterously take a stranglehold of your time.

I have finally learned to say no, to stop spreading myself too thin into multiple areas, and to be objectively focused in a prioritized manner. Being able to manage your time requires you to start by taking possession of your time!

Predictive Analytics Is Not the Only Entry Point into Analytics

Many organizations and consulting firms advocate that the primary entry point into the analytics discipline is through predictive analytics—the power to predict some critical or important event in the future. Most organizations start off with data mining and data science activities to find that elusive nugget of information that presents significant business value. We are often led to believe that developing a powerful predictive model is the ultimate goal, and hence, building such a model is the point where all our analytics endeavors and engagements should begin. While I have no reservations against embarking on the journey with predictive analytics, a few of my observations from the field are worth sharing:

- Building predictive models is not easy. Whether the predictive power of the model is good enough to inspire the organization to believe in its prophecies is neither definitive nor easy to achieve.
- Predictive models commonly must deal with issues around data availability and data quality, which is where the majority of the time is spent rather than focusing on building the model itself.
- It may not be the quickest hit to business value.

My experience leads me to believe that, at least in some industries more than others (for example, in the industrial and manufacturing space), it is critically and equally important to harness the potential of operational, or real-time, analytics. The point is to monitor the operational assets in real time to generate key performance metrics and manifest them into intuitive and interactive real-time infographic visualizations. Operational analytics often serves as the key to optimizing an asset's overall equipment effectiveness (OEE). Also, in many cases, it may turn out to be easier to generate key performance indicators (KPIs) and focus on their interactive real-time user experience rather than churning through months' and years' worth of data to generate a really insightful predictive model. Some of the reasons may be, but are not limited to, the following:

- Computing analytical metrics (for example, KPIs) in real time is definitive (that is, formulaic driven) by its very nature.
- Generating key metrics in real time offers the advantage of taking corrective actions as and when some critical operations are underway; that is, actions can be taken at the point of business impact.

So, while there is no takeaway from predictive analytics, we should also consider, as an example, the value propositions around real-time operational analytics as an equally powerful and value-driven entry point if deemed applicable in the industry context.

Leadership Can Be an Acquired Trait

As the adage goes, *leaders are born*. And they very well are. However, The Almighty is not too generous in encoding that into the genetic blueprint of all worldly entrants! So does that mean that the common man, like you and me, cannot become a leader? I used to think along similar lines until I picked up a *Harvard Business Review* article on leadership (Goleman 2004).

The summary of the message was that a leader must possess (if born with) or acquire (for someone like me) five essential leadership traits: *self-awareness, self-regulation, motivation, empathy,* and *social skills.* The article qualifies *self-awareness* as being aware of your own emotional traits, strengths, and weaknesses, along with being clear on drives, values, and goals; *self-regulation* as being in control of your impulsive reactions and redirecting them toward positive actions; *motivation* as your drive to achieve something worthwhile; *empathy* as your keenness to be compassionate about others' feelings when making a decision; and *social skills* as your ability to manage relationships effectively enough to seamlessly influence them to move in a desired direction.

The ability to practice these leadership traits, even after being thoroughly convinced and believing in them (as I have been), requires exercising a good dose of conscious free will. Since I was not born with natural leadership qualities, I had to consciously practice exercising these traits—some in a planned manner and some in a more ad hoc manner. Conscious exercising morphs into default and instinctive behavior, which becomes second nature—the power of habit!

Leadership traits can indeed be developed through conscious practice. As an architect, you are looked upon as a technical leader. You are expected not only to lead software development but also to engage in C-level discussions. You are the upcoming chief architect, chief technologist, or CTO; the leader in you will be called upon to shine in resplendence sooner rather than later!

Technology-Driven Architecture Is a Bad Idea

IT projects and initiatives have many different points for initiation. Some start purely from a set of business drivers and goals that require an IT System to take it to fruition; some others are incubated in IT as IT-driven initiatives that often include good ideas and intentions, but not always! I have seen many IT projects initiated in IT with the intention to try out some new things, some new technologies in the market, or some cool aids that someone may have read up on or thought were cool. Beware of the last type (that is, the cool aid drinkers) and ensure that any such initiative can be directly traced back to a business sponsor with clearly defined business objectives that it is expected to fulfill.

Many technical teams start by declaring the availability of a technology platform on which the system ought to be built. Architecture constraints and considerations are laid out based on the requirements, specifications, and constraints of the technologies that have been declared. In such settings, when business requirements are gathered, impedance to acceptance creeps in from the technical teams: technology constraints need to be violated to meet the requirements, for example, or the technology or product components may not be able to satisfy the required capabilities.

I'm happy to share a couple of my own experiences, illustrated in a short-story style:

- A business intelligence (BI) reporting tool or product was chosen to be a part of a technology stack before we understood the type of reporting needs expected from the system. When the requirements were gathered, there emerged a class of visual widgets that needed to visualize some operations data in real time; that is, when the data was flow-ing into the system; more and more of the visualization expectations started falling into this category. The BI reporting tool supported widgets that were only able to render and refresh the user interfaces by periodically querying a database; it did not have the capa-bility to render and refresh widgets from data that was streaming into the system. Big problem, bad idea! The team had to perform a deep technical analysis to arrive at the conclusion that an alternate visualization technology would be required to support the business needs. Declaring the use of an existing BI reporting tool to be the technology of choice was not a good idea after all.

- An enterprise chose a Hadoop platform with the expectation that it would satisfy all analytic needs and workloads. When the enterprise needed to develop a couple of com-plex predictive models for its manufacturing assembly line, the data scientists were put to the task of building the predictive models and running them against the data in the Hadoop cluster. Surprisingly enough, running the queries, which were required to train the statistical models, took an inordinate amount of time. It took up a lot of time, jump-ing through multiple layers of frustration, disgust, and finger-pointing contests, to finally figure out that the chosen Hadoop platform was not conducive to running complex queries on petabytes of data and expecting them to be adequately performant. Big prob-lem, bad idea! The team had to go back to the drawing board before finally figuring out that a database management system would be required to provision the relevant data sets needed to build and train the predictive model.

When you confront such scenarios, working through them is not only frustratingly painful but also quite detrimental to the image of IT in the eyes of the business. As an architect, you need to be aware of such scenarios and speak up with confidence and conviction to not put the tech-nology before the business needs. This is why it is critically important to start with a functional model of the solution architecture and align the functional needs to the technology capabilities and features. Yes, you can develop the functional and operational model in parallel; however, you should never declare the technology stack before the vetting process is completed to your satisfaction.

You may get lucky a few times, but just so many. The pitfalls become quite significant to warrant keeping an eye out for them!

Open Source Is Cool but to a Point

One of the best things that could have happened to the IT industry is the proliferation, accep-tance, and use of open source technologies. Consortiums such as the Apache Foundation and companies such as IBM, among others, innovating and then donating technologies to the open source community have remarkably transformed the nature of software development. Technol-ogy has reached the hands of the Millennials (that is, the new generation) far more ubiquitously than we have ever seen before. For example, the ten-year-old child of one of my colleagues competed in an advanced programming contest, built a JavaScript-based web application, and won the first prize!

Open source has fueled tremendous innovation in IT. Many organizations have embraced and adopted complete open source technology platforms. I play around with quite a few open source technologies on my own laptop and find them fascinatingly powerful.

However, there is one word of caution that I must not hesitate to throw out. While open source technology is fantastic for prototyping a new or innovative concept, fostering a *prove out quickly* or *fail fast* (if at all) paradigm, a careful, well-thought-out technical analysis needs to be exercised to ensure that applications built on open source technologies can be tested and certified as enterprise strength.

Let me share one of the examples I have come across:

- An innovative simulation modeling application that addresses a significant problem in the industry was built on an open source database engine (its name purposely obscured). While the system was powerful in demonstrating the art of the possible to multiple potential customers, it hit a snag when it was time to implement that system for a very large customer. The sheer weight of the data rendered the core simulation algorithms nearly useless because the open source database engine could not keep up with the query workloads in time for the simulations. The entire data model and data set had to be ported on to an industrial-strength database engine (which had database parallelization techniques, among other features) to make the system functional for the enterprise.

As an architect, you need to carefully analyze the use of open source technologies before formalizing them for enterprise-strength applications. As massively powerful as these open source technologies are, they may not all be able to run industry-strength applications supporting the expected nonfunctional requirements and metrics.

Write Them Up However Trivial They May Seem

You may find yourself doing some fun programming experiments that are so interesting that you just cannot get your mind off them until you're done. At other times, you may get stuck solving a problem that needs to be addressed in order for the proposed solution to be declared viable. Such problems can either manifest as programming or configuration or design problems; they are problems nonetheless.

You may invest some intense, long, often-frustrating hours before you finally and inevitably solve the problem. Now that the problem is solved, the dependent tasks that were stalled get to move again. Now what? Of course, you need to move on to address the next problem at hand. However, what if you first ask yourself "How difficult was it to solve the problem?" More often than not, the answer you hear from inside was that it was easy, something quite simple at the end.

Let me share a personal story with you. One day, some 15 years ago, one of my senior colleagues asked me how I finally solved a specific problem on which the team had been stuck for more than a week. The problem was how to configure a J2EE application server to work with a directory server for security (that is, authentication and authorization of users into an enterprise portal). I explained to my colleague that solving the problem ended up to be quite simple, and I laid down the steps I took to finally get it done. He listened to me quite intensely and then asked me: "Why don't you write it up as an article?" I thought he was crazy to ask me to write an article on this topic and publish it in a technical journal. He insisted that I write it up just the way I had explained it to him, and although I did not believe in its value, I went ahead and did it to gain some credibility with him.

The article got published in a technical journal as my first ever technical publication. It is hard for me to believe how, even today (although much less frequently than it used to be), I get emails and inquiries from IT professionals all over the world. They tell me how the article helped them to get ideas to solve similar problems they were faced with.

I had come to a startling realization: no matter how trivial you may think solving a particular problem could have been, there may be many individuals who are stuck with the same (or a similar) problem and who would benefit tremendously from your experiences.

I never stopped writing from the day I had that realization. Knowledge only grows if you share it with others. If you write and publish, not only will you be known and sought after, but also there will be a growing user community who will follow you. And in today's ubiquitous socially networked world, you don't even have to write a 10-page article to share your knowledge; just tweet it!

Think about some of the problems that you solved, restructure your solution in your mind or on paper, and then write it up. Publish it!

Baseline Your Architecture on Core Strengths of Technology Products

As a part of developing and defining a system's architecture, you will have to choose, in a certain phase, the appropriate technologies: middleware products and platforms, hardware, networks, among others.

Choosing the right or most appropriate technology can be a challenging if not a daunting task. Competing vendors may have similar products, each touting why theirs is better than the rest. Competition is steep, and vendors often are forced to add some capabilities to their products just to answer affirmatively "Yes, we do it too!" One of the challenges for architects and technology decision makers is to assess and evaluate vendor technologies to differentiate between the features that form the core and foundational elements of a product from the features that are just add-ons or bolt-ons in order to keep their products on par with competitive vendor products.

In my experience, it is always safe to choose a vendor that focuses on its core product strengths instead of trying to support a multitude of other features that do not really form the core product. While you are architecting a solution, it is even more important to base that solution on the core product strengths and not try to use each and every feature just because they exist. An architecture that is built on the core strengths of a set of technology products, along with a sound integration architecture facilitating data and information exchange between them, would inevitably be more robust and scalable than one in which all product features are used just because they are available. As an example, if you are evaluating a vendor technology to decide on a real-time stream computing engine, try to focus on its ability, scalability, and versatility to ingest data in volume and variety and from multiple data sources instead of focusing on a feature that states it also does predictive modeling!

Summary

I wish I could summarize a chapter wherein I took the liberty of sharing some of my experiences and reflections. There is no summary to them; they can only get more elaborate.

The only thing I may say is that it is important to take a step back once in a while, reflect on some of the experiences that you may have gathered or some nugget of wisdom you may have stumbled upon. Sharing your hard-earned experiences and wisdom with your colleagues and with the community at large is as philanthropic as it is satisfying.

I can only hope that you subscribe to this thinking and build your own fan following!

References

Goleman, Daniel. (2004, January). "What Makes a Leader," *Harvard Business Review*. Retrieved from http://www.zurichna.com/internet/zna/SiteCollectionDocuments/en/media/FINAL%20HBR%20what%20 makes%20a%20leader.pdf. This article illustrated the five traits of leadership that I mentioned.

25 Topic Goodies

As an architect participating in technical and related discussions, I have had my share of awkward moments when I don't have a clue about specific topics or questions that are discussed. My stress level rises in an uncanny anticipation that I may be asked to throw light on or share my point of view on those topics! Sound familiar?

In this appendix, I have picked 25 topics that I have frequently come across or I feel a software architect needs to have enough understanding and awareness of to be able to contribute to a discussion on such or related topics.

I do not claim that the ones I chose are the top 25 picks because *top* is a relative term; what seemed top to me may not be the same for you. I focused on topics that appeared to me to be supplemental and related to the overall topics of architecture, technology, and some aspects of analytics (because we dedicated a whole chapter to it in the book).

What Is the Difference Between Architecture and Design?

Architecture deals with the *structure* or *structures* of *systems* that are composed of software components, the external visible properties of those components, and the relationships among them. Design deals with the *configuration* and *customization* of *components and subcomponents* that adhere to an existing system environment and solution requirement.

What Is the Difference Between Architectural Patterns, Design Patterns, and a Framework?

An architectural pattern expresses a fundamental organization schema for software systems. It provides a set of predefined subsystems and components, specifies their responsibilities, and includes rules and guidelines for organizing the relationship between them.

A design pattern, according to the Gang of Four book titled *Design Patterns: Elements of Reusable Object-Oriented Software* (Gamma, Helm, Johnson, & Vlissides 1994), is the packaging of a set of participating classes and instances, their roles and collaborations, along with the distribution of responsibilities (between the classes and instances) to solve a general design problem in a particular context.

A framework, on the other hand, can be considered an implementation of a collection of architectural or design patterns based on a particular technology. As an example, Spring is a J2EE framework based on the Model View Controller (MVC) pattern implementation in Java.

How Can We Compare a Top-Down Functional Decomposition Technique and an Object-Oriented Analysis and Design (OOAD) Technique?

Top-down functional decomposition is a design methodology that deconstructs the problem from an abstract functional definition of the problem (top) to a detailed solution (bottom). It is a hierarchical approach in which a problem is divided and subdivided into functional subdomains or modules.

In a practical world of software development, no matter how hard you try to achieve completeness, requirements will always contain a varying degree of flux. The challenge with the functional decomposition technique is that it does not let the code be adaptable to possible changes in the future for a graceful evolution. With the focus being on functions and their decomposition into subfunctions, the problems that arise are low cohesion and very tight coupling between the original overarching main functional problem and its functional subdomains. This is a result of the ripple effect, which is quite common in a problem solution using functional decomposition in which the data set that the functions work on is possibly shared among the various functions. Changing a function or the data that is used by a function, hence, will require changes to be made in other pieces of the code, leading to a popular phenomenon in software development called the *unwanted side effect*. This effect quickly snowballs, and the effect often becomes drastic and unmanageable.

OOAD is a design methodology in which the deconstruction of a problem is in the form of objects. An object, which is an instance of a class, is a mapping of a real-world entity into the software domain. An object, conceptually, is an encapsulation of its own internal state and exposes a set of behaviors (through a set of methods or operations, which work on the object to change its internal state). The intent is to ensure that the only way to change the object's internal state is through the methods, the collection of which determines its behavior.

In OOAD, unlike top-down functional decomposition, no one single overarching function is responsible. The responsibility is encapsulated into these software building blocks called objects. This leads to a properly encapsulated system in which the data (that is, the object's state) is tightly integrated with the operations (which define the behavior) that manipulate the data. In turn, this leads to a system that is characterized by low coupling and high cohesion.

OOAD is very adaptable to changes. These changes do not touch the entire system; rather, they are localized in only the set of objects whose behaviors need to change in order to achieve the new functionality.

Note: An object is an instance of a class. While a class defines the entity, an object is an instance of the class. As an example, a Car is defined as class and a BMW is an object that is an instance of (that is, type of) the Car class.

What Is the Difference Between Conceptual, Specified, and Physical Models?

A conceptual model, as it applies to a functional model, represents a set of concepts, represented as entities, that have no affiliation to any technology. The entities represent constructs—for example, people, processes, and software systems, along with depicting their interactions. A conceptual model, as it applies to an operational model, represents only the application-level components that will ultimately need to be placed on a physical topology.

A specification-level model (which is what we have called the "specified" level model in this book), as it applies to a functional model, describes the externally visible aspects of each component (in the model)—for example, their interfaces and ways in which the interfaces interact across components. A specified model, as it applies to an operational model, represents a set of technical components that will ultimately host the application-level components and also support the interconnections and integrations between them; focus shifts into a logical view of the infrastructure.

A physical model, as it applies to a functional model, represents the internal aspects of the components as they relate to the implementation technology or platform—for example, whether a component may be implemented in a J2EE or a .NET technology. A physical model, as it applies to an operational model, defines the hardware configuration for each operational node, the functional components placed on each node, and the network connectivity details of how one physical compute node is interconnected with other nodes or users in the overall system.

How Do Architecture Principles Provide Both Flexibility and Resilience to Systems Architecture?

Architecture principles provide a set of rules, constraints, and guidelines that govern the development, maintenance, and use of a system's architecture. When a principle is expected to be adopted and followed across the lines of business that use the system, it provides the resilience of the architecture around its adherence. An example of such a principle may be the security mandate for all users, regardless of line of business or persona, to use consistent credentials to access the system. When a principle encourages extensibility, it provides room for the system to be flexible. An example of such a principle may be to adopt a baseline information model but allow for extensions specific to a set of applications used by a line of business.

Why Could the Development of the Physical Operational Model (POM) Be Broken into Iterations?

When you are developing the specified operational model (SOM), you are iteratively refining your understanding of the application-level components and also identifying the technical-level components that will ultimately support the application-level components.

If you have knowledge of the current IT landscape, vendor affinity of the customer, and the evolving architectural blueprint (with its principles and constraints), which are gained during the SOM analysis, you will be able to leverage informed judgment to start identifying the products and technologies required to build the physical operational model (POM). During this phase, a critical understanding of some of the NFRs (for example, availability, disaster recovery, and fault tolerance) may give clues into the final physical topology (for example, which middleware product or component needs to support a hot-cold standby operations mode and which ones will require an on-demand compute ramp-up). However, their detailed configurations may not be required at this point. Hence, it is quite natural to perform the *component selection* process of the POM in parallel with the SOM activities while leaving the *component configuration* activities for a later time. Initiating an iterative and parallel (with SOM) development of the POM is quite realistic, often practical, and timely.

What Is a Service-Oriented Architecture?

Service-oriented architecture (SOA) is an architecture style that aims at identifying a set of business-aligned services, each of which is directly aligned to one or more quantifiable business goals. By leveraging a set of techniques, the architecture style identifies one or more granular or atomic services that can be orchestrated in a *service dance*, so to speak, to realize one or more business services. At its core, the style advocates and fosters the implementation of services that are self-describable, searchable, and reusable (that is, they participate in the implementation of multiple business processes). The focus in SOA is on reusable entities or constructs called a *service*, which is business aligned.

A suite of technologies supports the implementation and deployment of services. For example, *Service registries* serve as repositories for services, Web Service Description Language (WSDL) provides a language to specify the metadata for the service descriptions, and Business Process Execution Language (BPEL) provides an orchestration language to invoke and integrate multiple services to implement business processes.

What Is an Event-Driven Architecture?

Event-driven architecture (EDA) was originally proposed by the Gartner analyst firm as a framework to orchestrate behavior around the production, detection, and consumption of events as well as the responses they generate. EDA is an event-centric architecture; the core element of EDA is an event, a first-class entity, that is typically generated asynchronously within or outside the address space of the system under consideration. Events may typically be aggregated, or brokered forms of multiple simpler events correlated both spatially (occurring in different locations) and temporally (occurring at different times) to formulate higher-order events that are relevant and contextual to trigger the execution of a business process.

EDA typically leverages some form of an ESB for the event receipt, event aggregation, and brokering; it also triggers business processes.

There have been philosophical debates regarding the use of SOA versus EDA. One simplified approach that has been tried is the unification of SOA and EDA into SOA 2.0.

What Is a Process Architecture?

There is a class of applications and systems, and arguably a class of enterprises, that is heavily process driven, some more so than others. Consider manufacturing and production companies that typically have to incur heavy operating costs due to design errors. The later these errors are caught in the process, the more costly is the undertaking. Such organizations need a framework to not only reduce the errors at every step of the process but also to be able to rapidly adapt parts of the business process to support dynamic and adaptable changes. A careful analysis of such process-centric enterprises may also reveal a strong causal relationship between a set of events that drive such process-centric systems: the sending and receiving of events triggers parts of or entire operational processes.

A process architecture typically has a business description, in process terms, as well as an underlying technology framework supporting its implementation. The business description provides a high-level specification of the participating set of processes, their interdependencies, and intercommunications. The technology framework not only defines an underlying technology foundation (which supports a set of events for which the receipt and triggering provide the interconnections and intercommunications between processes) but also provides appropriate tooling and a runtime to simulate how new processes may communicate with the existing processes and how new processes may react to events. The technology framework also defines interfaces for processes (a.k.a. process interfaces) defined in terms of events that a process may receive or send as well as how events define the communication conduit between processes—a communication architecture connecting processes with events using a distributed integration middleware.

Process architectures typically fall under the bigger umbrella of enterprise business architectures, the latter defining the enterprise value streams (represented as an outcome-driven collection of activities and tasks) and their relationships to both external and internal business entities and events.

If you look closely, you may be a bit confused as to why and how process architectures are different from EDA. The confusion is quite legitimate. One way to handle any confusion is to consider the perspective and lens through which you are looking at the problem. If you are talking to the business strategy community, it may be worthwhile to put the processes at the center of the conversation. If you are talking to production and operations users, it may be worthwhile to discuss the events that are central to the execution of the processes. As a software architect, you need to be cognizant of the user community you have to deal with and orient yourself to speak the lingo that the intended community is comfortable with. It is important, however, to document the individual business processes as well as their interactions. It is equally important to describe and define the events that enable them to react to anything that is external to the processes. In technology speak, it is critical to define the integration architecture that ties the processes to the events and their interconnections. As long as you are not perturbed by so many different architecture terms and instead focus on what needs to be solved and how to define an architecture to solve the "what," you can keep the confusion at bay.

What Is a Technology Architecture?

Architectures have multiple views and viewpoints and also have multiple renditions as they go through various phases of maturity—from concept to realization. One of the critical architecture formulation phases requires the functional architecture views to be mapped on to the operational architecture views. During such a mapping, the middleware software products, the hardware compute and its specifications, and the network topology need to be designed and defined; all these need to come together.

The technology architecture of a system defines the set of middleware products, their placement on well-specified hardware configurations, and the network topology that interconnects the servers to other parts of the system. A system's POM may be a good phase in the design to formulate and formalize the technology architecture.

What Is an Adapter?

In any nontrivial enterprise system, connectivity between multiple, possibly disparate systems is quite common. Such disparate systems may be built in different technologies, supporting different data formats and connectivity protocols. Data and information exchange between such disparate systems requires some means to adapt to each of those systems so that their language can be understood, so to speak.

An adapter is typically a piece of custom or packaged code that connects to such systems so as to streamline data and information exchange while abstracting the specificities of the particular (often proprietary or archaic) protocol and formats from the adapter's consumers. The adapter does all the magic of hiding those specificities while exposing an easy-to-use facade (interface) for communication and data exchange.

The adapter exposes a set of APIs used to interact with the underlying systems, which makes enterprise application integration (EAI) simpler!

What Is a Service Registry?

A service registry is a software component that provides a simple service registration capability, allowing service developers and service registrars to easily register new or existing business services into a service catalog. The component allows developers to browse the catalog to find a suitable service and then easily request to consume it by registering the application (which would consume the service).

Among others, the component may also optionally provide the following capabilities:

- Service-level requirements supporting a set of service-level agreements (SLAs)
- A service management profile for service governance and life-cycle management
- Bulk loading of services into the registry from various common sources (for example, Excel sheets and flat files)
- A simplified user interface to browse the metadata and specifications for the services

What Is a Network Switch Block?

A switch block is a collection of Access and Distribution layer network devices (refer to Chapter 10, "Infrastructure Matters") that connect multiple Access layer switches to a pair of Distribution layer devices. It is essentially a block of switches consisting of multiple Access layer switches, along with a pair of Distribution layer devices.

What Are Operational Data Warehouses?

Traditional data warehouses (a.k.a. enterprise data warehouses or EDWs) are designed for very efficient reads, for executing analytical queries on large data sets with a quick query response turnaround, and for aggregating data from multiple transactional and referential data sources. Their strength is in building a trusted source of enterprise data, typically across different lines of businesses and answering strategic after-the-fact business questions that span across multiple lines of businesses on data that is kept over relatively long periods of time such as multiple years. Such data warehouses are typically refreshed infrequently, perhaps once a day.

In the current era of big data, the volume at which data is being generated is staggering to say the least and, as per projections, is only going to grow exponentially. The need to harness analytical insights from data, in real time, requires a different paradigm. Data needs to be streamed from transactional systems into a data warehouse in near real time. Such data needs to be analytically processed and persisted into the data warehouse at the rate at which it is ingested. Analytics on the newly arrived data need to be generated immediately. An operational data warehouse involves technologies that allow a traditional data warehouse to preserve its traditional capabilities and areas of strengths but also support the following:

- Ingesting data at a high frequency or in a continuous steady-state stream (also known as trickle feeds)

- Writing data at a high frequency without compromising the performance of reads and analytical queries

- Generating analytics on the combination of high-frequency incoming data and the existing data sets

In essence, an operational data warehouse is a traditional high-performing enterprise data warehouse that can support very high-frequency refreshes with new data without compromising the strengths of the en'terprise data warehouse.

What Is the Difference Between Complex Event Processing (CEP) and Stream Computing?

To understand complex event processing (CEP), you need to first understand complex events. Complex events detect causal and temporal relationships and memberships of simpler individual or homogeneous events. Causal relationships between events can be horizontal or vertical in nature. Horizontal causality implies triggering of events at the same level (for example, one business meeting outcome being the decision to arrange another follow-up meeting), whereas vertical causality relates to how, in a hierarchy of events, higher-level events are traceable to one or more lower-level events and vice versa.

CEP is a set of techniques, packaged into a technology framework, used to detect patterns of complex events, actively monitor and trace their causal relationships (both horizontally and vertically) in real time, define the relationships of complex events to autonomous business processes, and take appropriate actions through the triggering of business processes upon complex event detection. CEP primarily deals with the real-time analysis of discrete business events.

Stream computing is a relatively newer concept and technology that can be traced back to the initial maturity timelines of big data. Stream computing is a programming paradigm, supported by a runtime platform, that supports the ingestion of a continuous stream of data (in discrete data packets); it performs complex and computationally intensive advanced analytics on the data in motion and in real time (that is, at the rate in which data is generated and is ingested into the stream computing platform).

While the vendor-specific product literature of both technologies claims to support real-time and ultra-low latency computations, the difference is in their quantitative degrees in rates of data processing and their qualitative nature of support for advanced analytics. The differences may include

- CEP engines expect *discrete* business events as data packets; stream computing supports a *continuous* stream of data packets.

- Stream computing is expected to support an order of scale higher *volume* of data processing in real time.

- Stream computing typically supports a wider *variety* of data (both structured and unstructured); CEP typically functions on structured data sets.

- CEP mostly leverages *rules-based* correlations of events; stream computing is expected to support simple to very *complex* and *advanced analytics* (for example, time series analysis, image and video analytics, complex mathematical techniques such as integrals and Fourier transforms on numerical data, data mining, and data filtering).

What Is the Difference Between *Schema at Read* and *Schema at Write* Techniques?

Schema at read and *schema at write* techniques have become discussion topics with the advent of Big Data processing. With the proliferation of unstructured data and its tremendous value as it pertains to analytical decision making, the need to persist data that is primarily unstructured in nature has gained a lot of importance.

Structured data has been around for more than four decades: using schema definitions to store structured data has been the most common technique to store data in database systems. A lot of upfront design work goes into the design and realization of the structured data, primarily because of the inherent structure in the data that requires it to be modeled before data persistence (that is, design of data schemas before data is written), and hence the name *schema at write*. The inherent nature of unstructured data implies that it carries no predefined structure; the variety of unstructured data (for example, text, images, videos) makes the investment of any effort to come up with a predefined structure quite impractical and cost prohibitive. Therefore, storage for unstructured data may be realized without any *a priori* schema definitions; it can be persisted in its native form. Processing (that is, retrieving, interpreting, and analyzing) unstructured data after its persistence requires significantly more investment in time and effort primarily because the nature, and more importantly the intended usage, of the unstructured data has to be known when it is retrieved for analysis—hence, the name *schema at read*.

Schema at write requires significant investment of time upfront to define the data schema before the data can be persisted but makes up for that time with fast and efficient reads. *Schema at read* requires a significant effort to understand the nature of the data at the time it is retrieved but makes up for that time with very fast and efficient data persistence. You give some, you get some!

What Is a Triple Store?

A Triple Store is a special type of database that stores data in a way that is more generic than a normal relational database. Its purpose is to store triples, which are short statements that associate two entities in the form subject-predicate-object—for example, Ants (*subject*) are destroying (*predicate*) the garden (*object*). The Triple Store can store semantic relationships between any pair of entities and record the nature of those relationships when they are stored. Triple stores are primarily used to store textual information after it undergoes lexical parsing, the outcome of which is a set of tuples.

One major advantage of a Triple Store database is that it does not need any structural changes to accommodate new entity types or new relationship types.

What Is a Massively Parallel Processing (MPP) System?

MPP is a technique in which a complex job is processed, in a coordinated manner, on multiple parallel and dedicated compute nodes (that is, processors that have their own hardware, memory, and storage, with the array of processors communicating with each other through a high-speed interconnection). The interconnection works as a data path to allow information exchange between the processor bank (that is, the array of processors). Owing to the nature of each processor dedicating its entire compute power to the assigned workload, MPP is also considered a *shared nothing* architecture.

MPP typically requires a coordinator that deconstructs a complex task into a set of subtasks and distributes the subtasks to an array of dedicated processors. They, in turn, process at extreme speeds (often in the hardware) and return the subtasks to the coordinator. The coordinator processes the subresults to form a single response. Check out IBM PureData® for Analytics and Oracle's Teradata as two popular MPPs.

IBM Watson Is Built on DeepQA Architecture. What Is DeepQA?

DeepQA, which stands for Deep Question Answer, is the foundation on which IBM Watson systems were originally built. The DeepQA project at IBM was intended to illustrate how the wide and growing body of natural language content, together with the integration and advancement of natural language processing, information retrieval, machine learning, knowledge representation, and reasoning techniques, plus massively parallel computation can drive open-domain autonomic Question Answering technology to a point where it clearly and consistently assists and will ultimately rival the best human performance.

DeepQA architecture is built on advanced natural language processing (NLP) techniques. NLP, by its very nature, is ambiguous and polysemous (having multiple meanings), with its meaning often being highly contextual. A system like IBM Watson needs to consider many possible meanings, attempting to find the inference paths that are most confidently supported by the data.

The primary computational principle supported by the DeepQA architecture is to assume and maintain multiple interpretations of the question, to generate many plausible answers or hypotheses for each interpretation, and to collect and process many different evidence streams that might support or refute those hypotheses. Each component in the system adds assumptions about what the question means or what the content means or what the answer might be or why it might be correct. "Candidate answers" are then formed. The candidate answers are scored, independently of any additional evidence, by deeper analysis algorithms. In cases in which the original question was deconstructed into smaller questions, which were independently subjected to the evidence-based hypothesis technique to generate the best possible answers, the answers to the question subparts are synthesized (using advanced synthesis algorithms) to form coherent final answers. In the final step, trained machine-learning techniques and algorithms are applied to rank the final answers. The entire technique is working on a corpus of data that surpasses the capacity of a human brain to hold and to process in a timely manner.

What Is the Difference Between Supervised and Unsupervised Learning Techniques?

The clue to understanding the difference between supervised and unsupervised learning lies in their names. Supervised implies there is some element of supervision; that is, the learning model is trained based on historical data in which every instance of a set of input events has a corresponding outcome, and the learned model is then expected to predict a future event based on what it learned from the correlation between the input events and the outcome (the target variable). Unsupervised implies that the learning model does not enjoy any prior supervision; that is, there is no associated outcome for a set of input events, and the model is expected to determine and derive a set of clusters or groups in the data set.

In supervised modeling, a model is trained with a set of historical data that has the form $y = \Omega(x_1, x_2, ..., x_n)$, where $\overline{X}$ is a vector represented by $(x_1, x_2, ..., x_n)$; that is, $\overline{X} = (x_1, x_2, ..., x_n)$ and for every instance of the $\overline{X}$ vector, there is a known value of y (the response or target variable); Ω is the mapping function. The trained model is expected to predict the value of y given a new and unknown instance of the $\overline{X}$ vector. Classification and regression are two classes of modeling techniques that use supervised learning techniques. Decision trees, neural networks, and regression are examples of supervised machine-learning techniques.

Unsupervised modeling lacks any response variable; therefore, it cannot be trained with historical data. The goal of unsupervised modeling is to understand the relationships between the elements of the $\overline{X}$ vector $(x_1, x_2, ..., x_n)$ and try to determine whether and how some subsets of the $\overline{X}$ vector fall into relatively distinct groups. Stated in a different way, unsupervised modeling tries to identify clusters of variables that tend to display similar characteristics that are different from other such clusters. Unsupervised modeling is also called cluster analysis. Segmentation of a user population based on certain attributes (for example, income, race, address, and so on) can cluster users into high income brackets and medium income brackets. K-means clustering, Kohonen clustering, and Outlier analysis are examples of unsupervised machine-learning techniques.

What Is the Difference Between Taxonomy and Ontology?

Taxonomies model a hierarchical tree-like structure representing elements and their containment or constituents (that is, a parent-to-child relationship). Traversal of the tree results in narrowing down the domain of description. For example, *Universe -> Milky Way -> Solar System -> Sun -> Earth -> Mountains* is a taxonomy representation. Taxonomies often leave the meaning of the relationships between the parent and child elements loosely defined, owing to the inherent inability to depict relationships between the elements.

Ontologies, on the other hand, are taxonomies that are associated with rules on how elements are related semantically. The rules are expressed in the form of tuples: a subject-object-predicate relationship (for example, *Barack Obama is the US President)*. The tuples offer different perspective meanings to a subject based on the context (the tuple itself) in which it is used. The well-ordered tuples form the basis of knowledge induction; that is, the tuples form the basis from which the relationships can be reasoned and inferred.

What Is Spark and How Does It Work?

Spark, an Apache project, is a fast, general-purpose *shared nothing* MPP engine leveraging highly optimized runtime architecture of a cluster computing system for large-scale data processing. It supports fast startup times and leverages aggressively cached in-memory distributed computing and dedicated processes that are available even when no jobs are running.

The general-purpose Spark platform covers a wide range of workloads—for example, SQL, stream computing, machine learning, graph-based data processing, as well as leveraging the capabilities of Hadoop (although it is expected to be higher performing than Hadoop's Map Reduce).

The Spark platform is very flexible because it is written in Scala, an object-oriented programming language, and also easier to use than, for example, programming in Map Reduce. It has support for Scala, Java, and Python APIs. As of this writing, it is a significant advancement over the traditional Hadoop ecosystem, primarily gaining a significant edge over Map Reduce, through the availability of powerful interactive shells to analyze data dynamically and in real time.

The anatomy of the current Spark platform can be described by the following concepts of Spark:

- **Context** represents a connection to the Spark cluster. An application can initiate a context before submitting one or more jobs. The jobs can be either sequential or parallel, batch mode or interactive, or may also be long running, thereby serving continuous requests.

- **Driver** represents a program or a process running the Spark context that is responsible for running the jobs over the cluster and converting the application processing into a set of tasks.

- **Job**, represented by a query or a query plan, is a piece of code that will take some input from the application, perform some computations (transformations and actions), and generate some output.

- **Stage** is a subset of a job.
- **Tasks** are the constituents of a stage. Each task is executed on one partition (of the data) and processed by one executor.
- **Executor** is the process that is responsible for executing a task on a worker node.

Figure A.1 provides a visual depiction of the various components of Spark.

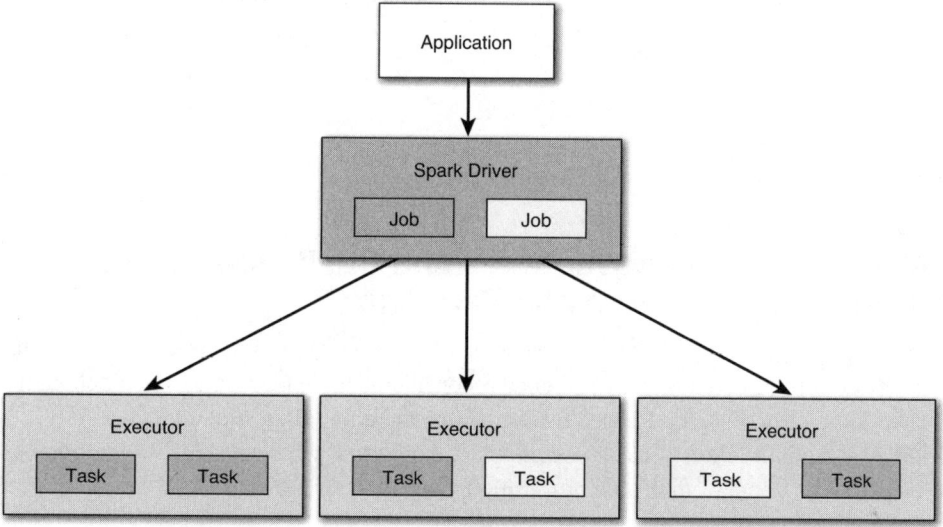

Figure A.1 The anatomy of how an application is executed on the Spark platform.

Each Spark application runs as a set of processes coordinated by the Spark context, which is the driver program. Figure A.2 provides a depiction of the same.

As shown in Figure A.2, each application gets its own executor processes, which stay up for the duration of the whole application and run tasks in multiple threads. This has the benefit of isolating applications from each other on both the scheduling side (each driver schedules its own tasks) and executor side (tasks from different applications running in different execution spaces—for example, different Java Virtual Machines). However, it also means that data cannot be shared across different Spark applications, which are instances of the Spark context, without writing it to an external storage system.

At the time of writing, Spark is gaining tremendous popularity, supported by rapid adoption, and is being touted as the next-generation integrated advanced analytics platform.

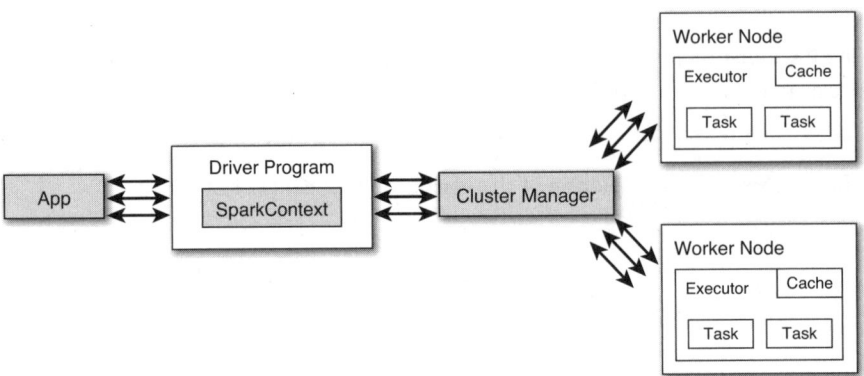

Figure A.2　Clustered execution of Spark applications.

What Are Some of the Advantages and Challenges of the Cloud Computing Platform and Paradigm?

Cloud computing is a relatively new paradigm that has caught on immensely quickly in the industry. In fact, any enterprise that has an IT presence is considered to be lagging quite far behind if it does not have some form of a cloud-based infrastructure and computing strategy.

Cloud computing obviously has some distinct advantages, which makes it such a powerful value proposition. Some of the value propositions, but obviously not limited to these, are the following:

- **Reduced capital and operational cost**—Infrastructure and computational needs can typically be requested and made available on demand with the elasticity to grow or shrink on an as-needed basis. Setting up the infrastructure, regardless of its usage and monitoring and maintaining its usage do not require any upfront locked-in costs. The billing model supports pay per use; the infrastructure is not purchased, thus lowering maintenance; both initial and recurring expenses are much lower than traditional computing.

- **Massive data storage**—Storage and maintenance of large volumes of data on an elastic compute platform are possible. Sudden workload spikes are also managed effectively and efficiently on the cloud, owing to its dynamic and on-demand scalability.

- **Flexibility**—Enterprises need to continuously adapt even more rapidly to changing business conditions. Speed to deliver is critical, requiring rapid application development that is made possible by assembling the most appropriate infrastructure, platform, and software building blocks on the cloud platform.

However, some inherent challenges ought to be addressed. Some of the challenges stem from the following:

- **Data security** is a crucial element because enterprises are skeptical of exposing their data outside their enterprise perimeter; they fear losing data to the competition and failing to protect the data confidentiality of their consumers. While enterprise networks traditionally put the necessary network infrastructures in place to protect the data, the cloud model assumes the cloud service providers to be responsible for maintaining data security on behalf of the enterprises.

- **Data recoverability and availability** require business applications to support, often stringent, SLAs. Appropriate clustering and failover, disaster recovery, capacity and performance management, systems monitoring, and maintenance become critical. The cloud service provider needs to support all of these elements; their failure could mean severe damage and impact to the enterprise.

- **Management capabilities** will continue to challenge the current techniques and will require pushing the envelope toward more autonomic scaling and load-balancing features; these requirements for features are far more sophisticated and demanding than what the current cloud providers can support.

- **Regulatory and compliance restrictions** place stringent laws around making sensitive personal information (SPI) available outside country borders. Pervasive cloud hosting would become a challenge because not all cloud providers have data centers in all countries and regions.

However, the advantages of cloud computing are lucrative enough to outweigh the challenges and hence make cloud computing a significant value proposition to fuel its exponential growth of adoption.

What Are the Different Cloud Deployment Models?

As of this writing, most cloud service providers support essentially three cloud deployment model options. You therefore can determine the right solution for any given enterprise. The three options are public cloud, private cloud, and hybrid cloud.

- **Public cloud**—Owned and operated by cloud service providers, this option allows service providers to deliver superior economies of scale to their customers primarily because the infrastructure costs are distributed (and hence shared) across a set of enterprises that are hosted in the same physical infrastructure through a multitenancy operating model. The shared cost fosters an attractive low-cost, "pay-as-you-go" cost model. This rental model allows customers to account for their costs as an operational expense (OpEx) spread over multiple years as opposed to an upfront capital expense (CapEx). An added advantage is the extreme elasticity of compute and storage available on demand as and when the system workload demands it. However, in this scenario, a customer's applications that share the same infrastructure pool do not have too much flexibility for personalized configuration, security protections, and availability.

- **Private Cloud**—Private clouds are built exclusively for a single enterprise, often owing to regulatory reasons, security policies, the need to protect intellectual property, or simply a client's desire. They aim to address concerns on data security and offer greater control, which is typically lacking in a public cloud. There are two variations to a private cloud:

  - **On-premise Private Cloud**—Also known as an internal or intranet cloud, it is hosted within an enterprise's own data center. This model provides a more standardized process and protection, but is limited in its elasticity of size and scalability. IT departments also need to incur both capital and operational costs for the physical resources. This option is best suited for applications that require complete control and configurability of the infrastructure and security.

  - **Externally Hosted Private Cloud**—This type of cloud is hosted externally with a cloud service provider, where the provider facilitates an exclusive cloud environment with a full guarantee of privacy and dedicated infrastructure. This option is best suited for enterprises that do not prefer a public cloud due to sharing of physical resources.

- **Hybrid Cloud**—This option combines both public and private cloud models. In this model, enterprises can utilize third-party cloud service providers in a full or partial manner, thus increasing the flexibility of computing. The hybrid cloud environment can be offered on an on-demand, externally provisioned scale and hence supports compute elasticity. In this hybrid setup, the private cloud capacity model may be augmented with the resources of a public cloud to manage any unexpected surges in workload. Applications and systems that require strict compliance can operate on the private cloud instance, whereas the suite of applications that can run under lesser constrained environments can operate on the public cloud instance with a dedicated interconnection between the private and public cloud environments.

What Is Docker Technology?

Docker is technology that was developed as a part of the Apache Open Source consortium. As of this writing, Docker is built as a portable, lightweight application runtime and packaging tool that is built on top of the core Linux container primitives. It also extends Linux's common container format called Linux Containers (LXC). The Docker container comes with tools that can package an application and all its dependencies into a virtual container that can be deployed on servers supporting most, if not all, Linux distributions. Once packaged, the self-contained application can run anywhere without any additional effort.

The virtualization in Docker is lightweight because it does not package its own version of the operating system; rather, it leverages the same instance of the underlying OS. This is different from standard virtualization techniques in which each virtual machine has its own instance of

OS, which highlights one perceived advantage of standard virtual machines: each VM can have a different OS, implying one VM can be on Linux, whereas the other can be on Windows server.

A Docker container is an isolated user or application space within a running Linux OS with multiple containers sharing the Linux kernel, and each application (along with its codebase, required packages, and data) has isolated runtimes (saved as file systems). Figure A.3 shows the way containers are isolated and running application instances.

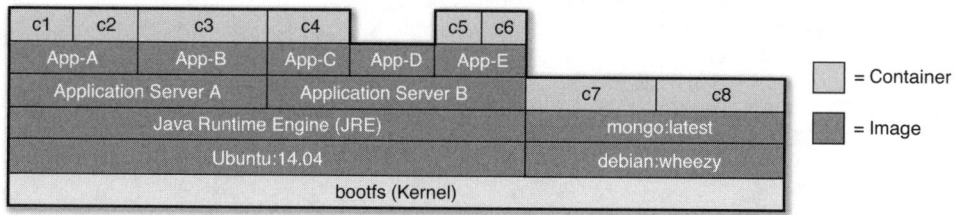

Figure A.3   A schematic of a Docker container stack.

Summary

In this appendix, I discussed a collection of concepts that I have encountered as an architect and modern-day technologist.

I have had my fair share of conversations and meetings in which some of the topics discussed here were not very well known to me, and although I was able to avoid embarrassment, internally, I did not feel too well until I went back to research and learn the concept or technique and got to apply it in real-world engagements.

I realize that discussing just 25 topics is not exhaustive; I easily could have discussed and highlighted another 25 topics. However, that would have distorted the main theme of the book a bit too much.

References

Gamma, E., Helm, R., Johnson, R., & Vlissides, J. (1994). *Design patterns: Elements of reusable object-oriented software.* Boston: Addison-Wesley Professional.

Elixir Functional Model (Continued)

This appendix picks up from where we left the functional model of Elixir in Chapter 7!

Logical Level

Component Identification

The components for the first subsystem—that is, Asset Onboarding Management—were covered in Chapter 7. Tables B.1 through B.4 cover the identified components for the remaining subsystems.

Table B.1   Responsibilities of the KPI Manager Component

Subsystem ID:	SUBSYS-02
Component ID:	COMP-02-01
Component Name:	KPI Manager
Component Responsibilities:	The responsibilities include
	• Detect the machine type for which data is received.
	• Calculate machine-specific KPIs based on incoming data.
	• Store the calculated KPIs in a persistent store (database).

Table B.2   Responsibilities of the Alert Manager Component

Subsystem ID:	SUBSYS-02
Component ID:	COMP-02-02
Component Name:	Alert Manager
Component Responsibilities:	The responsibilities include • Determine whether a computed KPI falls outside of the configurable thresholds. • Construct machine-specific alerts. • Dispatch alerts to an integration bus.

Table B.3   Responsibilities of the Failure Analysis Manager Component

Subsystem ID:	SUBSYS-03
Component ID:	COMP-03-01
Component Name:	Failure Analysis Manager
Component Responsibilities:	The responsibilities include • Detect the closest possible mode of failure related to a given KPI-based alarm. • Determine the most optimum recommendation (that is, remediation or mitigation action) for any machine condition that warrants attention.

Table B.4   Responsibilities of the Report Manager Component

Subsystem ID:	SUBSYS-04
Component ID:	COMP-04-01
Component Name:	Report Manager
Component Responsibilities:	The responsibilities include • Generate productivity reports for each machine. • Generated roll-up reports from assets to regions and to geographies. • Generate comparative analysis reports between two or more regions.

Apart from the list of components illustrated here, two components were identified: Error Logger and Security Manager. These components are, respectively, responsible for logging all application or system errors into a file system or database and managing the authentication and authorization of users accessing the Elixir system.

Component Collaboration

Figures B.1 and B.2 illustrate the following two component collaborations for Elixir:

- Generate Machine Alerts
- Recommend Work Orders

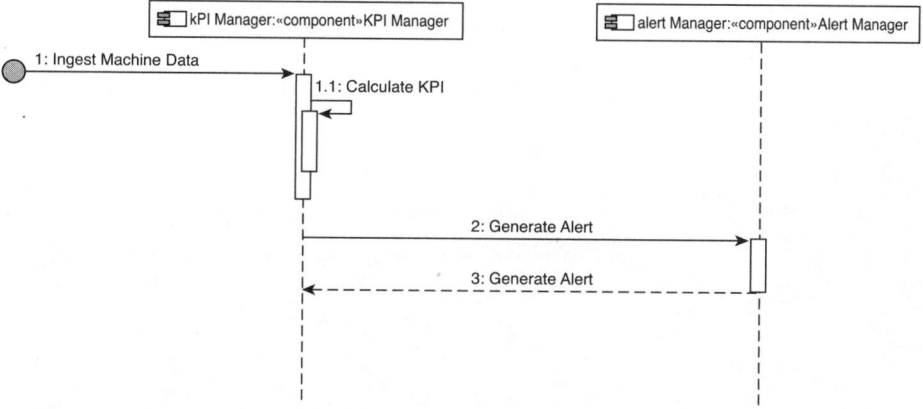

Figure B.1   Component collaboration for Generate Machine Alerts use case.

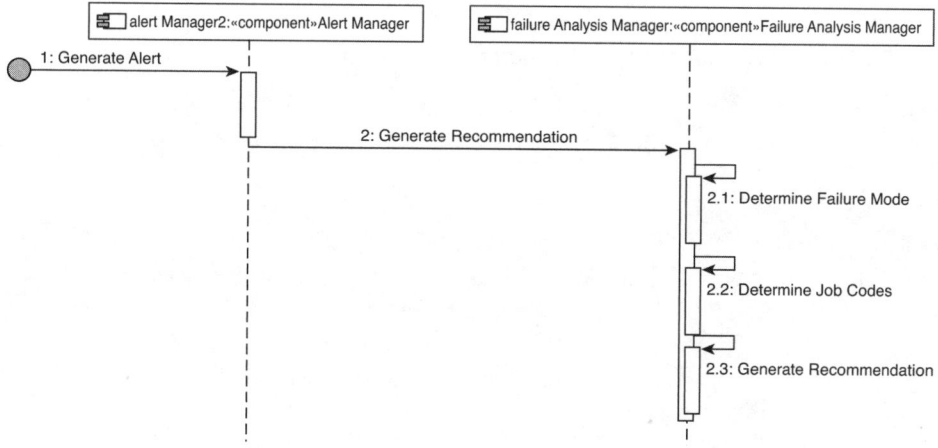

Figure B.2   Component collaboration for Recommend Work Orders use case.

Specified Level

Component Responsibility Matrix

The components for the first subsystem—that is, Asset Onboarding Management—were covered in Chapter 7. This section covers the components for the remaining subsystems.

Note: Tables B.5 through B.8 are similar to the corresponding tables illustrated earlier in this appendix. The only difference is that these tables augment the component responsibilities with the nonfunctional requirements. For the sake of brevity, the existing responsibilities (illustrated in the earlier tables) are not repeated.

Table B.5   Component Responsibility of the KPI Manager Component

Subsystem ID:	SUBSYS-02
Component ID:	COMP-02-01
Component Name:	KPI Manager
Component Responsibilities:	<<Existing Responsibilities, See Table B.1>>
	NFR-03—System should be able to compute 50 KPIs on each machine on a per second basis.
	NFR-04—System should be able to support 100 concurrent machine data feeds.
	BRC-002—If more than 5 KPIs on any one of the machine subcomponents have exceeded the normal operating thresholds within a span of 1 minute, the system is deemed to be potentially malfunctioning, and a warning should be generated.

Table B.6   Component Responsibility of the Alert Manager Component

Subsystem ID:	SUBSYS-02
Component ID:	COMP-02-02
Component Name:	Alert Manager
Component Responsibilities:	<<Existing Responsibilities, See Table B.2>>
	NFR-05—System should be able to visualize all alerts as and when they are generated, with near zero latency in the user experience.
	BRC-003—Alerts from lower-level subcomponents are inherited by the containing component. A critical alert on a subcomponent implies the containing component is under the same alert condition.

Table B.7   Component Responsibility of the Failure Analysis Manager Component

Subsystem ID:	SUBSYS-03
Component ID:	COMP-03-01
Component Name:	Failure Analysis Manager
Component Responsibilities:	<<Existing Responsibilities, See Table B.3>>
	NFR-06—System should be able to process up to an average of 100 concurrent alerts every minute.
	BRC-004—A failure mode maps to one or more probable causes (of failure). Each probable cause has a sequence of job codes for failure remediation. (The list of all failure modes, probable causes, and job code sequences is omitted for the sake of brevity and to preserve anonymity of any manufacturer-specific details.)

Table B.8   Component Responsibility of the Report Manager Component

Subsystem ID:	SUBSYS-04
Component ID:	COMP-04-01
Component Name:	Report Manager
Component Responsibilities:	<<Existing Responsibilities, See Table B.4>>
	NFR-07—Reports would be accessed by a total of 1,000 users and with 100 concurrent users at peak load.

Interface Specification

The interfaces for the components in the first subsystem—that is, Asset Onboarding Management—were covered in Chapter 7. Tables B.9 through B.11 cover the component interfaces for the remaining subsystems.

Table B.9   Specification for the KPI Calculation Interface

Component ID (interface belongs to)	COMP-02-01
Interface Name and ID	Name: KPI Calculation
	ID: IF-02-01-01
Interface Operations	1. Boolean registerKPIs(machineType: String, kpiList: <List> KPIProfile)
	2. String KPI_ID createKPI (kpi: KPIProfile)
	3. void calculateKPIs(machineID:String, kpiList: <List> KPI_ID)

Table B.10   Specification for the Alerting Interface

Component ID (interface belongs to)	COMP-02-02
Interface Name and ID	Name: Alerting ID: IF-02-02-02
Interface Operations	1. Alert createAlert(machineID: String, kpiID: String) 2. Boolean dispatchAlert(alert:Alert)

Table B.11   Specification for the Recommender Interface

Component ID (interface belongs to)	COMP-03-01
Interface Name and ID	Name: Recommender ID: IF-03-01-01
Interface Operations	1. Recommendation createRecommendation(alert:Alert) 2. Boolean acceptMaintenanceFeedback(feedback:String)

The Reporting Manager component would be implemented by a COTS product, so a custom interface on the component is not deemed of much value.

Two technical components were identified in this step: Security Manager and Error Logger. Figure B.3 provides a diagrammatic representation of the components and their interfaces.

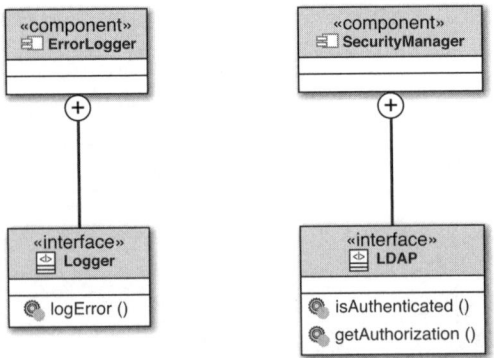

Figure B.3   The two technical components of Elixir and their interfaces.

Note: The SecurityManager component can either be considered as a technical component or as a functional component, based on the architect's choice! However, capturing its specifications is independent of its classification.

Associate Data Entries with Subsystems

The association of core data entities to the subsystems of Elixir was addressed in Chapter 7. However, a few data entities were not owned by the functional subsystems. These data entities are actually owned by the two technical components: the Security Manager and the Error Logger (see Figure B.4).

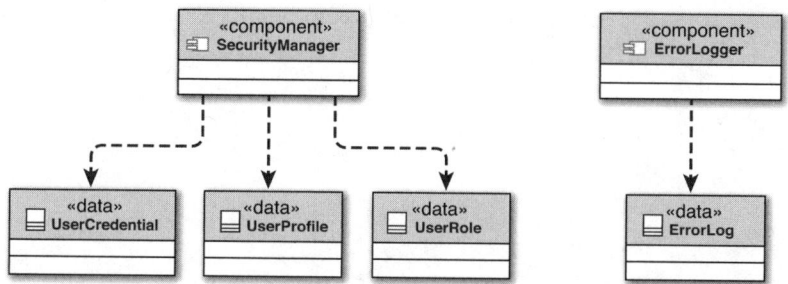

Figure B.4 Associating data entities to the technical components of Elixir.

Component Assignment to Layers

Because all the components were assigned to the Layered view as covered in Chapter 7, there are no additional artifacts to address.

Physical Level

Because all the components were assigned to an infrastructure topology as covered in Chapter 7, there are no additional artifacts to address.

Index